From WAR TO PEACE
OUR GLOBAL RESPONSIBILITY
Fourteen years of silent screams

FARIDA AHMADI

Supported by: Fritt ord and Norla

By Farida Ahmadi

Translated from Norwegian by Farida Ahmadi and Einar Grønnvoll

Copyright © Farida Ahmadi 2024

All rights reserved by author. No part of this publication may be reproduced, stored in a retrieval system or transmitted in any form or by any means, electronic, mechanical, photocopying, recording or otherwise, without the prior permission of the author. Although every precaution has been taken to verify the accuracy of the information contained herein, the publisher assumes no responsibility for any errors or omissions. No liability is assumed for damages that may result from the use of information contained within.

BlueRose Publishers takes no responsibility for any damages, losses, or liabilities that may arise from the use or misuse of the information, products, or services provided in this publication.

For permissions requests or inquiries regarding this publication,
please contact:
Global Happiness
www.faridaahmadi.com
sistersfarida@gmail.com

BLUEROSE PUBLISHERS
www.BlueRoseONE.com
info@bluerosepublishers.com
+91 8882 898 898
+4407342408967

ISBN: 978-93-5989-084-5

Cover design: **Farida Ahmadi (Global Happiness)**

Typesetting: Global Happiness and BlueRose

First Edition: February 2024

The children of Adam, human beings
are each other's limbs,
created, as they are, from the same core.
When time inflicts pain in one limb
the others can find no rest.
If you do not care about the suffering of others
you do not deserve to be called human[1].

Contents

Foreword by the Author vi
Foreword by Thomas Hylland Eriksen xi
Foreword by Rune Flikke xv
Foreword by Peter Hervik xvii
Foreword by Prof. M. Nazif Mohib Shahrani xxii
Introduction 1
1. Norway: The World's most Inclusive Society? 7
2. Lives of Suffering 16
3. The Multicultural Society and Multiculturalism 40
4. Life in a Ghetto 75
5. Women, War, Pain and Intimacy 88
6. Male Dominance and Social Control 108
7. Life in the Media vs. Minority Women's Everyday Life 119
8. Minority Women's Experience: A Guide to Reforming the Content and Organization of Norwegian Institutions 131
9. Globalization and its Abject 157
10. The Way Out: Minority Women's Hope 167
11. Let us rise up for peace and happiness 180
Terminology 212
List of References 233

Foreword by the Author

The history of humanity is a shared struggle for recognition, encompassing basic needs like love, rights, and solidarity. In my book "From War to Peace: Our Global Responsibility," I explore how pain and suffering arise from various factors such as poverty, unemployment, insecurity, and a sense of not belonging. My research suggests that multiculturalism, with its focus on diversity in religion, culture, ethnicity, and national identity, can also lead to pain, suffering, and even war by fostering a "us versus them" mentality. Globalization often acts as a catalyst, intensifying the us versus them. Many conflicts and wars today find their origins in this divisive perspective.

In the midst of our current dark times dominated by global pain, suffering, and war, the Norwegian King's hopeful New Year message for 2024 shines brightly. He emphasizes a shift in our community concept from "us and them" to a unified we ". Anger and frustration, damages the sense of community. To strengthen the community, one must listen and speak truthfully to build trust. In the part of the speech addressing the darkness and sorrowful loss of human lives in wars and conflicts, he recommends seeking help and invites us citizens to use our voices.

For me, the King's New Year's speech shines brightly because he recognizes that categorization of people of "Us and Them" damage the sense of unity of the community as a nation. The kings voice reflected my research which I wrote 14 years ago that Us and Them create pain and sufferings for the immigrant people as they excluded from the nation.

To have a strong community in Norway is not enough in our globalized world. I believe that we need to create a strong global community. Personally, my home isn't just Afghanistan and Norway; our shared home is our planet Earth. It's time to transform the global spread of pain and suffering into a global spread of peace and happiness. We know that the UN was the result of the second world war. Now, we need to develop a new UN which cover the needs of our time. We must create a global consciousness as a new UN institution.

We need more peacemakers like Gandhi. Let's work towards a new reality where Earth is recognized as our collective home, and let's create laws to prohibit war in our home earth.

Farida Ahmadi, January 2024

Blurbs from International Researchers
Blurbs from International Researchers

"Silent Screams delves into the physical and psychological pain borne by many women who have emigrated from countries in the throes of was and conflict. The book shows how pain stems from various conditions such as foreign intervention in their homeland, religion, male domination and poverty. Furthermore, they encounter and actual policy in Norway that treats women as members of a group and not as individuals. Farida Ahmadi bases her study on her own life experience and on her professional expertise and a social anthropologist. The book is both an important historical document as well as a social study. It is of general interest for those who are interested in the development of a multicultural society in Norway, and also provides special insights for those who work within the health and social services."

Knut Kjeldstadli, Professor of Modern History, University of Oslo

It has been a great privilege to follow Farida Ahmadis life and work over the past two decades. Silent Screams is a culmination of her life, her pain, her experiences and her research. She gives a voice to the thousands of women who have been silenced forever or continue to bear the burden of their pain in silence. Her courage to break the silence and speak out paves the path for women of migrant origin who are often unseen, unheard and dismissed. Her work sheds light on a subject that has a significant impact on the lives of many yet scarcely dealt with in depth. 'Silent Screams' provides valuable insights to health professionals, and Ahmadi's reflection, analysis and reflexivity will enable researchers to delve further in an unknown landscape- Ahmadi unique amalgamation showcases her prowess as a writer and researcher. Norway has been described as the 'haven of gender equality' by the UN. Though Norway has been declared as a gender superpower, migrant women are often left behind their Norwegian sisters. Migration is a defining issue of our times and diversity is here to stay hence it cannot be ignored. Ahmadis' powerful rendition is witness to the strength and resilience of migrant women, often seen as only as victims. Her work is both timely and relevant for decision makers to ensure that no one is left behind in multicultural societies. Ahmadis work will be appreciated for generations to come.

Prof. (Dr). Bernadette Nirmal Kumar, MD, Phd.
Special Advisor, Division for Health Services, Norwegian Institute of Public Health

Chair Global Society on Migration, Ethnicity, Race and Health

Vice President Women in Global Health Norway

"With this book, Farida Ahmadi reveals very important experiences in Norwegian society."

Elisabeth Eide, Professor of Journalism, Oslo and Akershus University

"Farida Ahmadi's book is a valuable contribution to current debates over the prospects of multiculturalism in a world of increasing polarization and xenophobia. Ahmadi's subject is the predicament of women whose voices go unheard; women who on grounds of their foreign ethnic, religious, and national background constitute a minority in a society where the majority essentializes the "otherness" they represent as cultural and religious givens, thus generalizing the individuals making up a most heterogeneous group and erecting barriers between "us" and "them". Ahmadi's book gives a voice that cannot be ignored to these women considered as so many individuals."

Arne Johan Vetlesen, professor of filosofi, Universitetet in Oslo.

Farida Ahmadi's crystallized insight into the lives of immigrant women – caught in the cross- fire between, on the one hand, a state apparatus unable to relate to their needs as individuals, and, on the other hand, immigrant cultures that constrain movement, participation and expression – is a painful gift to us all. With deep empathy, Ahmadi has engaged women who struggle, and she presents us with unpleasant, but undisputable, facts that ought to alter our understanding.

Kristian Berg Harpviken, Research Professor, Peace Research Institute Oslo (PRIO).

Silent Screams gives a much-needed subaltern view of Norwegian society through the lenses of Muslim women. Farida Ahmadi has written a brave ethnographic study where an analytical approach to pain is used as the entry point for a compassionate study of the suffering experienced by minority women as they struggle to deal with the patriarchal values of their male spokespersons, a Norwegian majority that rarely treats them as equals, and well-meaning integration efforts. Ahmadi has penned an audacious, thought provoking, critical attack on the multicultural mindset, which interact in the lives of these women in painful ways that are not recognized in their interaction with the welfare state and NGOs. Silent Screams is a pertinent work that deserves a wide readership among social scientists, policymakers, healthcare- and social workers.

Rune Flikke. Professor Department of social anthropology, University of Oslo

No one knows better than Farida Ahmadi how the predicament of women from the global south has been construed for multiple social and political purposes in today's European societies. Farida's message to regard these women, and all people, as individuals, not 'others', is a resounding affirmation of our shared humanity. Silent Screams is a challenge to all those who fail to recognize the strength in diversity. Her argument about multiculturalism is provocative and should be taken on board by policy makers, social workers, teachers as well as anyone wishing to be better informed about immigration.

Rachel Lehr Department of Geography, University of Colorado Boulder author of The Carpetbaggers of Kabul and other American Afghan Entanglements with Jennifer Fluri.

Foreword by Thomas Hylland Eriksen

Today's political struggles are not only about ownership of means of production, but ownership of identity and self-definition. Ethnonationalists confront cosmopolitanism; political movements based on religion oppose secular tendencies; and human rights organizations must fight against the idea that people have rights based on where they were born and their passports' colour.

Since the nineteenth century, European nation-building has focused on producing cultural homogeneity as a basis for social solidarity. This focus has been under increasing pressure through the power of globalization and its new cultural patterns, which have changed the demographic composition of many European countries and elsewhere. This happens especially in the big cities, due to migration. The new identity politics is a result of a greater awareness of cultural rights and the right to respect and recognition and can be seen as a reaction to cultural influence and the weakening of national borders.

This forms the backdrop for Farida Ahmadi's sensitive and passionate study of minority women in Oslo. With a focus on women's health problems and concerns regarding well-being and satisfaction, Ahmadi shows problems with multiculturalism using an ethnographic approach. She does this through a detailed description of the women's lives and difficulties, combined with statistical overviews and theoretical discussions. Ahmadi argues that "unofficial multiculturalism" permeates Norwegian social institutions, which makes it difficult for minority women to be perceived as unique individuals, and not as members of an ethnic, religious, or national group. Although their right to cultural identity is unquestionable, they also have the rights of equality. This is a real dilemma, which Ahmadi is well aware of. On the one hand, there is a gross multiculturalist policy that links individuals to their respective groups, and which can impose an undesirable cultural identity. This may, in spite of good intentions, help to justify oppression. On the other hand, there are those who deny that cultural variation deserves respect, those who show complete indifference to cultural diversity, following the motto that everyone should be treated in the same way. This indifference can silence and obscure the unique and specific problems that precarious groups such as minority women face. The problems are differing, not only from those of other minority women, but also from the Norwegian majority.

The fundamental dilemma for ethnically complex societies can be formulated as follows: On the one hand, all members of a liberal democracy (in principle, if not in practice) are entitled to equal rights and opportunities. On the other hand, all members of a liberal democracy also have the right to be different from each other. In our time and in our society, minority groups increasingly fight for the upholding of their rights to maintain and promote their cultural specificity, to be visible in the public sphere, in the media, on the school curriculum and so on. A crucial challenge for ethnically and culturally complex societies is therefore to open up to cultural differences, without violating socially defined rights. In other words, the challenge is to find a viable compromise, both for the state and for the citizens. A compromise between equal rights and the right to be different, which makes it important to strike the balance between difference and equality. Many immigrants find themselves at the short end of the stick: They are offered similarity where they want difference (e.g. with respect to religion), and are offered difference where they demand equality (full inclusion in society)

This contradiction is as old as nationalism itself. Nationalism, the ideology that claims that the state should be culturally homogenous, has a double origin. On the one hand, we find French Enlightenment theory, which emphasizes cultural (and often ethnic) uniformity, shared territory and citizenship as the basis for national integration and the source of political legitimacy. According to classical Enlightenment theory, there has been a universal human civilization, theoretically accessible to all people. On the other hand, in German romanticism, defined and championed by the philosopher Johann Gottfried Herder (1744-1803), people have, first of all, the right to defend their cultural and linguistic character. This way of viewing culture, developed primarily as a defence against French universalism, became a form of cultural imperialism at the local level (most likely without specific justification).

Currently, this perspective and its following are carried through ideologies highlighting the importance of cultural homogeneity for maintaining political identity. This applies even when the ideologies are nationalist and fight for homogenized states, and when they are ethno-political and insist that there should be ethnic-based rights for minorities within existing states. It is therefore not only multiculturalism that creates an obstacle to fair and equal treatment of all citizens, but culturalism itself, which is represented through the majority in addition to the minority.

There is no easy solution to this challenge. Instead, if we accept that diversity exists, but that it is wrong and misleading to inscribe it onto groups, it becomes important not only to see people as unique individuals with their own specific stories, but also to accept that not all people who live in a particular place, like Norway, necessarily have the same experiences and challenges. There is, as Ahmadi says, a need for shared standards and values, and a need to identifying diversity in society. We can look at the solution, which apparently identifies conflicting goals, as pluralistic universalism. The road to this cosmopolitan vision is irregular and uneven, but Farida Ahmadi's study sheds light on society's challenges and problems and helps us moving forward.

Ahmadi's vision is not just a proposal for a more convincing inclusion of minorities in complex societies. It can also be read as a recipe for peace. The perspective I read out of this book could be glossed as a form of universalist particularism. We must agree on rules and norms in order to have a society based on trust. But at the same time, we must respect our mutual differences and see them as an asset rather than an obstacle. A great deal of anger and aggression would have been avoided if this attitude, based on trust rather than suspicion, had been the default way of entering into a world of difference, similarity and complexity.

It has been a few years since this book was first published, but it has never been more relevant than now, as heated debates about identity politics, structural racism and freedom of expression have gained a dominant place in the public sphere and politics, in Norway and other places. This book deserves a wide readership.

Thomas Hylland Eriksen, Oslo, spring 2024

Professor of Social Anthropology, University of Oslo

Foreword by Rune Flikke

Through good empirical examples, clear and thorough arguments, Ahmadi invites the reader to think through the problematic sides of what she describes as an "unofficial multiculturalism" affecting the Norwegian public. Despite the good intentions, it becomes quickly obvious that the Muslim minority women, interviewed by Ahmadi, experience multiculturalism as a burden. The book is carrying the proximity between Ahmadi and these women, with all of the variations in experiences and positioning taken into consideration with empathy, insight and respect– it is not at all a homogenous field she is describing.

As a woman, born and grown up in Afghanistan, and with the experiences she has carried with herself as an immigrant living in a Norwegian suburb, Ahmadi is exceptionally well positioned for this project. Not only has she access to open the spheres of experiences and give a voice to a part of the Norwegian society that usually remains unheard, but she also draws on her experiences gathered as a medicine student, working in the Afghan countryside. A central question in the book is how the women's fates and experiences in war-torn Afghanistan have so much in common with those of the minority women whom she met as an anthropologist within the Norwegian welfare society.

For Ahmadi two perspectives are important to answer this question. Firstly, how politics and the media understand and treat culture, and further trace it within everyday activities. Here, Ahmadi is drawing on the well-known Indian anthropologist Veena Das who has pointed to the ways cultural differences are treated and how suffering spreads out unevenly throughout a society. Secondly, "the voice" is becoming a central topic underlining this: Who is talking for whom? What are the practical consequences of whom is given voice and recognition within the Norwegian public? This is made visible through compelling ways on many levels within the text.

Throughout the book, Ahmadi is continuously balancing oppositional approaches, between group and individual rights. On the one hand, it is the realization of equality that is central in her argument. As individuals, we have the same rights and duties. She makes clear that this is leading to specific difficulties, in this case for the minority women, which are remaining unnoticed. On the other hand, we are meeting the root of her critique of the Norwegian multiculturalism; the focus on religious and cultural differences creates a situation where minority women are being ignored and reduced to an identity and societal role in which they are not comfortable. This is the origin of the pain expressed by her respondents. Ahmadi is delivering us a row of thoughtful examples how originally well-meaning actions can place minority women at the margins of society and thereby prevent them to build up the knowledge and experience they needed to integrate into Norwegian society. One challenge that Ahmadi is discussing in depth is that the marginalization along these lines leads some of her respondents closer toward a cultural and religious identity and others toward resignation and unwanted disability benefits. They all have the experiences of pain in common, a pain that the Norwegian health system cannot alleviate.

The book shows a thorough theory and method and a clever, insightful contribution to one of the biggest contemporary political topics. My hope is that it receives a wide readership and that it continues to influence the public debates throughout the next years.

Rune Flikke

Professor and leader of the Department of Social Anthropology

University of Oslo

Foreword by Peter Hervik

A student who attended a course on nationalism, which I had taught at the University of Oslo several years ago, recently approached me. She asked me if I remembered her, the enthusiastic student who used to sit in the front row during lectures, and I did. I remembered her story about the experiences she had before she came to Norway and her first months in the country. This student was Farida Ahmadi. I consider teaching an educational experience for both the students and myself. Farida's history induced a degree of seriousness and challenge in teaching, something I have appreciated to this day. Now I am learning from her new book, revised and translated into many languages.

I do not necessarily agree with everything Farida writes, but as a whole, I am happy and excited about her book. The old but empirically strong concept of multiculturalism can serve as a driving force for a destructive understanding of the differences between and diversity among people, especially in the media and social media commentary. "Culture as small islands" is a concept that considers human identity as created by the same, all-encompassing culture from birth to the grave. This contributes to strong beliefs and practices that determine who is included and excluded, in addition to generating ideas of incompatible traits, where real differences are transformed into social hierarchies based on subordination and superiority. The point here is that people do not come from isolated islands, but are rather shaped through interactions, mobility and exchange. This means that people have much more in common with each other, than differences that divide them.

Her reflections are well built and based on real experiences, which she in turn places and analyzes in a larger framework. Again, it is not my job to agree or disagree. The interplay between Farida's own experiences, her education in anthropology, her dedication to listening to the experiences of other women and her thorough analysis, all transform her individual thinking into a book that I encourage and support. In this support also lies my personal experience and awareness. The Western paradigm of science needs more works with understanding of what Eurocentrism entails and how we can put an end to it. Farida offers an important and positive approach, an approach that builds a bridge between Afghan and Norwegian perspectives. A similar presentation can be found in the scientific collaboration between Nielsen and Hervik in Women in Post-revolutionary Egypt (Nielsen and Hervik 2017), a work that addresses women throughout Egypt after the 2011 revolution. Through her research, Farida interacts with women of migrant and refugee background in Norway, who are in particularly vulnerable positions. She talks to the poor, the uneducated and the oppressed, and concludes that each person has something to talk about ongoing experiences of discrimination as well as other stories that are often very intimate. Some women are vulnerable due to rigid social control, mostly exercised by men; control based on an informal, traditional way of thinking about the relationship between women and men. Other women are either not aware of their rights, or are simply critical of the man's power, but afraid of losing their husbands. This dynamic evokes a picture of how men can be good husbands and citizens in Norway.

In her work, Farida discovers the pain, suffering, scars and trauma in the language of people who have come to Norway. These various forms of pain and suffering are carried abroad from war zones. In several cases, this pain and suffering reproduces, and sometimes even new dimensions form through experiences and interactions with Norwegian authorities and people. Identifying and documenting this pain is the first, most important step to further analysis. Then Farida draws attention to the multiple layers of this pain, and the social spheres associated with it. My interpretation is that the pain and suffering that Farida is referring to can be even more destructive to society than what the academic sphere already recognized. Pain grows, pain persists, and pain is eventually transformed into fear and anger. Anger leads to guilt and can further develop into moral indignation, which is the basis for violent acts and reactions that accompany nationalism. If recognized correctly, such reactions can be transformed into dedicated, constructive, innovative and positive action-oriented initiatives, which Farida is striving for. The fact is, however, that we live in an era of pain, as previously discussed by the Indian author Pankaj Mishra in his thought- provoking and easy-to-read book.

One of the strengths of Farida's approach is that she starts with the real experiences of people. She focuses on their lived experiences, and she is critical of approaches where individuals appear as an anonymous entity, where the "individual" collapses into the group. This is important, almost trivial, but still only a few academics do this. An example is the category "non-western" which was established by the UN as a statistical category, but which is now also used as an ethnic category. Despite the great variety Farida encounters through her research, all "non-Norwegian" people are placed together in this category when they have only one thing in common; they are all considered non-Norwegian based on their appearance. Not being recognized and the incorrect assessment have a devastating effect on minority women and men in Norway.

When I read the book, it becomes clear that it is the same concept of culture (culture as an island) as the backdrop and condition for both, nationalism and multiculturalism. Both are concerned with equality and inequality; the nationalist always considers himself unique and superior, which reminds us that identity and power cannot be separated from each other. The fundamental values attached to nationalist approaches are, in my opinion, merely examples and the very structure of authoritarianism. According to linguist and neurologist Georg Lakoff, national, familial and masculine values are closely inter-linked, and in the American context they can be boiled down to the image of a "strict father" (the authoritarian father). In a "wicked world," and in a game of winners and losers, the father seeks to protect his children. He teaches them about right and wrong, uses punishment as an incentive to achieve the "right" way of thinking and acting. The strict father knows what is best for his children (and for the country) and uses physical discipline, more than the use of dialogue, as a guideline in raising children in his own image. One of the problems is that he neither knows, nor accepts alternative ways of dealing with conflict in the family and the nation. On the other hand, we find the "caring parent" model, by which the children are brought up to be caring, friendly and empathetic towards other children and citizens. They learn through explanations and through boundary setting. If they do something wrong, they learn to make amends. Built into the "strict father" model, and not into the "caring parent" model, we find the traditional masculine values. In the "caring parent" model, father and mother take on the same parental role.

More than a century ago, W.E.B. du Bois was on a mission to visit the infamous, black, problematic ghettos in Philadelphia on the American South Coast, to find out what was wrong with the "Negroes" because there was so much poverty, crime, unemployment, and so on. After considerable empirical effort, he wrote in the book *The Philadelphia Negro* that it was not in question what was wrong with the "Negroes." Instead of taking this categorical and stereotypical point of departure, the question should rather be seen in the light of structural conditions, specific circumstances and forced pathology. The category "negro" was about questioning what it means to be a human being. In light of the traumatic experiences of minority and immigrant women from conflict zones and human security in Norway, we can see that this is the right question and starting point in Farida's book that helps us on the way to understanding.

At the core of Farida Ahmadi's call for a stronger global community united in peace by a shared awareness of a profound sense of humanness and human suffering. Such awareness has no divisiveness, no US and THEM. Divisiveness is a sign that people have lost their heart and are lost in distractions. Some of us have been teaching peace and conflict studies with seminar groups consisting of people embodying the very conflicts we deal with. For this, we need to start from basics. Basic humanness. What it means to be a human being. We are in this together also because people are suffering, collective suffering, whether war crimes, forced gang rapes, massacres, and genocide. There is only one point of departure. Farida's contribution to this purpose is exceptional, extraordinary, urgent and so welcomed.

References

Du Bois, W. E. B. (1899). *The Philadelphia Negro.* New York: Lippincott.
Lakoff, George. 2004. *Don't Think of an Elephant! Know Your Values and Frame the Debate.* White River Junction, VT.: Chelsea Green Publishing

Mishra, Pankaj. 2017. *The Age of Anger. A History of the Present.* New York: Farrar, Straus and Giroux Nielsen, Mette Toft and Hervik, Peter. 2017. *Can Behaviour Be Controlled? Women in Post- Revolutionary Egypt.* Frankfurt am Main: Peter Lang.

Foreword by Prof. M. Nazif Mohib Shahrani

Farida Ahmadi's book is a remarkably empathetic, self-reflexive and intimate ethnographic accounts of the pains, longings, and desires of some 300 women, primarily Muslims, forced into taking refuge in Norway, because of the wars and violence perpetrated by the West on the Third World, what the book calls the "Third World War". The fact that these Silent Screams are reported from Norway, reputedly, a most welcoming host country for refugees, at least since 1970s, with liberal and inclusive policies towards their growing non-European resettled compatriots.

The author, Farida Ahmadi, is a Norwegian-Afghan who studied medicine in Kabul during the 1980s and was involved in the provision health services to the Afghan villagers. When she became a refugee herself in Norway, she lived in a ghetto in Eastern part of the city of Oslo. She was surprised to encounter refugee women among her neighbours in Oslo, from the war-ravaged countries in the Middle East and Africa (including Afghanistan), complaining from the same physical and mental illnesses she had encountered in rural Afghanistan. When Farida began studying anthropology as a graduate student in Oslo, she wanted to understand the reasons for such unexpected similarities between the refugee women in Oslo and the village women she knew in rural Afghanistan.

She quickly discovered that the debilitating pains (both physical and mental) of war and violence at their places of origins as well as oppressive customs and cultural practices amounting to gendered discrimination such as exclusion of women from public arena, their powerlessness within the family and society, among others, had not only accompanied them to Norway, but intensified further in Norway. She blames, at least partly, the adoption of multiculturalism as a slogan by the Norwegian government which has created a space for heightening cultural "otherness" of non-native Norwegians. That is ideals of multiculturalism spoken but not practiced, she says have caused intensification of cultural boundaries rather than drawing the immigrant community closer as citizens with equal rights and access to resources.

For immigrant women suffering ailments (physical and mental) the stringent biomedical approach to health services which readily dispenses pain killers without listening or willing to understand their individual life histories and stories, has brought no relief to them. Their repeated visits to the doctors for the same illnesses has frustrated both the doctors and the patients. The doctors have started blaming the victims, the immigrants— i.e., their religion and culture--for not getting well. An unfortunate reality which has resulted in refugee women's withdrawal from the larger Norwegian society. A process, aggravated by the daily media coverage of "wars on terror", has led to mutual distrust, invisible walls of mutual indifference and/or hate resulting in a vicious outcome of exclusion, non-recognition or acknowledgement of immigrant women as individual human beings, leaving them with no options but resorting to Silent Screams!

One may not agree with everything in this remarkable book, but the author's real intention to bring the plight of these women to the attention of the violently globalizing world, and especially to the attention of policy communities in Norway cannot be denied. Farida Ahmadi, in this well documented and analyzed volume, does not only make the Silent Screams of these suffering women heard, but also suggests critically important ways and means to alleviate the causes of such harm. Her book should be read widely by scholars, policy makers and social services professionals, especially in the health services sector, so that they can acknowledge the dignity of these women's personhood and understand the historical and violent societal conditions that have made them scream, even if silently.

M. Nazif Mohib Shahrani

Professor of Anthropology, Central Asian & Middle Eastern Studies

Departments of Anthropology, CEUS & MELC

Hamilton Lugar School of Global and International Studies (HLS)

355 Jordan Avenue

Indiana University Bloomington, Indiana 47401

Introduction

About the content of this book

In this book, you will encounter a group of minority women. These women come from various countries, have different backgrounds and worldviews, but they all belong to a category of people Norwegian authorities and statisticians call "non-Western immigrants". This book is not about all women in this category. It is about those among them who are not well. Those whose life and presence in Norway is difficult for themselves and for the Norwegian authorities.

I wish that "Ezat", "Nasrin", "Shaeen", "Tajeba", "Arezo", "Belquis", "Elisabeth", "Kamille", "Baarin" and "Shogofa" could have told their own stories openly and under their own names. But that is not possible. It has been necessary to anonymize all the women in this book who have opened up their lives to me. They have given me honest and detailed insights into their private lives and their experiences under employment in the Norwegian labor market. In addition, they have dared to criticize aspects of Norwegian society. For some of them, being recognized could create problems in their relations with their husbands, ex-husbands, and the community; others fear they may lose their jobs. For the same reasons, I have chosen to use the pseudonym "Angarudd" when speaking of the part of Oslo where some of these women live.

My respondents also came from the majority population; Norwegians who work with these women in three Norwegian institutions providing services to immigrants in Oslo. I interviewed and observed leaders and employees at the Jacob Center, the "Knowledge Center" and at the Psychosocial Center for Refugees. I also talked with doctors working at the Tøyen Health Center where many of the patients are women from Norway's minority population. I have chosen to anonymize two of these institutions, the Jacob Center and the "Knowledge Center". The most important reason for this is that this enabled the women to tell me openly about their meetings and experiences in these centers without fear of being recognized or being perceived as ungrateful and critical of the very institutions that were trying to help them. I have chosen to do so also to protect the employees and leaders at these centers, as these are people who do their jobs with the very best of intentions. Both centers offer several valuable services for immigrants. Nevertheless, I feel it is important to identify and discuss how various forms of institutionalized discrimination manifest and are played out in some Norwegian institutions providing services, specifically those for immigrant women.

After having spoken with several hundred people I was left with an enormous amount of data on the daily life situation of Oslo's minority population. Although my research was conducted in Oslo, I believe that the women I have used as examples in this book are representative of many of those I have met, i.e., those having problems that minority women elsewhere will recognize from their own experiences.

As for myself, I am from Afghanistan. I grew up in Kabul, where I also lived the first part of my adult life. I have also spent a lot of time in the Afghan countryside as a young medical student hoping to help educate the rural population on the health of women and children. It may seem strange to some that I compare minority women living in a ghetto area in Oslo with women living in the Afghan countryside. Listening to and learning from the women I met in the Afghan countryside and to the stories of my beloved Afghan grandmother and well-educated women and politicians during the Soviet occupation, as well as observing the emergence of fundamentalism – all this has given me insights into real issues and needs. I experienced how a lid was put over the needs and dreams of Afghan women during the Cold War and I saw with my own eyes how religion, ethnicity and culture gained an increasingly prominent role in Afghanistan. Memories of and nostalgia for Afghanistan came over me when I listened to conversations among women in the laundry room in the apartment block in a suburb outside the center of Oslo when I first came to Norway.

I was surprised that the same issues which I observed in Afghanistan also affected the lives of these women. Their needs and dreams were being ignored and neglected. When I later started my fieldwork in social anthropology at the University of Oslo, I thought more and more about how the pain and suffering of minority women in Oslo has remained invisible in public discussions and public policy, while these very same problems became more acute in Norway. Within this context the issue wasn't the Taliban and lack of knowledge, but rather what I will call a constructed unofficial multiculturalism in the democratic country of Norway. I encountered many views about how women within supposedly homogenous religious and cultural groups thought and wanted to live. At the same time, I also encountered the prejudiced and generalized views of minority women on the society they now live in. Not to see the individuals behind cultural, religious and ethnic categories is the most serious violation of humanity. To cling to generalizations and categorization is a source of conflict that we have to do something about.

Pain is a central concept in this book. For me, pain has many dimensions: physical, psychological, psychosomatic and social. I experienced that this concept of pain was one with which those I talked to understood. At the same time pain can be many things. For some, pain was a "knot" in their body that would not go away. For many others, pain had to do with being feeling like losers in their social relations, both privately and publicly, and how this led to experiences of powerlessness and paralysis as well as physical pain. This kind of pain is an illness with symptoms that many go to the doctor for a cure, but its cause remains hidden. My goal has been to explore the complexity of causes that lies behind the layers of pain that have "accumulated" in the bodies of my respondents. My claim is that the causes are complex, but that we nevertheless can see a red line running through all of it. It in- volves a widespread and rigid attitude towards the category "non-West- ern immigrants" that those thus labeled suffer under – also physically. In addition, it involves the life situation of women within this category in present day Norway, whether they have a job, education, a network, a decent standard of living and close, good and safe relationships. As the reader will see, the pain of minority women in Oslo is, at the core, about experiences of violations encountered on many levels.

The starting point for this book was my master's thesis in social anthropology from 2006. I wanted to understand how it was possible that so many immigrant women in the social democratic country of Norway could be suffering to the extent that the statistics actually showed. This was a mystery to me. I started out as a feminist who saw male dominance as the most important explanation for these disorders. But during my fieldwork I had to nuance my view. Men alongside women are caught up in multiculturalism. The pain of sufferings of man is not so visible and it's the consequences of multiculturalism too. For example, group rights and duty. The imbalance between paradoxid rights and duties in Norwegian society. They experience other pressures as well such as poverty, unemployment and lack of belonging. Multiculturalism as a misleading policy is producing a domino effect. I had to correct my views after conducting interviews with men.

This edition has also been complemented with a completely new chapter (Chapter 11), which is an update on what has happened in the last 12 years in within the theme of pain and multiculturalism. Since this book was first published in 2008, I see that the dimension of pain worsened in some ways but improved in others. Every time I travel abroad and return, I experience a stronger sense of belonging to Norway. I am proud to live in a country with so many great institutions that preserve the rights of the individual. Nevertheless, within this chapter, I want to shed light on the things which are not working so well, and which continue to create pain and insecurity among minorities, and thereby further impacts the majority population as well.

The big question for me, how to turn globalization of pain suffering and war to globalization of peace, justice, and happiness. Therefore, I named this English edition from war to peace: Our global responsibility. We must work together to forbid the war and make a law prohibition of war.

At the end of my book the different concept and terminology I used; I gave explanation.

Thank you to those of you, who have made this book possible.

Thanks to economic support from the Norwegian organizations, "Fritt Ord" and "NORLA", my goal was realized: I was able to communicate my knowledge about the painful lives of many minority women to a larger audience. Thanks to Kari Ann Kvamme for help in expressing what I meant in Norwegian. For me, working with this book has felt like being handed a gift. I also had the opportunity to ponder what possibilities there are for creating a genuinely inclusive society.

This book could not have been written without the many people who gave me their trust and let me into their lives. Therefore, my first thanks go to all my respondents, both from the majority and the minority group, including the three institutions that allowed me to do my fieldwork at their premises. I learned a lot from all of them and the book could not have been written without their stories and opinions. There are too many names to be mentioned – those not mentioned are not forgotten.

I wish to thank my supervisor and consultant professor, Thomas Hylland Eriksen, a very engaged and knowledgeable human being. From him I received a lot of inspiration, encouragement and strength to follow my own way of thinking. Professor of History Knut Kjeldstadli has also been of considerable support in the work with the thesis, which is the genesis of this book. He also encouraged me to formulate my own thoughts and ideas.

Professor of Philosophy Arne J. Vetlesen's perspective on pain has been important in my work. I also wish to thank Professor of Political Science Hege Skjeie and Professor of Criminology Kjersti Ericsson for interesting discussions and encouragement.

Thanks for academic help also go to Marianne Gullestad. As a scientist studying the Norwegian majority population, she was an inspiration. Marianne Gullestad was unique and irreplaceable. Her death is a great sorrow and a big loss for Norwegian anthropology. Thanks also to Professor Hallvard Vike and Rune Flikke and to psychiatrist Solveig Dahl for useful discussions in connection with the chapter concerning women's intimacy.

I am an optimist. With this book, I hope to contribute towards placing the real needs of immigrant women at the center. My wish is that knowledge about the situation of these women will increase, and that the conflicts connected to issues concerning their lives will lessen. Only then can we create a more harmonious society, a society where globalized pain can be turned into a globalization of knowledge, happiness and peace.

Oslo, 2024
Farida Ahmadi

1. Norway: The World's most Inclusive Society?

"Pain is not in my body, all my thoughts are painful," Ezat said. "Pain and being female are two sides of the same coin," Nasrin told me. "Culture is our invisible pain," Kamilla said more precisely. "When I see mullah Krekar on TV, I get a headache," Shaeen complained. "The pain from being unemployed is worse than the pain from circumcision," Tajeba noted. "Exclusion from the employed community makes me paralyzed," Elisabeth summed up.

Ezat, Nasrin, Kamille, Shaeen, Tajeba and Elisabeth are only a small sample of the women I have met and who described their pain and their lives to me. These six women are quite different from each other. They have different levels of education, belong to different religions and have different views on integration. Because of their differences, they chose separate strategies in order to live a dignified life. But they have something in common: they all experience, more or less, unmanageable pain. And they live what I call a difficult life. It is precisely what they have in common that makes them representatives for hundreds of minority women I have met in Norway during the last ten years.

This book deals with those minority women who belong to the lowest social class in Norway today. It deals with how bad health affects their lives - a situation marked by lack of power. Lack of self-esteem, lack of a sense of control over their own lives, and numerous experiences of violations mark the daily life of these women to such an extent that I am convinced that it must be seen as an important cause for their bad health.

Several years ago, I started to study anthropology with the intention of writing about the difficult situation of women in Afghanistan. But as I became aware of the situation for minority women here in Norway, I discovered, surprisingly, many similarities between the women I met here and the women I had met in the countryside in my country of origin. Throughout my adolescence in Kabul, and in particular through my work as a student of medicine and a grown woman under the Soviet occupation in the countryside in Afghanistan, I had met a lot of women with bad health - and many of these complained about strong pains. However, the hopelessness in their situation was apparent; they lived in an occupied country, there was a lack of money and a lack of mod- ern health facilities. They were overloaded by responsibility because their husbands often were involved in the war, and they were worried. Both their bad health and their feeling of powerlessness were directly connected to exterior circumstances: occupation, war, poverty, religious fundamentalism, lack of knowledge and lack of modern health facilities.

When I later met many minority women in Norway, I was surprised that they did not have a better life than they actually had. Most of the external circumstances I had seen in Afghanistan that led to powerless- ness among women and their complex problems, should not exist in a modern democracy like Norway. Just the same, I encountered many of the same symptoms: depression and strong pains that could not always be defined and categorized - that did not have a simple physiological explanation.

Questions about why there were such similarities between women in a country ravaged by war and poverty and women in a modern democratic country like Norway, was interesting. Statistical studies have for several years shown that minority women in Norway have health problems. But why? Norway is a modern democracy with an exceptionally well-developed healthcare system. Why were so many of the women I met suffering from work disability? Why is such an overwhelming majority of these non-Western women in so much pain that it affects their quality of life?

In 2002, the Norwegian Institute of Public Health published a major health survey that studied how variables such as sex, age, residence, education, employment situation and place of birth influence health conditions. The results show a clear overrepresentation of both mental and physical illness among non-Western women.[1] What lies behind these numbers? Why do these women experience more pain than other groups in society? What are the causes of their suffering? Do the main causes lie in bad experiences in their country of origin and the strain of moving from their original home? Or can their bad health simply be related to lack of integration?

The feeling of powerlessness among the minority women I met, and still meet, is striking. The possibility to influence and improve their own situations seems to be missing. Do these two things - powerlessness and pain - have a connection? Can lack of power in itself cause bad health? If so, what is the cause of the powerlessness of these women?

Powerlessness in a New Life

To gain power and control over one's own life and daily existence, it is first necessary to acknowledge one's own individuality and needs. Many of the women I met in Norway, like those in Afghanistan, have a daily existence in which they have so much responsibility for others that they forget about and ignore themselves. They work all day to satisfy the needs of their husband, and, in particular, their children - for food, for clothes and for the "things" that a child in a Western society is expected to have. Many minority women are at the bottom rung of the social ladder in Norway. They are trapped in poverty - also here in our Western democracy. Many of them lack important knowledge about how the society they live in works - for example, how to relate to the healthcare, tax and school system. This increases their feelings of powerlessness. They are not always able to identify who has both the economic and categorical power over them. All the time, they encounter situations, views, and not the least, institutions that both define and partially rule their daily lives. How does the system for social security benefits actually work? What is the meaning behind a possible yes or no from this system? And what is needed to get out of the situation they are in? Without a necessary overview, many of these women struggle to find strategies that work to gain control over their own situation.[2]

The big difference between women in Afghanistan and minority

women I have met in Norway is that the latter live in a society where the majority consider women as equal to men. This is of great advantage when considering the possibilities for change. Particularly in a Norwegian society where there are unique possibilities for the recognition of minority women as individuals, as well as equals. What are the obstacles that stand in the way?

Many of the women I met feel almost personally assaulted when they hear about generalizations concerning their own culture, and especially that it suppresses women. To practice a policy where a focus on religious and cultural differences become prominent both in public discourse and many institutions, worsens the quality of life of these women. The multicultural way of thinking, founded on the idea of difference, is, hence, a wrong strategy. It is, among other things, a hindrance for these women to acquire the knowledge necessary to enable them to change their lives. When thoughts about fundamental cultural differences are transformed into politics, the consequences are that women on one side accept the situation they are in, while the majority on the other side, blame culture and religion. Their pain is silenced, both in the public domain and in private. This is the most important reason I chose the topic Silent Screams for the background of my book title "From war to peace, our global responsibility". The women suffer from not being seen as individuals. They have needs comparable to those of the ethnic Norwegian women. They need basic recognition in their close relations and in their encounters with society. But they often feel ignored, and actually violated, both by the minority society they belong to, and the majority. And they usually do not have a voice when the discourse is about them. Their pain is often connected to this: not being seen and understood. The lack of recognition of individuality - and individual needs - constitutes much of the pain minority women feel in Norway today.

I discovered that the women I met often struggled with a combination of physical, mental and psychosomatic illnesses. They were often exhausted, tired, and had back and stomach problems. Many were unable to work. Several were obviously depressed. Many of them were on strong medication, and most of them had been to numerous consultations and examinations. Their illnesses were complex, and their encounters with the Norwegian healthcare system had often been un- successful, filled with conflict and of little use.

We know that there are big social health differences in Norway, but is there a willingness to look at the complexity in this picture and find the real causes? Are we willing to try to manage a continually growing problem for the welfare system in an adequate way? One thing is sure, we cannot go on looking at the situation of these women just from a biomedical perspective that isolates their health issues as fragmented physical or mental problems. Another thing is also sure, their health problems are not something they just brought with them when they came to Norway. When I met these women, it became clear to me that it is their new life that is most painful. First of all, we must understand their form of suffering is not private, but they have three dimensions: local, national and global accumulated in their body and mind of an immigrant woman which is difficult for the Norwegian health system to understand. We must do two things at the same time: we have to extend the concept of pain and illness, and we have to look at the relation between these women and the society they live in. What are the elements that make up their new lives? The health authority, welfare society of Norway must think in global health or look after the global issue which is dominated of suffering illness and war. How does democratic Norway function for minority women in our globalized world?

The World's most Inclusive Society?

At the beginning of 2006 Prime Minister Jens Stoltenberg who is now the head of NATO presented the idea of Norway as "the world's most inclusive society".[3] Stoltenberg pointed to riots in the French suburbs as an example of what can happen when immigrants are excluded and marginalized. To create the world's most inclusive society, everybody has to be on the team. The target for integration is that "those who live in this country can experience a sense of belonging and membership in the community, with all the possibilities this offers". Stoltenberg started by writing that the creation of the Directorate of Integration and Diversity (IMDi) marks the recognition that we have to rethink immigration policy. When the Red-Green parties formed a government, they ensured that the districts were represented, and that the balance between the genders was in place. Immigrants, however, were ignored. Eventually, after strong criticism from the media and professionals, the Labor Party appointed an immigrant with an Indian background, Krishna Chudasama, as a ministerial state secretary. She had a radical suggestion to solve the problems of minority women, namely that minority children should get priority when it came to places in the kindergarten.

The "immigrant alibi" Chudasama was, after a while, replaced by Hadia Tajik, who eventually gained real power as an advisor to the prime minister.[4] In the fall of 2007, there was another ray of light. The Norwegian government had its first minister with a non-Norwegian background, Manuela Ramin-Osmundsen. The joy was short lived.

Exclusion of immigrants and minorities from the political process is nothing new. Political Norway separates between "us" and "them", between majority and minority.[5] And even if this way of thinking accepts minorities being included in the political process, their participation is limited to being representatives for "the others". When it comes to issues more directly affecting "us" - the national majority - they are often marginalized. In comparison with earlier Norwegian governments, it seems that politicians under the so-called Soria Moria discussions were concerned with forming a government adapted to the majority society. What the government imagined as the community, the Norwegian nation, is identified with ethnic Norwegian persons. Minorities do not belong to this community in the same way.

This exclusion reflects the political situation for minorities more generally. They had lack of influence and real power. When minorities are encouraged to speak in public, it is about their religion and issues Norwegian politicians attach to their culture, such as circumcision, imams and re- pression of women. General allocation policy, housing policy and the Norwegian healthcare system are issues that minorities typically do not comment on, but that mostly concerns them. Minorities are looked upon as "sand in the gears", as a disturbing element in the imagined Norwegian society.[6] There is still much resistance against looking at the globalized reality: that the Norwegian society has changed. Norway has, during a few decades, become a totally new society with a different mix, but many are not able to get rid of the term ethnic Norwegian as a main character in the national concept.

The Norwegian public is, in various ways, dominated by a clear distinction between "us" and "the others", where minorities are looked upon as a fundamentally different group of people. The real contribution of minorities to the Norwegian society has been made invisible. On the surface, especially as presented by the press, it looks like they often exploit "our" welfare system. The single individual and his or her particular immigration story with causes that lies beyond the individual, disappears to the advantage of a concept of large groups who themselves have chosen to come to the Norwegian welfare state - as if the individual made this choice based on many options. Again, they privatized the problem of immigration such an individual choice to come to Norway. Many women talked to me that they just came here due to escape from war since the war pushed them to become an immigrant rather to their choice.

The prime minister is concerned about integration in the neighbourhood, in the football team and during the lunch break, but for this to work, the state has to use its power to define and include - not ignore. The positive Nordic social-democratic thought of everybody being on the same team, created optimism. But it has to be combined with the will not to reduce people to statistical images of cultures, religions and nationalities. If we make real the idea of equality and solidarity for all, we are well on our way to actually creating the world's most inclusive society together.

Basic Human Rights and Opportunity

The Norwegian social anthropologist, Unni Wikan, already in 2002, raised the question of how we can ensure equal possibilities for immigrants and their children. Today, Norwegian authorities and scientists still lack an answer to this question. Wikan pointed to a decisive principle that has to be realized if equal opportunities are to become a reality, namely that we recognize the basic and universal rights of each individual. She writes: "I argue a universal discourse that recognizes the basic integrity of each separate human individual and the irreplaceable value of respect for human rights."[7] The recent riots in France show the possible consequences of a purely universalistic way of thinking and an indifference concerning the difficult situation of minorities. For a universalistic way of thinking to work, I think we first have to ensure the basic needs of people, i.e., psychological needs as well as the need for economic and legal security. This is a prerequisite for the development of human opportunities. The perspective of Wikan is problematic because the asymmetric relation between majority and minority is ignored. The reality is that minorities in Norway do not have the opportunity to compete on the same terms as the majority - for example, they have less power, lower education, weaker economy, larger problems related to illness, and they often lack a social network.

To compete on equal terms means a society without differences. But there are big differences in Norway, also among ethnic Norwegians. "The Norwegian society is divided by class in many areas. Everything from income to health is characterized by social background."[8] In this community, minority women often find themselves at the bottom.

The Pain of Minority Women: A Question of Quality of Life

An optimal condition of health can be defined as a condition of physical, mental and social wellbeing.[9] Good health is about quality of life, and quality of life has an obvious connection with the total situation of the individual. My respondents lacked this quality of life.[10]

The German philosopher Axel Honneth puts forward three forms of recognition that are fundamental aspects of a normative idea of the good life. The first form of recognition can be achieved privately, in the closest of relationships. Here, love is given and received, so that people have the opportunity to develop confidence in themselves, their abilities and values, i.e., self-esteem. The other sphere for recognition is as a legal entity and citizen in a democratic society. The general respect embodied in having rights in the society we live in, confers legitimacy to our own needs. This gives us self-respect. The third sphere for recognition is the cultural, political and occupational community. Here one is part of a community with common values that at the same time is open to diversity. This gives us a sense of our own value.

The opposite of recognition is violation. When the three fundamental needs for recognition are ignored, this creates conflict. Various forms of violation, in private and in public, created the background for a completely necessary struggle for recognition. Recognition on different levels is, thereby, not only a prerequisite for the good life, but also for a well-integrated society.

I believe Honneth's understanding of the political battle of today as a fight for recognition is highly relevant when one looks at the relation between the majority and the minority in Norwegian society, and, especially, if one looks at the situation of minority women. But where Honneth sees a condition similar to a depression as a symptom of the circumstances not being right for attaining recognition, I also see an undefined and extensive pain.

Pain is the barometer of the human body, an expression of how you really are. Pain is a subjective feeling that can have many causes. It can be a reaction to a physiological illness the doctor can see and confirm from examining the patient and various test results. But pain can also be so much more: an expression of a lack of feeling well, physically, mentally or socially. Consequently, pain is an expression for what kind of life we live.

To find out how minority women in today's Norway actually feel, we have to look at how they live. Their total situation is formed by the social field individuals are in, the environment that makes up the living space of people.[11] Some of these spheres are connected to negative values, while others are positive. What value we put in these social fields, often has to do with our relationship to other people in the particular arena. For most people, it is necessary for their interaction with others to give a good feeling of togetherness, to understand and find meaning in what is happening, and to be able to predict and have influence on what is happening. When an individual "loses" in his or her relations - in terms of not attaining recognition and communication - those individual feels powerlessness. Then pain often invades the body and becomes dominant. Powerlessness become large symptom of our globalized world.

To find out more about the lives of these minority women, we therefore have to look closer at the social fields they are in, where do they live? What relations do they have? What institutions do they relate to? How do they settle down in their new Norwegian life?

2. Lives of Suffering

Arezo, Belquis, Elisabeth, Baarin, Shogofa, Shaeen, Nasrin, Tajeba, Kamille and Ezat tell stories about themselves and their life that have important similarities with the stories and experiences of many other minority women. Most of the women in my story have a Muslim background, but two of them are not personally religious. They all came to Norway as adults, from Chile, Afghanistan, Somalia, Pakistan, Iran, Morocco and Sudan. Four came as refugees, one came to her husband through family reunion, and one came together with her husband who was an immigrant worker. The rest of them have immigrated to Norway for various reasons. They are all between 30 and 48 years of age, they all have children, and most of them are married or have been so. Baarin was studying. Shaeen has a tertiary education, Shogofa is a teacher, while Belquis, Arezo and Tajeba only went to school for a few years. When I met them, nobody had a job. Shogofa later got work, and Belquis and Shaeen had been working, but were unemployed at the time.

Arezo's story

I call her Arezo, "hope" in Persian. This name helped me to write about her life. Arezo is in her late thirties and has three children. She has lived in Norway for more than 21 years. She was born in a small and isolated village in Pakistan. She has only a partial primary education from her homeland. She came here after being married at the age of 16, as a second wife to her husband. Despite just taking a short course in Norwegian, she speaks the language well.

Arezo's life is difficult. It revolves around family duties, coping financially and preserving the family honor. Also, the life of her family is demanding. They have worked all the time since they came to Norway, but still are living in constant poverty. Since Arezo came to the country, she has worked in the shop of her husband. She is also responsible for her parents-in-law who are in need of care and who live together with her and her husband. In addition, she is responsible for her mother in Pakistan who is ill. I asked her why her mother- and father-in-law did not apply for a place at a retirement home. She answered that it was out of the question. In traditional Pakistani family culture, it is a great shame if parents move to a retirement home. As for herself, she thinks that also Pakistani families - especially women - need the kind of relief nursing and retirement homes can provide.

Arezo has worked hard for many years, both at home and in the shop. Her body is worn out. She has a lot of pain, and in addition, she obviously struggles with depression. Currently, she is ill and goes from one doctor to the next and from one health institution to the other. She cries and says: "Today I didn't manage to hold my teacup. I have so much pain. My doctor doesn't understand me."

Arezo takes a lot of painkillers. She struggles with having her pain accepted in the Norwegian bureaucratic health and welfare system because what she describes does not fall into the criteria for diagnosis that social security uses. She also struggles with making the doctor understand that she is actually ill because there is no good physiological explanation for the pain she experiences.

Despite having worked hard in Norway all her adult life, Arezo, officially, has never had any work. She has never been registered as an employee. The reason is twofold: When Arezo immigrated to Norway in the early 1980's, she became linked to the private sphere of her husband

- both by her husband and by the Norwegian authorities. Consequently, she became invisible in official Norway. Nor did the Norwegian authorities recognize Pakistani women as independent individuals. They were looked upon as "helpers" to the Pakistani man, completely accepted as inferiors who should only assist their husbands in being good workers in their new homeland. Consequently, the work of Pakistani women was never recognized, neither privately nor officially.

Arezo has extremely limited knowledge concerning the laws and regulations of Norway, and how the society works. The result was that she understood too late how important it was to be registered as an employee when she was actually working. This lack of knowledge about modern institutions makes her life difficult in general and prevents her from improving her situation. It is worth noting that Arezo has this in common with a lot of minority women. The consequence is that they, now as when they came, are economically dependent on their husbands. This results in them not having earned any pension points for their retirement, even if they have actually worked hard all their lives. Furthermore, the consequence for Arezo is that her request for disability benefits is also denied.

The financial dependency on their husbands of many minority women, lead to them having to give in to the demands of the strongly patriarchal and traditional family life of their husbands and their families. It is a fact of life for Arezo. Her life unfolds within the four walls of the apartment. She cares for the old and sick in the family. She has sole responsibility for the children.

Arezo is burdened with worries. She feels strongly denigrated when the social welfare office tells her that she has never worked. "I want disability benefits, but the social welfare office does not accept it." Arezo is obviously too sick to work. In reality, she doesn't even have the capacity to take care of her parents-in-law. In addition, her parents-in-law function as an extension of her husband's authority and controls her. They ensure that she behaves as a traditional chaste woman, according to their understanding. Her husband, who is considerably older, is happy that his parents have taken on this policing function - it helps him to control her.

Arezo is like Nora in Ibsen's "A Doll's House", but with a hijab. She struggles against the suppressed female role her husband and his family try to put her into. Like Nora, she does not wish to be trapped at home. She wants to break free from a husband who doesn't understand her needs. She mourns a lot over the 21 years she has lost being married and dominated by her husband. "When I married him, my miserable life began."

Despite her rebellious attitude concerning the traditional patriarchal family structure, she is unable to react as she has no means to do so. She does not understand the Norwegian welfare system, and she is "punished" for not having learnt how it works. She does not know her own rights or how to act to oppose decisions she feels are wrong. Her attitude is fatalistic and resigned: "We are immigrants," she says, "they think we only come to take money from the welfare system, which is why we get no help. They forget that we also have participated in building Norway. My family has worked many years in various jobs in NSB (the Norwegian Railways), so that the trains can travel from one end of Norway to the other. But when Norwegians sit comfortably on the train to Northern-Norway, they forget this."

I met Arezo the first time in a Norwegian Christian organization I shall call the Jacob Center. This organization wanted to help minority women, and formed, probably with the best of intentions, a Quran Group. Arezo participated in the Quran Group, and we sat together and talked during the breaks. She told me that she had come to the group "to find peace and quiet" in her life. "I want to do something else than being at home all the time," she said, "I'm escaping from my pain." Her search for peace and quiet was connected to getting away from her difficult life, a search for thinking about something else other than the tiresome job in the shop of her husband and family problems. She had come to the Quran Group because she didn't know any other services. Just the same, after visiting this organization twice, once in the Quran Group and once in an exercise group, she concluded that it didn't help her. She thought the Quran teacher talked too much about punishment: "Just like my mother-in-law: Everything is about punishment, 'God punishes us, God sends illnesses upon us'. Why does God send all illnesses and punishments to the Muslims? Everybody in the Muslim world experiences such misery and poverty."

Arezo seemed to be an insecure woman, and she was very tired the

first time we met. Like many other women I met, she didn't just de- scribe her body as filled with pain, but also her thoughts. She was in a hopeless situation, both in terms of her health and her economy. And, I would venture to claim, lack of knowledge made it impossible for her to move on in life. Knowledge is also about power, and lack of knowledge often leads to powerlessness.

It is interesting to note that Arezo looked for a Norwegian institution to get away from her troublesome daily life. This was not a place where she wanted to confirm her own culture or religion. But what she met was exactly what she didn't like, and what she was escaping from: thoughts about sin, punishment and honor.

Belquis's story

I first met Belquis when we stood together and made zometza - an Arabic dish - at a Ramadan celebration at the Jacob Center. It was difficult and labor-intensive to make zometza, and while I struggled to keep up with the pace, Belquis had no problems at all. On the contrary, she loved the actual work involved in making the dish. When she saw how much I struggled, she laughed and asked me if my mother hadn't taught med anything about household chores. I told her that my mother died when I was young, and she came over full of sympathy (and dough on her hands) and gave me a big hug - the ice was broken. The hard work made her warmup, and after a quick glance for men nearby, she took off her hijab. I said: "Oh, you are so beautiful without your hijab." She laughed and said: "Yes, I remember my husband said the same thing", with a voice filled with both happiness and sorrow. "We were taught to show the most beautiful part of our body only to our husband."

Belquis is in her forties, has three children and comes from Sudan.

She is a single mother after her husband died a few years ago. One of her children is chronically ill. She worked for many years as a cleaner in a company in Oslo. She has no education and is very religious. Her identity as a "Muslim" is very important to her.

Belquis's three children are between 11 and 20 years of age. It is very difficult to fulfill both their material and emotional needs. Belquis has to function both as a mother and a father, despite the fact that she has been taught to think of these roles as fundamentally different. For Belquis, many of her tasks are traditionally the work of the man. She thinks that the situation she is in is the will of God and struggles to do her best. "I do not want the children to feel that I'm mourning," she says.

She has worked hard because she wanted a better life, and because she wanted her children to get an education. She thinks a good education might prevent them from experiencing the same hate she feels against herself in Norway. Belquis is convinced that Norwegians don't like her. Most of the time, she feels totally isolated from Norwegian society.

Belquis's situation was and is generally difficult. When I first met her, she had a stressful and unsatisfying job in addition to being in conflict with her boss. She felt that her boss was a racist, and that she disliked her. Belquis got up at five in the morning, fixed breakfast for her children and went off to work before they went to school. Even if her job was hard, the wage was very poor, but she didn't dare to complain. "If you say anything against the boss or complain, you will be replaced," she said. She had to wash 33 toilets and several long corridors in a very short time, corridors where the employee's used scooters because they were so long. While she talked about her difficult situation at work she started to cry. When she came home from work, she was very tired. Her daughter's chronic illness compounded her worries. She didn't have any energy left to cook for her children or help them with their homework. This made her very sad. She was also very unhappy because she was in such a bad mood when she came home to her children. "I say to my children that they must go to their room" - she looks at her bed and continues: "while I go to my grave and throw myself in it".

In addition to the work itself being difficult and not particularly satisfying, the continually growing conflict with her boss made her working days even worse for Belquis. She told me that she cried several times on her way from work while she thought: "One day God will punish my boss." To me, she compared her boss to Sharon and Bush.

In the beginning, she didn't know that she had rights as a worker, among which was the right to be organized in a union. After a while she contacted the LO (workers union) and joined up. The union came in as a negotiating partner in the conflict between her and her boss. Despite this, when they didn't come to any agreement, Belquis was told it was better if she took sick leave. The boss had also accused her of doing a poor job. She showed me a worn work testimonial from a lady she used to clean for. This was now the only proof that she had ever worked in a proper and honest way.

While she was on sick leave because of the problematic working relation, Belquis suffered an accident that made it difficult for her to move. Because of this, she is not able to work any longer. In contrast to Arezo, Belquis does not want to get disability benefits. She wants to get well so that she can start working again. She owns her own apartment and has to cope with the mortgage payments. She also thinks it is important to work, so that she can later acquire a better pension. Belquis has a lot of pain, and like Arezo, she doesn't feel she gets any help when she sees the doctor. She has problems sleeping and feels far from rested in the morning when she wakes up.

Since she no longer trusts her doctors, she chooses to read a part of a hadith instead of taking her sleeping pills. Belquis shows me a hadith where she finds a citation that she reads 30 times each evening. A hadith is a passage of scripture about the statements and deeds of the prophet. She feels calmer after the reading. "If every Muslim reads this, everything will be fine," she says.

Belquis has had and has a life with a lot of stress. As a single mother, she has to learn to cope in her encounters with Norwegian reality.

Despite Belquis having managed to acquire knowledge about Norwegian society in the years of living in the country, this knowledge is fragmented and incomplete. This is the case for both the Norwegian system and what Norwegians in general stand for.

The thoughts of Belquis are, to a considerable extent, created by the media, by how they serve up reality on the TV screen in her own living room. She lives in isolation and feels excluded from the society at large, while the nuances in the real world disappear. Why does Belquis, who isn't even from Palestine herself, associate the conflict with her boss with the conflict in the Middle East? In the same way as she feels that she is being exposed to simplified beliefs concerning immigrants, she herself uses simplifications and beliefs about conflict when she de- scribes her reality. To her, many Norwegians are racists. She is not able to see that the society she lives in, compared to other countries, is the best country when it comes to welfare, prosperity and protection of the rights and needs of the individual. In her experience, this is not the case.

What the Numbers Tell Us: The Social Distribution of Illness in Oslo

Norway is a country with considerable differences in the population's health. At the same time, Norway is often portrayed as a society without big social differences. But for several years we have known about major health problems among minority women. Do we not also know something about the causes?

As mentioned, in 2002 the National Health Institute published a health study for Oslo (the HUBRO survey)[1]. The publication was based on a big health survey in Oslo municipality, where a big representative sample of the adult population participated. The survey showed clearly how variables such as gender, age, residence, education, employment situation and country of birth influenced health conditions. The survey also showed that the immigrant population had worse health than the population defined as ethnic Norwegian.

Figure 1: Different distribution of pain for men and women

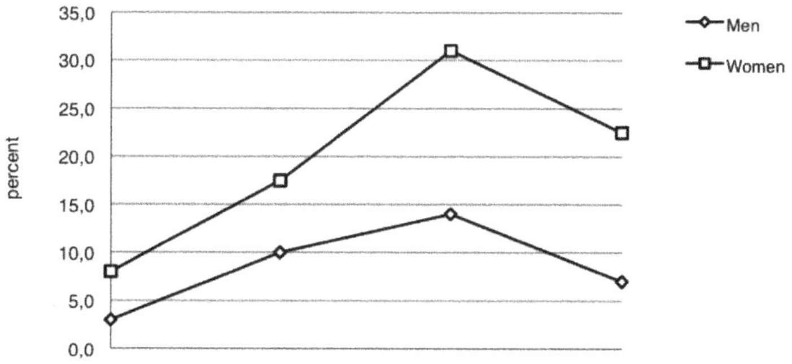

30 years   40+ 45 years   59–60 years   75–76 years

Source: HUBRO

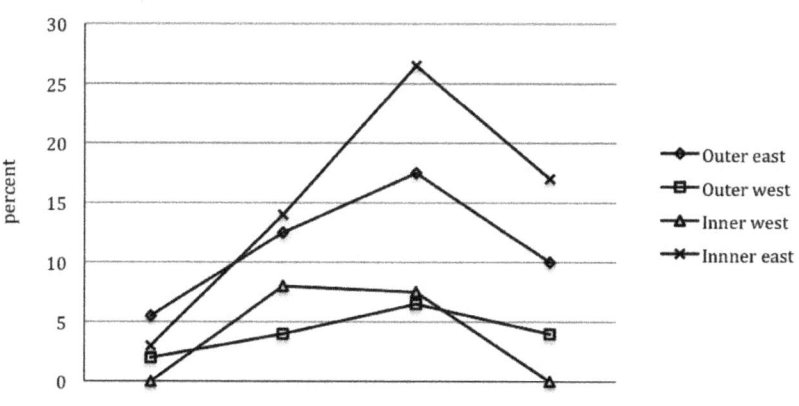

Figure 2: Men reporting pain

30 years   40+ 45 years   59–60 years 75–76 years

Source: HUBRO

The data in this study is confirmed by the stories of my respondents. For example, the study showed that highly educated women handled pain better than those with low education, and pain and illness was, to a lesser extent, part of daily life for those with a permanent job.

Figure 3: Women reporting pain

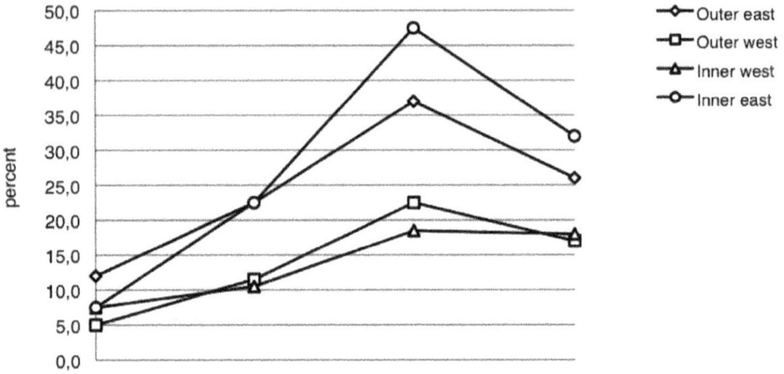

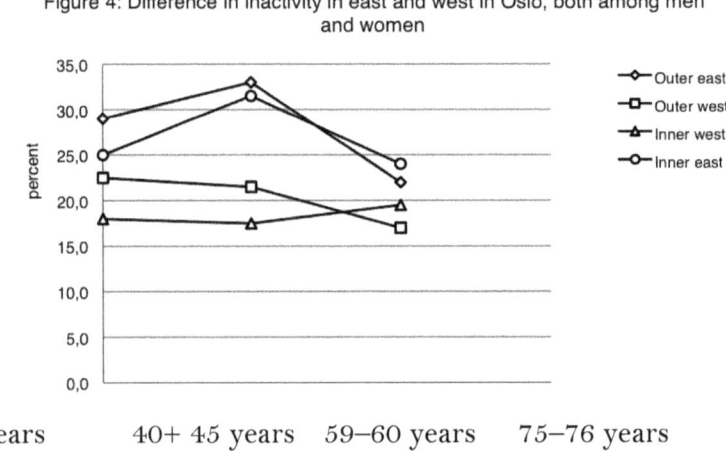

Source: HUBRO

Figure 4: Difference in inactivity in east and west in Oslo, both among men and women

Source: HUBRO

Among women with work and many children, stress was a factor that created pain in another way. The most common condition among women with- out a job was a feeling of hopelessness and lack of meaning.

Figure 5: Difference in inactivity in east and west in Oslo, only women

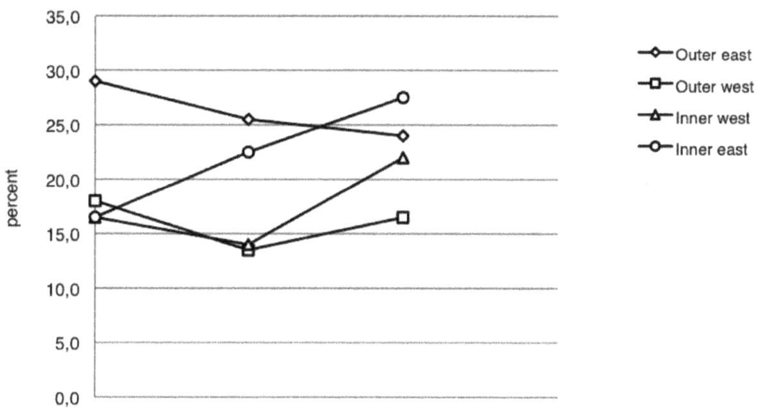

30 years   40+ 45 years   59–60 years   75–76 years

Source: HUBRO

The study used the term "non-Western immigrants". This category is problematic because it emphasizes ethnic affiliation in a way that conceals socioeconomic conditions.[2] On one hand, there are "non-Western immigrants" with higher education and work, and among these, health conditions are different. On the other hand, it is very difficult for non-Western immigrants to get a job in Norway and other Western countries. This also applies to immigrants with higher education.

What is interesting about this important study is that the category "non-Western immigrant" can be seen in relation to other variables. Only in this way we can find out more about the causes for the poor health of non-Western minority women.

Health conditions are not neutral. They are in no way connected solely to individual conditions. From quantitative studies and statistics, we know that health conditions often are associated with socioeconomic and social conditions. This not only applies to minorities and immigrants, but also "Norwegians". For example, the health profile of Oslo shows great variations in health between persons living in western Oslo and eastern Oslo, in addition to variations between genders.

In the health profile for Oslo, pain was one of the categories the respondents of the study were asked about. Most importantly, this part of the study shows a clearly different distribution of pain for women and men (see figure 1).

Women, regardless of religion, culture and nationality, have more pain than adult men. The quantitative study also shows us that the number of people who identify their suffering as pain is far greater in the eastern part of town than in the western part.

The study shows that 48 percent of older adult women in the city's inner east side say that they suffer from pain, against only 18 percent in the inner west side -a difference of 30 percent. The difference between older adult men in the city's inner east side and inner west side is 18 percent.

This tells us that the area of residence is a startlingly crucial factor, and that the difference between women and men is amplified further by the environment. In the survey, we find a further wide difference in lack of activity in the eastern part compared to the western part of Oslo. Physical activity is undeniably an important factor connected to people's health.

Figure 6: Physically inactive. Oslo 2000 - 2001. In percent. Chi-square method is used to calculate p-value (* $0.01 < p \leq 0.05$, *** $p \leq 0.001$, ns no significance). Source: HUBRO.

	30 years		40+ 45 years		59- 60 years	
	Women	Men	Women	Men	Women	Men
All	22	25	20	28	22	21
Education						
Primary school	44	30	38	42	29	20
Secondary school	35	35	25	29	21	23
University/college	18	23	16	26	18	20
Statistic sign.	***	***	***	***	***	ns
Employment						
Non-profit work	30	22	28	35	25	20
Part time	24	28	17	33	19	19
Full time	20	25	19	27	21	21
Statistic sign.	***	ns	***	*	*	ns
Marital status						
Living together with spouse or partner	23	27	19	29	21	20
Single with or without children	21	20	24	25	32	22
Statistic sign.	ns	ns	*	ns	*	ns
Country of birth						
Norway	19	23	17	24	21	20
Western-Europe, North- America or Australia	16	28	12	25	21	17
"Non-Western"	45	42	49	49	49	34
Statistic sign.	***	***	***	***	***	****

Figure 7: Persons afflicted with a lot of pain/stiffness in muscles and joints. Oslo 2000- 2001. In percent. Chi-square method is used to calculate p-value (*** p ≤ 0.001, ns no significance). Source: HUBRO.

	30 years		40+ 45 years		59- 60 years	
	Women	Men	Women	Men	Women	Men
All	9	4	18	10	31	14
Education						
Primary school	20	2	38	19	40	25
Secondary school	14	9	22	14	33	17
University/college	7	2	13	7	23	7
Statistic sign.	***	***	***	***	***	***
Employment						
Non-profit work	15	10	39	27	50	35
Part time	12	5	14	19	30	17
Full time	7	3	13	7	20	8
Statistic sign.	***	***	***	***	***	***
Marital status						
Living together with spouse or partner	8	4	16	9	30	13
Single with or without children	8	3	26	11	36	17
Statistic sign.	ns	ns	***	ns	ns	ns
Country of birth						
Norway	6	2	14	6	30	12
Western-Europe, North- America or Australia	10	2	11	6	23	13
"Non-Western"	23	16	42	30	54	40
Statistic sign.	***	***	***	***	***	***

According to the study, women in Oslo are generally more inactive than men. The eastern districts of the city where most non-Western immigrants live have the highest proportion of inactive men and women.[3] The proportion of inactive inhabitants is considerably higher among non-Western immigrants than among the Norwegian population and Western immigrants.

In addition to inactivity being connected to an area of residence, we see that it is also directly connected to the level of education, employment and country of origin (see figure 6). "Non-Western women" like "non-Western men", are, as mentioned, far less active than those belonging in the other categories. They also have a lower level of education and a lower employment rate.

Area of residence, education and employment influence the total life situation for most of us because they also impact our financial situation. The HUBRO study showed a clear connection between these important factors of the kind of life situation people actually have, and whether they are afflicted by a lot of pain (see figure 7).

In addition, numbers from the Central Bureau of Statistics show that the registered unemployment rate among immigrants is high (5.6 per- cent among immigrants compared to 1.7 percent among the majority). Immigrants from Somalia and Afghanistan are among the groups with the lowest employment rate, being 31.7 percent and 41.7 percent respectively in 2006.[4] Unemployment is an important cause of poverty. A report from the Central Bureau of Statistics sums up: "Non-Western immigrants make up just over 6 percent of the population, but 32 per- cent of them live below the minimum income level in the EU. If the EU definition of 'poverty' is used, then persons in non-Western immigrant households have three times as high a probability of belonging to the low-income group compared to the population as a whole."[5]

Also concerning employment, there is a big difference between the genders among immigrants, especially for immigrants from Pakistan, Afghanistan and Somalia. The Central Bureau of Statistics reports that the rate of employment among women from Pakistan is 29.1 percent, while the rate is 62.2 for the men. For Afghans, the employment rate is 23.8 percent for women compared to 54.1 percent for men, while Somalis have an employment rate of 40.4 percent for men and only 21.4 percent for women.[6] Immigrants mainly live in the eastern part of Oslo. In general, we see that the population there has lower education, higher unemployment and, obviously, weaker health than those living in the western part of Oslo.

The statistics show exactly the same pattern when it comes to pain and stiffness in muscles and joints, as well as for diabetes, accidents and injuries, mental health and suicide.[7] According to the psychiatrist, Edvard Hauff, who has studied the figures from the previously mentioned health study, immigrants and refugees from non-Western countries have more than twice as high a risk of developing mental problems as the rest of the population or immigrants from Western countries. "It seems that financial well-being is what protects best against anxiety and depression." Hauff finds some differences between women and men: "Not to work and feeling discriminated in the employment market is what wears most on the men, in addition to trauma from their home country."

Also, when it comes to women, he sees a connection between mental problems and lack of paid work, but women struggle especially with the feeling of being discriminated against in the housing market.[8]

Whether or not one has good health is, consequently, connected to the factors that make up our total situation in life. Where and how one lives, whether or not one has a job and, consequently, money, and whether or not one has the opportunity to have an education, are fac- tors we know are absolutely decisive for how we feel. This has been known from statistical material for years. Norway is a country with great social health differences.

When the various figures are collated, the study also shows that "non-Western" women have the most problems with their health. And we know that these women often stay in apartments that are more cramped than what Norwegians like, and in places and in apartment blocks where Norwegians don't want to live. We know many of them have low education, and we know only a few of them have jobs - and from this, we can infer that many also are financially weak. If something is to be done about their health, it is obvious that we have to change some of these factors in their lives. Is this possible? And is it enough?

Edvard Hauff thinks that even if the previously mentioned health study deals with the population of Oslo, the results would be about the same in the country as a whole. According to Hauff, the Norwegian government has to do something about the social and economic differences that are about to develop between the majority population and minority groups in Norway: "The Norwegian health care system has not, in particular, taken into account that Norway has become multicultural. In many Western countries, subgroups are formed where ethnicity and poor living conditions go hand in hand. We ought to prevent the same pattern from taking root in Norway."[9]

Many of the women I met wanted to work. They thought education was important but were not in a situation where it was possible for them to study. However, they wanted their children to have that opportunity. Those who had an education seldom made anything of it in terms of work. Several of the women had been advised to be more active. They themselves knew that this was important and wanted to improve their health condition somewhat, but they had problems accomplishing this in practice. I saw the figures tallied in the statistics being "lived" as a vicious circle where causes and effects could not be separated: unemployment, poor living conditions, lack of education and knowledge, inactivity, a feeling of hopelessness, illness, pain and depression, weak financial situation.

But I also saw something more fundamental. I saw, again and again, that the feeling of powerlessness had its own dynamics. For when these women seek help, they often experience that the situation only becomes worse. In their encounters with the institutions of the society at large, they seldom feel understood, and they seldom feel that their needs are acknowledged. Their ability to take control and get an understanding of their own situation, and to do something about it, was not changed. And the lack of recognition was constant.

In spite of the health conditions of many being so obviously connected to how they lived and how they felt in a wider perspective, I experienced that many of the women I met, did not choose constructive strategies to improve the circumstances of their lives - the reality surrounding them and their relation to it. They had a clear feeling of their own situation being hopeless. In spite of this, they didn't manage to change the situation to the extent that it was helpful.

Basically, they all sought out the same kind of help as ethnic Norwegian women did, the doctor.

Common for the women I met was that they had been to the doctor countless times, and that many of them felt they had no credibility left in the eyes of their GP (doctor). After hearing countless stories about consultations filled with conflict with their GP, I am convinced that minority women have a far more problematic encounter with the health care system than Norwegian women. One of the most important institutions minority women encounter in Norway is the health care system. It is therefore crucial to look closer at what these encounters full of conflict are all about.

Arezo at the Doctor's Office

Arezo explains her failed visit to the doctor like this: "My doctor gives me painkillers that only work short term. Norwegian doctors are strange. When I visit him, he is occupied with his computer. He doesn't look at me but asks questions about where I live and writes this on his computer. I miss a doctor who talks to me and who has enough time to listen to me. There is no time to explain that I cannot go to the gym."

"Maybe this is my destiny," she adds in a depressed tone. "Even if I pray five times a day, maybe it is a punishment from God, you never know."

Within Western biomedicine, a rational and individualistic way of thinking and practice is used. Social aspects of illnesses are, to a very small extent, taken into account.[9] My respondents, on their side, come to get help for pain that, to a large extent, is caused by social conditions. I think this is the main reason why they are often dissatisfied with their doctors, and that the relation to the doctor, so often, is characterized by conflict.[10] The doctors, on their side, are often dissatisfied with patients like Arezo. Professor in general medicine Kirsti Malterud puts it this way, after many years' experience with research on the health of women: "Medical theories and practices have an obligation to challenge their lack of recognition. Today, it is usually the woman who gets the blame for the doctor's lack of understanding."[11]

In an interview with the doctor at the Tøyen Health Center in Oslo, who works a lot with minority women, I was told that minority women themselves are responsible for their health. The doctor also believed that these women did not listen to recommendations: "They don't want to become better," she said.

Arezo experiences the same attitude from her doctor: "In the end the doctor said that he couldn't give me any more help. I had to find out how I could cope with my life, he said, and live with the pain." Ideally, Arezo should be able to find better solutions. But do we progress any further by insisting that health is an individual responsibility?

Arezo complained that her doctor had little time to actually listen to what she says. The current GP system has little room for spending the necessary time on many patients. The demands on efficiency and earnings lead to doctors having limited opportunity to evaluate the total life situation of each patient, even if it is stated in the Report to the Storting no. 49 (2003-2004) that health services must take this into account.[12] However, it is not noted who must take this into consideration, or in what way.

Another of the women I met, Shaeen, told me that she had tried everything the doctor had offered her without success. In the end, she too was told that she had to "cope" with her life and learn to live with the pain. Both she and Arezo were advised to exercise. But there are obstacles in the way for such individualistic measures to be implemented and to become effective. Both for finding the causes and for taking the measures to get better, we must dare to look at the social structures involved in creating the pain and suffering that people like Arezo and Shaeen experience - and then to do something about them. The first step on the way to getting a better insight of the causes might be looking at factors such as understanding, responsiveness, and recognition.

The health care system, as it functions today, only to a limited degree captures the problems minority women struggle with most. The physical body is at the center of these problems. Physical examinations involve X-rays and blood samples, while the solution is often medication. The biomedical perspective doesn't in any way cover a complete understanding of human health problems. In the meeting with minority women, an exclusive focus on biomedicine becomes fatal. Medication pacifies while an active awareness of the root of the problems becomes continually more pressing.

We cannot choose to ignore this. Non-Western minority women in Norway have startlingly poor health. We cannot progress any further if we exclusively look at this as an individual problem that can be solved by individual means. To solve the problem, we have to put the whole human being and its quality of life into focus.

Arezo, Shaeen and many others have a quality of life most people from the majority of the Norwegian population would consider very poor: shortage of money for the most essential products, illness, disability, frustration and isolation.

We must dare to look on how Norwegian society functions - or not function - for these women. These are people who don't do well but are unable to communicate with the one person they're most likely to meet from the majority society, their GP.

The needs of these women are complex. But the solutions are neither, exclusively, to offer individual solutions that require surplus energy, such as physical activity, nor to connect their pain to culture, religion and ethnicity, as the doctor in Tøyen did.[13]

The doctor says that "they" do not want to become better and makes it clear that "they" means non-Western women from Muslim societies. Nor is medication the only solution. Many of my respondents tell me that the medication they get only makes them more passive. Consequently, the result is that the public agency they sought out for help, pacify them even more. In this way these women become an even bigger "burden" to the Norwegian welfare state.

Passive Coping Strategies (Belquis)

Passive coping strategies are strategies that don't identify the real causes of suffering and pain.[14] The tell-tale sign of passive coping strategies is simply that they don't work, and in some cases, contribute toward reproducing the pain and the difficult situation. Instead of raising awareness they lead to acceptance and resignation of the situation. In a way, we can say that this is what happens both on an institutional and an individual level. The health care system doesn't address the complex causes of the serious health problems of these women. This is a kind of institutional resignation. But the same thing happens also on an individual level, among the women themselves. One example is Belquis reading the Quran every night. Belquis has a lot of pain and has problems sleeping. The doctor has given her sleeping pills, but "I don't take the medication," she says.

The pills make her too sleepy in the morning. "I read a religious text. The text is about how a man came to the prophet Mohammed to get advice concerning how to cope with his pains. The prophet Mohammed told him to read a hadith about moral actions 30 times a day. Then he would be able to sleep and have a happy life. The prophet also said that pain is a punishment from God, and people, therefore, have to act morally right to avoid it." It is this text Belquis reads 30 times every night in the hope of making her better. She has received the text from the Jacob Center.

The efforts of Belquis to be a good and moral Muslim combined with the problems she faces in her painful social environment, becomes a contradiction whereby she is unable to find effective coping strategies. It becomes an unmanageable conflict between how she feels she "should" live, according to the Quran, and how she actually has the possibility to live.15 When she goes to bed, these contradictory and chaotic thoughts manifest themselves so strongly that it becomes impossible for her to sleep. The fact that she sets high standards for herself creates much of the frustration that makes her ill.

Christmas, summer vacation and Easter are often characterized by conflict and sadness among minority families, especially the children. The holiday period, which is of great importance to most Norwegians, is stressful. The whole of December, the children participate in Christmas preparations at school and are affected by the joyful atmosphere of Christmas. It is quite a contrast to come home for them. Belquis perceives Christmas as a Christian tradition, while her children take joy in Christmas regardless of what tradition it is.

Around Christmas time, I got a phone call from Belquis. She was very unhappy and told me that she wasn't able to sleep even after reading various religious texts 60 times. She had quarreled with her children who wanted a Christmas tree, but she had refused because Christmas was a Christian celebration. She was also worried that she was losing control over her children. Since she hadn't slept, she was very tired and irritable, and she had yelled at her children, something she regretted deeply now. She was in despair, and the children were very unhappy.

She told me that she hadn't managed to cook or do anything for her children, and she was paralyzed to act. I invited her over to eat good halal food. Not long after she arrived, our children played together and sang Christmas songs they had learned at school.

I had a Christmas tree for the sake of my children. I am also not a Christian, but the tree was something I had because it made my children happy. Belquis saw that the children were happy and agreed it was right. "Look, my Habibi! Look how happy he is!" Still, she felt that she could not do the same. I was not religious, she said, but she was, and this was a Christian celebration. Still, at least one problem was solved. The children had the pleasure of celebrating Christmas without Belquis having to embrace what she considered religious symbols of "the others".

Even if a lot of research shows that religion can help people to handle difficult situations, it can also lead to a sort of fatalism and resignation concerning problems. This leads to people not taking practical steps or not being able to see practical solutions to their problems. The passive coping strategy of Belquis did not address the actual conditions creating the stressful situation she was in. Belquis had a lot of problems that, primarily, had to be solved practically, but she chose to pray more and more. After a while, she did this not in addition to, but instead of, finding practical solutions. She identified herself more and more with the religious mindset. At the same time, her encounters with other religious traditions became more filled with conflict. She experienced that by giving in to the wishes of her children, she had been "invaded" in her own home - by the belief of the majority.

The dilemma of Belquis rises partly because she belongs to a marginalized group, a group where the boundaries to "the others" both feel too absolute and too vague.[16] The Christmas tree was a symbol belonging to "the others", and by taking it into her home it would cross a boundary. It would become threatening.[17]

She tried to find a solution by reading passages from the Quran twice as many times as normal. In addition to the Quran, she also read other religious texts repeatedly. Even after two or three at night, she couldn't sleep.

Belquis experienced that moral conflicts were "locked" as an unmanageable knot in her mind. Many of the women I met experienced something similar. Practical, financial and ethical problems became completely unsolvable. Encounters with the institutions where they sought a solution, like the health care system, welfare office or religious organizations, often made this feeling worse. Passive coping strategies were often chosen, and they were often connected to religion. At the same time, the unresolved knot remained a part of their minds. And after a while, it spread to their bodies and manifested as physical pain.

What Options Women Have

To see the options available, one has to know which options exist. My work with women in the villages of Afghanistan during the Soviet occupation taught me that practical advice related to the situations people live in, and the options that actually exists, are what helps. This is also the case for minority women in Norway. However, most of them have had little experience with a well-functioning democratic society based on the balance between rights and duties and made up of various institutions with different functions. This has to be learned! The social democratic balance between what you give and what you get is not obvious.

Everybody has a potential for learning. But this implies both the opportunity to learn and the opportunity to use what is learned. To increase one's knowledge about society, one has to live in it, not adjacent to and outside of it. This is also the precondition for being able to choose freely. And if one does not have the opportunity to choose, one also lacks substantive rights.

We have to believe that minority women in Norway today are able to acquire knowledge about the society they live in. Many of those who struggle are just middle-aged. To ignore them and their needs would be to give them up. This causes increased pain and more illness, and in addition, they become bad role models for their children.

To live with prolonged pain and suffering that is not acknowledged, like my respondents do, have consequences for the ability to react sensibly. This leads to loss of hope and an inability to act.18 Passivity when it comes to getting out of a difficult situation often reproduces the differences already there within the society, we live in.

Both Arezo and Belquis had great problems orienting themselves in the Norwegian system. The result is, among other things, that they culturalize the problem by using religion as a solution. In addition, their problem is culturalized by the society at large, one that continually refers to the religion and traditional culture of the women. In this way, a layer of religion and culture will cover the actual social circumstances, which then becomes a part of the problems of these women. The HUBRO study is quite clear on this point: education, finances, and area of residence are social factors that play an important role for people's health. And in addition, I will say, we are dealing with something even more fundamental. The women I met had experienced a lack of recognition of the most important areas in life: in close relations and in vulnerable situations, for example when they sought assistance because of illness.

A problematic social environment also leads to a problematic social

body – that is what we can denote as social suffering and pain. The pains these women experience are often pains connected to their situation as women and minorities. The pains they present to their GP are, consequently, often a condensed and physical expression for extensive problems that to a large extent lies outside them. And to be met with a lack of understanding just makes these problems worse.

To some, the women I describe will appear as complaining, dissatisfied and critical – and tempting to ignore. I think this is a dangerous way to view the issue. Instead of saying they have to do something themselves, I think we have to consider how we can empower them to do so. As a society, we must be able to deal with their pain and weakness. And we also have to admit to the impotence of the institutions that the women encounter – among others, the health care system.

Common for the women I met, is that they first consult a GP. Here, the powerlessness of the patient often meets the powerlessness of the doctor. The Leader of Eastern Norway Regional Health Authority, Pål

Gulbrandsen, expresses it thus: "Health workers are educated to handle illness. Many of them are probably naïve and unprepared for the daily challenges. Often, they cannot fix the problems they encounter. This leads to helplessness, a discomfort we seek to avoid. Among the coping strategies, we find rejection, and simplifying and choosing among tasks if possible."[19] Health care workers also have their own passive coping strategies. When both parties, both the doctor and the patient, avoid and bypass the real problem of the patient, it is unlikely the problem of weak health among minority women is solvable. "Lack of empathy humiliates people every day in the Norwegian health care system, often quietly. Diagnoses are ignored, sufferers are not heard. The system measures productivity, not quality."[20] Pål Gulbrandsen more than suggests that this is a structural problem. In our multicultural society, we have to be willing to look closer at the structural problems of Norwegian institutions. In addition, we have to investigate the life of the minorities in their social environments. But first, we have to look at what basic attitudes the majority society has toward minorities - and vice versa.

3. The Multicultural Society and Multiculturalism

Immigration and the growth of the multicultural society are linked to global processes and relations. Immigration should therefore not be individualized. It is not just the choices of individuals that led to the multicultural society. There are social, political and economic reasons for people emigrating from their countries. Immigration as a process can, consequently, not be understood at an individual or local level. It must be understood as a global phenomenon. We can therefore not hold individual immigrants responsible for the situations they have stumbled into.

The Norwegian public discourse is often characterized by an unrealistic perspective on immigrants. On the one hand it is believed that immigrants, to a considerable extent, have chosen to come here themselves - that individuals are themselves responsible for the situations they are in. On the other hand, the actual immigration story of each immigrant is ignored. The individual's life experiences as an immigrant are almost non-existent in Norwegian public discourse.

The story of an immigrant is precise the story of being robbed of the right to choose. To begin with, most of them could not choose to stay where they were. But in Norway, very few know much about the Cold War and its many negative consequences, or how life really is in Pakistan, Afghanistan or Somalia. Norwegians know that Norwegian history and the contemporary (peaceful) political situation is important in their lives. But the immigrant's often direct experience with historical and international political events is being ignored. They are perceived almost as people without a personal story.

Non-Western immigrants are often perceived as people with a lot of culture and religion. They are perceived as parts of some cultural, ethnic and religious groups. From the time of the first wave of immigration in the 1970s, the relationship between the minority and the majority in Norway has been debated seriously - both politically and officially. They have debated how to integrate and handle groups of people with religious and cultural expressions different from and alien to "what is Norwegian". Does this mean that the Norwegian state has had, politically, a clear and official standpoint concerning immigration?

It has mostly been agreed that integration in some areas is necessary, and that assimilation is not desired. But a coherent policy concerning how the relationship between the majority and the minority ideally should be, has never been presented, neither have the measures been put in place to achieve this. I think Norway has a coherent political strategy, but it is unofficial. I will also argue that this political strategy has a number of negative consequences. I will argue that there is an unofficial multicultural mindset that dominates across the landscape of institutions, political parties, as well as public arenas and discourses.

A multicultural way of thinking is concerned with cultural, religious, and ethnic differences and how these can be safeguarded and financed. A multicultural political strategy is a policy facilitating the preservation of different cultures within Norwegian society. The watchword is cultural diversity. But at what cost? I will argue that there has been, consistently, too much focus on culture, religion and ethnicity - and their differences. This exaggerated concept about differences transforms the "they" who have immigrated to Norway, so that they become fundamentally different from "us", i.e., ethnic Norwegians. The result is a barrier of differences that cannot be crossed. "The others", the immigrants, meet this, both on the mental, social and institutional plane. In reality the individual is vanishing behind the categories of religion, culture, and ethnicity.

As mentioned, I think we can use the philosopher Axel Honneth's concept of recognition to rethink Norwegian integration policy. We are different, but at the same time so alike that we both can recognize our own needs in others, and, not least, that we can acknowledge the other. Honneth takes the three dimensions, love, justice and solidarity, and shows how real recognition is necessary at all these levels to live what most people would call a good life. If we use Honneth's view on recognition of immigrants in Western societies today, I will say that one manages to acknowledge "they" superficially as a group or groups, but not as individuals in line with the majority. This is, unfortunately, no real recognition. Norwegians have to recognize that their minority population wishes to have the same benefits and rights as they have. Only then, will human rights and the rights of women come to the fore.

Multicultural thinking prevents immigrants from achieving a sense of inclusion in Norwegian society. Hence, conflicts arise between majority and minority communities - where the majority has the power, and the minority feels powerless. When minority women tell me about the attitudes they meet, how they live, how difficult it is to get a job, and what is happening to them when encountering a number of Norwegian institutions, I see how this dominating unofficial multicultural- ism manifests itself in a raft of conflicts between majority and minority.

To be perceived everywhere as part of a religious and cultural group that Norwegians have distinctive views on, is generally a burden. On one side, we have a control system and public media with an exaggerated preoccupation with differences. On the other side, as a reaction and consequence, the immigrants have their own preoccupation with cultural differences. This combination, which is quite distinct in Norwegian society, promotes the conservation of cultural differences and conflicts. To understand the consequences of being so preoccupied with differences, we have to look at how these differences actually are perceived. What do we think of those different from us? And how does "the other" experience being perceived so differently from the majority?

In 1966, Mary Douglas published the book Purity and Danger. Here she shows how "matter out of place", meaning material residing in the wrong place in relation to established moral and symbolic systems, is experienced as threatening and polluting. Various scientists have drawn this argument further through showing how groups experiencing a threat, reinforce and support the boundaries separating them from the imagined others.[1] The sociologist, Zygmunt Bauman, has done research on and written a lot about purity and the setting of boundaries. He also points at how globalization has led to a problemization of individual and collective identities.[2] These perspectives are relevant to both the majority and minority in Norway.

Difference is recognized by both parties, while it is increasingly perceived as a threat against ethnic identity, religious values or an imagined national community. I think this is a very important perspective for understanding why Norwegian policy concerning immigrants is based on a categorical distinction between "us" and "they". In Norway, there is an attitude to "the other" that can be found in postcolonial studies, even if Norway has not been a colonial power like, for example, France.[3] This division marks official policy and discourse, but also private opinions and attitudes, and it is not only the Norwegian majority who think along these terms, the minority do so as well.

It is on this premise that we should understand the emergence of the particularistic identities of the minority population, that is, the feeling of identity connected to religion, culture, ethnicity and origin. In his introduction to Bauman, the sociologist Benedetto Vecchi couples this problematic and limiting way of thinking about individual and collective identity directly to the appeal of religious fundamentalism in today's society. He explains how the need for a feeling of identity can be exploited politically thus:

> *The various religious fundamentalisms are nothing more than the transpo- sition of identity on to politics by cynical apprentice magicians. The decep- tion behind this transposition can only be uncovered if you reconstruct the crossover from the individual dimension, which identity always has, to its codification as a social convention. This, I believe, is the central question.*[4]

Belquis is a living example of Vecchi's contention. She coupled her individual identity to the political and religious polarization at the global level. She compared her former boss with Bush and Sharon. As we will see, she also prays for bin Laden to come and make Norway and the world a fair place. We find another example in the story of Shaeen and her rage against the way Norwegian authorities treat the mullah Krekar case.

Because Norwegian authorities and the Norwegian press transform mullah Krekar to a representative for immigrants, they create an enormous polarization in the Norwegian society. In debates, he gets the opportunity to represent something more than himself and his case; he represents the "danger" of immigration. In various ways, this has to do with rigid notions about identity, connected to religion - or more specifically "to being a Muslim" - as the only identity marker. Shaeen feels that the way the media portrays mullah Krekar is a direct violation of her own identity, as a particularly bad and oversimplified representative of something much more diverse. This is the rationale for her complaint: "When I see mullah Krekar on TV, I get a headache."

Mulla Krekar is known as the 'Kurdish bin Laden' and is a wahhabist from Kurdistan. Earlier he had been a teacher at the Peshawar University in Pakistan and had also been running a guesthouse for fighters who travelled to Afghanistan to fight against the Soviet occupation. He came to Norway in 1991 as a refugee together with his family, and even though he was a refugee in Norway, he travelled back and forth to Kurdistan to whip the Kurdish society and burn thousands of books deemed inappropriate, through the rebel group Ansar al-Islam[5]. Krekar has now been convicted and linked to IS, and on March 26 he was deported to Italy. Here he has been convicted of planning terror activities in the West.

Multiculturalism as Political Strategy

The multicultural way of thinking has always been part of a political struggle. When Charles Taylor formulated his philosophy about multiculturalism, it was to secure the rights of the French-speaking people in Quebec in Canada. It was, from the beginning, a political question. Now the concept has undergone a historical evolution.

Today, we see that multiculturalism in the world is taken up and used by strongly conservative religious forces who spark conflicts. In turn, this thinking particularly discriminates against women. Women are losing the battle of getting their rights recognized in Norwegian society. Minority women cannot apply laws in the same way as ethnic Norwegian women because they are remotely controlled by religious forces, imams, their families, and even themselves. Everything to preserve religion, culture, identity and established norms in one's own culture. Therefore, the need for recognition becomes an incomprehensible and difficult struggle.

Multiculturalism is today a contested concept, but it usually refers to one or more political strategies that are used to tackle problems connect- ed to diversity in a multicultural society. In the same way that there exist various multicultural societies, there are many types of multicultural strategies. The focus of multiculturalism is to maintain cultural identity markers. Multicultural policy facilitates the conservation of cultural differences. Often, this is justified by the idea that these differences can be connected to the identity of various ethnic groups. Such facilitation can be, for example, the economic support of various religious communities and allowing them to establish autonomous institutions. The consequence of this may be that one chooses not to get involved with the kind of attitudes the imam expresses towards women, or to take an official standpoint when it comes to practices that the majority does not regard as right or good for its community members.

Most of the various forms of multiculturalism that, for example,

Stuart Hall defines can be found, at least in part, in the Norwegian political landscape and in official discourse. Liberal multiculturalism for example, is an ideal about integrating various cultural groups into a common political framework based on universal and individual citizenship. Pluralist multiculturalism in its turn celebrates differences and erects boundaries between groups based on their cultures. Commercial multiculturalism is based on the belief in markets: As long as people consume in accordance with their culture, all practical difficulties and conflicts connected to cultural differences will dissolve without the need of a more extensive redistribution of resources and power. What Hall calls critical or revolutionary multiculturalism, represents a wish of being multivocal, i.e., having many voices. It fights against power, hegemonies and oppressive hierarchies.[6]

To me, multiculturalism is the political strategy that concerns the institutionalization of differences based on ethnicity, religion and culture, and that institutions based on these categories become autonomous entities in society. In this perspective, to distribute information material in many languages is not multiculturalism. It is just a way to ensure that all citizens in the society have identical information. Education in their native language in school does not need to be part of a multicultural strategy if it is an option that is in addition to learning Norwegian well.

But if it replaces the main focus on Norwegian language, then it can be part of a multicultural strategy and an instrument for maintaining a problematic diversity.

On the homepage of the Center for Studies of Holocaust and Religious Minorities, multiculturalism is defined thus: "Multiculturalism is based on the idea that cultural differences are important to preserve. The more cultures a society encompasses, the richer it is. The problem of placing too much emphasis on cultural differences is that these differences can create boundaries that prevent contact." Later, how this way of thinking is connected to integration is explained: "Multiculturalism is a certain idea for integration. The core in multiculturalism is acceptance of differences. Citizens should have some values in common, but these do not need to involve laws and rules. Cultural or religious philosophy can vary significantly. According to multiculturalism a society can be well integrated and harmonious even if the individuals in the society have very different ideas of what a good life is. A multicultural social order is, in other words, a society where the minorities participate with equal rights and duties without having to give up their national, cultural or religious characteristics."

This is a pretty precise definition of what multiculturalism is. But when the text ends by telling how the Norwegian government handles multiculturalism, the formulations are highly imprecise: "Integration must happen without destroying cultural differences, with the government agreeing to religious and political diversity. Just the same, multi- culturalism is rejected as a political ideology in Norway based on the idea that if a group achieves special rights, then cultural boundaries and differences solidify instead of the result of a natural form of integration." This is wrong. Both economic support and the attitudes of politicians are focused precisely on religious, cultural and ethnic minority groups. The notion of how different we are, leads to a certain way of looking at the relation between "Norwegians" on one side and minorities on the other. This notion also characterizes political Norway.

Religious and cultural differences appear as something objective, something that exists in each immigrant, and is used as an explanation of their situation and the problems concerning immigration in general. The multicultural way of thinking is also based on the idea of the nation as a marker of the boundary between "us" and "them".[7] The ethnic, cultural and religious groups being defined are just not part of "the national". This can again be connected to Norwegian history and be understood in relation to the development of Norwegian national identity. In his book, *Mistenkelige utlendinger- og andre "fremmede" i norsk presse* (Suspicious foreigners and other "strangers" in the Norwegian press), Elisabeth Eide and Anne Hege Simonsen clarify this link to the national: "Mistrust in the other can be placed in connection with a wide variety of conditions, not least the growing nationalism that became the dominating political movement in Europe while Norway still had a union with Sweden. Several researchers on nationalism show how the idea of a national state had a strong organizing character. It arranged the difference between us and them into a system and led to thinking about differences in institutions and bureaucracy".[8] To define something as different and worthy of preserving, can, in some cases, be necessary. But a universal thinking about otherness is, just the same, not fruitful. Also, throughout Norwegian history, many people have not been included in the larger community. Who are included, and who are excluded today, and by what mechanisms?

I think we must substitute multicultural thinking with equality and recognition. In spite of it being possible to argue that this is also a goal in multicultural theory and political practice, it is time to admit that the strategy is on the wrong track. Such all-encompassing thinking about differences is not compatible with equality. To understand who are excluded today, we must be willing to look at who actually experiences infringement. And do they experience this infringement as a group, or to a greater extent, as individuals?

Multiculturalism cannot work as a solution to conflicts. On the contrary, it is a source of conflict in Western societies today, in my view. As Bauman and Vecchi show, for example, the concept of fixed individual identities is brought into an aggravated political arena. A concrete example of this is the polarized debate about freedom of speech between Muslim extremists and Christian fundamentalists in connection with the Muhammad caricatures. People on both sides of the divide came with the wrong standpoints on the issue of religious freedom. Institutions played a decisive role, for example, the Islamic Council, which traveled to the Middle East at the expense of the welfare state to "solve" the conflict.

My respondents are not interested in caricatures, only in their daily struggle. They are frustrated, and consequently, are easier to manipulate to participate in demonstrations against the society they live in. They are "caught up" in acute major conflicts that apparently deal with the West and Muslims.

The Norwegian multicultural attitude apparently tries to recognize and make minority women equal, but paradoxically, it does the opposite - that is, it violates their need for recognition of individuality. The problem is that ignorance comes with a set of rights. The "right" to think and act completely different from the majority or the "right" to think and act as the majority believes each specific ethnic, cultural or religious group should think and act.

In my country of origin, Afghanistan, women fight against oppression and fundamentalism, and they know who the enemy is. The problem in Norway is that oppression comes commingled with what is presented as "free choices" by Muslim women. In Norway, one is unable to sort out and identify what one should fight against. At the same time, people experience that they are looked upon as strangers in all connections - also, at the institutional level.

Organizations such as Islamic Council represent a fusion of Muslim conservative men and the multiculturalism of the Norwegian state. To think that this council has anything constructive to add in questions concerning minority women only because they are Muslims is a multicultural attitude that is intolerable. The Islamic Council presents itself as the "representative" of women and talk about how "Muslim women can choose for themselves". The leaders in these organizations belong to a privileged class in the minority and have nothing to do with most of the minority population. A multicultural attitude that actually lies behind the financial support of this organization, only serves a small elite of the minorities, and none of the women I did research on. On the contrary, the organization now represents institutionalized social control over women in Norway. In the Norwegian public, it is the male spokesmen from the Islamic Council and similar organizations that, time after time, get the power to define and tell the Norwegian people what is right and what is wrong according to the Quran.

Multicultural thinking does not solve conflicts but enhances them.

The philosophy of recognition, on the contrary, can help us to understand the seeds of conflicts and to find a possible way out of them. My claim is that the focus on religion, culture and ethnicity camouflages the causes of the conflicts. It hides the truth about human needs. Multiculturalism implies making religion, ethnicity and culture more essential.

The "religious" and the "cultural" or the "ethnic", are large designations constructed from a series of terms few of the individual women I met can identify with. To understand their problems in particular, and to understand conflicts in general, it is useless to start with these large designations and to try to find out what they "really" are - in reality, they are diverse individuals. So, when, for example, healthcare workers try to find out how they can solve conflicts with minorities by studying how Muslims think, this is the wrong strategy to follow. One has to ask each individual how he or she feels and thinks - and how these feelings and thoughts are met with.

One of my respondents, Shogofa from Afghanistan, told me that she was once asked to stand in front of medical students at the Psychosocial Centre for Refugees and to talk about her own experiences as a refugee and mental patient. She said to me that, for the first time, she felt dignified. It reminded her of the time when she was a teacher and imparted her knowledge in Afghanistan. She talked about something she knew a lot about. She had individual experiences of great importance.

To understand conflicts in society, we have to start with the individual and his or her experience of violation.[9] It is when we ignore the basic needs of each other that the seed of conflict arises. The basic needs of humans are love, justice and solidarity. The emotional part of these needs is closeness and intimacy with the partner, children and other family members or close friends. One of the examples Honneth gives of the need for love and recognition of this is the relationship between mother and child. When the child cries, it expresses a need - maybe it is hungry, maybe the diaper is wet, or it is in pain. The mother then goes to the child to see what it needs. Her love for the child makes her sensitive to its needs. The first form of ignorance that lays a seed of conflict is neither to give nor receive love. Emotions increase the level of conflicts. War often causes this need of love in one way or another to be ignored. Most of the women I met had experienced this. Other needs have to be satisfied first to survive, such as food and clothes, and there is no place for love. When reality becomes hard and difficult, people ignore their own need for love. This situation can arise in war and persist in the circumstance of the immigrant.

To avoid conflicts, Honneth thinks we need a moral grammar in society. He compares the recognition of human needs to grammar in language. For a language to function, it needs a grammar, and in the same way, society needs a moral grammar to avoid conflict. Honneth was interested in how the German nation should function when he wrote this in 1992. When I read Honneth, I noticed that he formulated himself very precisely, but I also observed that the same thoughts have been mentioned by Eastern poets and philosophers like Attar (1145-1220), Sana'i (1080-1131 / 1141)[10] and Rumi (1207-1273)[11]. They too were concerned with the human need for love and erfan which is known within Sufism. Erfan is a way to understand the truth within Eastern and Islamic philosophy. We can see that these three thinkers conveyed the same message as Honneth, but through poems that are unknown to many in the West. We have to extend the theory of recognition to a global level while thinking about how to behave locally. Recognition of human needs must apply locally, nationally and globally.

To avoid conflicts, I think we need a global conscience combined with the knowledge we have about how minority women actually feel. In this global conscience, meeting Honneth's human fundamental needs must be central: the need for love, legal rights and solidarity.

In my study of pain among minority women, I discovered that multiculturalism hides fundamental human needs, especially female needs. It "gives rights" to categories of people. Instead of placing the individual at the center, it places its culture, religion and ethnicity at the center. In this way, the basic needs of recognition both privately and publicly for each individual is hidden behind constructed needs such as culture, religion and ethnicity. This construction has erected a wall that prevents us from seeing what minority women in Norway really need today.

A Historical Perspective on "Us" and "Them"

European notions about "the others", "the strangers", emerged during an asymmetrical power relation during the colonial era. Notions of "strange", "exotic", "wild" and "uncivilized" were used in the construction of the European self-image as "civilized".[12] This was a legitimization of Western power through what Edward Said calls orientalism[13].

As mentioned, we can also see a link between the development of the European self-image and the growth of nationalism in Europe. Ordinarily, we separate between a German and a French concept of nationhood. The French concept denotes a political nation. The nation consisted of those who wanted to join the political community. In principle, they could be born anywhere. Their background was irrelevant, in that they were treated alike, and that they could not demand any special rights or respect for their own cultural background. The French model was universal and assimilatory. Those who joined the community would become French.[14]

The German model arose as a reaction to this universalism, especially during the period when France under Napoleon occupied the German states. Contrary to the French, the German model was particularistic and culture relativistic. It emphasized the particularity of each nation. This way of thinking was linked to the German national Romanticism that considered each people as a unique unit with a special character or "spirit". This model is called a cultural nation. The idea was that there existed an inner connection between a people, a culture and the territory where these people lived. Common language, history and origin were emphasized. People were born German; they could not become German.

European immigration policy is influenced by these two models. The German Romanticism and nation building identify "culture" and "the people" with geographic limited national borders and lineage. And it is in relation to these boundary markers that the concept of "strangers" and minorities attained a new dimension. In the French universalistic model, there was no link between the immigrant population and the state.

England and France were the leading colonial powers. They practiced two different political models on the colonies. The English strategy resembled the German nationalism; Englishmen thought that they achieved the best form of ruling system by keeping the local culture, religion and local governments. Therefore, religious and ethnic leaders were used as links between the state and the colonial population. When people from the colonies moved to England, the government kept this strategy for the immigrant population.[15] The territorial principle is central in French policy, and therefore, they continued their assimilatory and universalistic policy towards the new immigrant population. When you are born in France, you are French. In England the principle of lineage ruled, and the English model was, as the German, cultural relativistic.

Nation and nationalism are linked to the emergence of capitalism

and the breakdown of the feudal agricultural society.[16] Benedict Anderson has a good definition of nation: An imagined ethnic community.[17] Norway is a young nation, and because of this, the emphasis on the Norwegian and the national community is understandable. Just the same, it is time to expand the concept of nation with something new and something more.

Primordialism is an anthropological concept of "the original" about each individual. Characteristics such as place of birth, ethnicity, religion and mother tongue are primordial aspects of a human being. These aspects are both attributed by others and used as a self-description by the individual. In homogenous societies, these are latent aspects that are not reflected upon. But when people with different primordial traits meet, they are problematized. The problem arises when these attributes are problematized in an objectified way. They are essentialized. They are referred to as static categories, and as the most important aspects of a human being. Consequently, I will not, for example, first and foremost be considered a social anthropologist and a mother, but an Afghan. The latent aspects are revitalized and become important identity markers in many multicultural societies. The instant you see a person with dark skin, you automatically ask if she is a Muslim or not, or where she comes from originally. The primordial attributes are incorporated into the power structure and become the basis for policy.

Multiculturalism is the essentialization of the primordial attributes of culture, religion and ethnicity. Multiculturalism is a policy that transfers the focus on these primordial traits to institutions, for example, the media. Those with power to define get the opportunity to talk about others and on the behalf of others in the media, and in various debate programs where, according to my respondents, they appear to "enjoy themselves" with the various characteristics. The state becomes a spectator to the conflicts, as in the cartoon controversy. When Shaeen saw a TV debate in the aftermath of the killing of three sisters at Kaldbakken in Oslo, she saw that representatives from various organizations who fight for minorities participated, and that all of them got involved in the multicultural discourse. She sighed and said: "They are like vultures who quarrel over three dead, innocent girls."

To use primordial traits lying latent in each individual as something objective is the source of conflict. Integration measures in the form of funding for voluntary organizations based on these factors, are heading in the wrong direction.

Multiculturalism in Norway Today

The consequence of thinking that we, first and foremost, are different, that the "culturally foreign" person is so foreign that he doesn't even induce pity, was expressed openly when two ambulance drivers left a man of African origin with a brain hemorrhage in Sofienberg Park in Oslo in August 2007. Such ideas about differences have a long history in the West.

Nationalism is, in my opinion, the first error in the construction of a social community in the global world of today. Nationalism makes us blind to the increasingly close relations between the local, national and global. "When the builder places the first brick skewed, the rest of the construction rises skewed to the sky," is an old Persian proverb.[18] The idea of a narrow national community tied to ethnicity is the first error in the construction.

Tordis Borchgrevink places the Norwegian policy between the French and the German model.[19] She says that, formally, Norway has a French model where there is equality between the native population and immigrants, but, informally, Norway has kept the German model where lineage is important. Marianne Gullestad agrees that the distinction between "us" and "them" is still deeply rooted in the Norwegian population but adds "skin color" as a crucial symbolic marker.[20] She points out that the European colonial power description of the "white" and the "black" still exist in our thoughts and attitudes. In Generous Betrayal, Unni Wikan strongly criticizes the dichotomy in "us" and "them".[21] She starts with a young immigrant girl - Aisha, born and raised in Norway - and how the Norwegian authorities and institutions classify her as one of "the others". She shows explicitly how this can result in racist practices and how Aisha's rights are violated.

Even if Norway does not have a clear official multicultural policy, the dichotomy between "us" and "them", is still present in the Norwegian population and influences institutional and political practices. We can gain insight into how the state thinks by reading the white papers published in various areas[21]. By doing so, we see that, for example, a child born of immigrant parents is called "descendant of immigrants". This supports Wikan's claims concerning the division between "us" and "them" as a way of classifying people in the Norwegian national state. [22]

In theory, such categories may seem necessary, and also useful, but in everyday speech and practice, they often function, and are experienced, as stigmatizing and derogatory in nature. In my material, children felt a sense of being stigmatized and excluded from the community because their parents came from another country. "Where do you come from?" is a question many "descendants of immigrants" really struggle with. The experience of a lack of original belonging is reinforced by this exclusionary question. A young girl told me she whined her way into a French private school. She did this to avoid feeling excluded from a "Norwegian" school milieu she considered impossible to become a part of. This is actually also one of many reasons many Pakistani parents choose to send their children to English schools in Pakistan.

Categories connected to culture, religion and ethnicity are usually

always artificial and place people in static and imagined homogenous groups, independent of often considerable, differences in experiences and situations in life. These are, for example, regularly used in the media. The contrast erected in the media between "us Norwegians" and "the others", together with the conflicting dramaturgy of the media, definitely plays a part in inducing anxiety about the minorities becoming a majority in Norway. Another example of this multicultural thinking in Norway is the tendency to exoticize immigrants. I witnessed this myself during a visit from a Member of Parliament at the Jacob Center. The Somali employees and the clients of the center were asked to dress in their national costumes and prepare food from their home country. When the Member of Parliament arrived, the clients were placed in a row dressed in clothes from their "own culture", in a solemn and expectant mood - while the Member of Parliament regarded them, tasted the food and praised "the colorful community". I couldn't avoid being reminded of tourism and the entertainment aspect of colonialism, where the exotic others were simply exhibited.

Multiculturalism is also expressed by institutional divisions between

the institutions of the majority and those of the minorities and the way these are used. 56 percent of Pakistani parents with children spend their leisure activities in religious communities.[23] This applies primarily to the poor and poorly educated, and there is no doubt that this practice is linked to strong social control and group pressure. In spite of this, the practice is widely accepted. However, financial support for minority institutions that maintain culture and identity is not a policy that helps minority women to gain greater freedom. Instead, it is a policy that consolidates and enlarges the divide between "us" and "them" even more in the Norwegian community.

This is about structural power, and this power is connected to the way the Norwegian state uses its power of definition. Grete Brochmann has studied how power creates attitudes.[24] Power to exclude or include, and power to ignore. Brochmann shows how various definitions of power lies implicit when thinking of "us" and "them". Brochmann calls this institutional racism.[25] It is important to realize that there are institutions that have been built with support from the state to begin with and are funded based on a multicultural way of thinking that is controlling and oppressive of minorities themselves. Among the majority, these organizations and their leaders are perceived as representatives of the minorities, without really being so. This contributes toward widening the already wide minority-majority gap, and further leads to even more stigma and helplessness among minorities. I choose to call this unofficial multiculturalism because I think it is important to show how this policy, which is often presented as well intentioned and an opportunity to make members of Norwegian society equal and a solution to disagreement and conflict, has the exact opposite effect. In addition, it is important to look at this as both about policy at a community level and attitudes at an individual level.

In today's media that create attitudes among people, minorities are very often presented as a problem. Forced marriages, circumcision and potential social clients are recurring themes. The media contributes to the creation of attitudes and has a big responsibility.[26] What the media says about immigration and the population in general is based on multicultural thinking where real structural factors - for example, class or extensive exclusion - is not seen or taken into account. The killing of women is, for example, discussed as a phenomenon linked to ethnicity and culture. We seldom see an analysis of the economic or social conditions that actually reflect the life of these minority women who are particularly exposed to violence and homicide.

Not wanting to see the whole picture but maintaining minorities as "the other" and not full members of the national community, is the discrimination of our time. And it is maintained even after minority persons have lived for generations in Norway.

Unni Wikan talks about "a conspiracy of silence". She thinks this silence "has already torn apart the lives of many immigrants and their children."[27] We have to realize that this is the core of the pain of minority women, just to be "the other" with all that this implies of exclusion and lack of recognition. In this way, they are also implicitly excluded from the resources needed to live a life full of meaning and rich in quality. This, in the end, is also an issue of health.

The Difference between Constructed and Objective Reality

Many misconceptions concerning minorities exist in Norway today. To understand the difference between real and constructed reality, we can use an example from biology. When we see a leaf on a beautiful tulip, we observe that it is green. Green is (a part of) reality. The truth behind the color is chlorophyll and the photosynthesis that occurs there. But you can never see or feel this, and furthermore, it is a process in continual change. When you meet a woman with a headscarf and of Asian appearance on the bus, you (probably) see a Muslim woman. The headscarf is part of objective reality. But in Norway today you have an idea of the truth about the attitudes and opinions of this woman, as if it is possible to see this truth. This idea may come from what you read in the newspapers and see on TV about "the category" Muslims. But it is a constructed truth.

One day I witnessed a conversation between a Somali woman and the leader of a project aimed at understanding and doing something about the situation of inmates in Norwegian prisons.[28] Many of the relevant inmates were young Somali boys (older teenagers). The leader of the project asked the Somali woman if she had any idea about why so many Somalis became criminals and ended up in jail. "Is it something in Somali culture that turns so many into criminals?" The woman answered, embarrassed, that "in our culture we fiercely condemn breaking the law. There is no acceptance for criminality in Somali culture".

When we speak about ethnic Norwegian criminals, I have never heard anyone talk about explanations linked to "Norwegian culture". The young Somali boys came from a country ravaged by war. Many had been robbed of the opportunity to go to school. They have no experience in basic concepts like democracy, and consequently, lack the prerequisites for succeeding in Norwegian society. War is the greatest violation an individual can be exposed to. In conversations between the Somali women and the leader of the project with young inmates, both the past of each boy and his total situation in life at present were ignored. Instead, focus was put on a question of culture. The Somali woman in her turn tried to defend the "Somali culture" by emphasizing that crime was strictly condemned in her culture.

Multiculturalism also permeates large parts of academia. In the article "Liberty, rights and the sex of orthodox priests" by the expert on religion, Berit Thorbjørnsrud, we can see a manifestation of this multicultural discourse.[29] Many religious communities assign the sexes different roles and rights, contrary to what the Norwegian law of gender equality requires. The article of Thorbjørnrud discusses the issue of whether political rights can overrule religious convictions. Through the debate concerning the issue that only men are allowed to be ordained as priests in the orthodox church, which is contrary to Norwegian gender equality law, she wants to show that secular laws cannot (always) overrule religious ones. She acknowledges discrimination against women as a serious problem but thinks that not all differential treatment of the sexes is discriminating. She claims that in some cases, like the one concerning female priests in the orthodox church, the women in the religious community don't consider it a problem that they are not allowed to be ordained as priests. She asks: "Who will then decide if religious concepts concerning gender represent acceptable differential treatment or unacceptable discrimination? Can we, for example, overrule religious women in their evaluation of their own situation in life? What will then happen with their experience of their own liberty?"[30] But who are these women Thorbjørnsrud is referring to? Is she a spokesperson for these women? In my study, "women of faith" say the opposite. They are for equality. And in reality, haven't many Norwegian conservative religious women been in the same situation? But in that case, the Norwegian public fought for equality!

I think Torbjørnsrud is blind to the power perspective in her analysis. We cannot make freedom relative in the way that there are "different ideas about what freedom is". Freedom is the right to love, justice and solidarity, and toward full recognition in Norwegian society. Torbjørnsrud's idea of "orthodox women" who don't want fundamental freedom is a construct.

There are many examples of the consequences of multiculturalism in Norway, on many levels. Often, it is the women who are affected. For years, Norwegian authorities supported the organization, Health and Welfare, run by a conservative Pakistani man. Several times, he invited an imam from England to talk about sharia at the Park Hotel. Paradoxically, the bill was paid by the Children and Equality Department. I participated on these seminars. Among other subjects discussed, was one on how a Norwegian divorce is not accepted by Pakistani authorities, and how a Muslim must behave in order to get a divorce. At the seminar, I met Pakistani women who struggled to get a divorce. They said quite explicitly that they wanted Health and Welfare to turn to Norwegian and Pakistani authorities to find solutions so that they would not be stigmatized and could freely travel and visit family in Pakistan without any pressure. But nothing was done and the whole issue was kept within a conservative religious context. Even the brochures of the MiRA Resource Centre for Immigrant and Refugee Women provide the contact information of mosques when they "inform" women of how they can get help concerning divorce. It is a big problem for many minority women who live in difficult, and even violent, marriages that the whole discussion concerning the right to divorce is connected to an idea of their "religious culture". This is one of many examples of how multiculturalism leads to discrimination, and how this policy is not compatible with the full recognition of minority women and their needs as legal subjects, as individuals and as women, that is women with a need to get out of a painful marriage devoid of love.

Consequences of Multiculturalism

Multiculturalism is a misunderstood political strategy because it creates an imbalance in the social contract[31], which is part of the basis of democracy as we know it today. The social contract deals with the rights and duties of the state and the individual; the state shall protect the rights of the individual while the individual achieves its protection and freedom by complying with the law.

Multiculturalism, as a political management strategy, is widespread in today's globalized world. This creates the imbalance between rights and duties, and at the same time weakens the power of the state. Philosopher and professor at the University of Guelph, Monique Deveaux (2010) [32] points out how granting rights to groups, such as the right to practice one's own culture and religion, can create a breeding ground for limiting personal autonomy through authority and social influence. Fortunately, there are brave women who take to the streets and help steer development in a positive direction. The women's uprising[33] that took place in a Somali mosque in Norway is a current example of this. These women were tired of not being allowed to attend the important meetings regarding the mosque, but that they were put to wash and clean instead. One of the women, Lul Abdis, stated: "We are tired of just washing, cooking and paying, we also have rights. This is Norway. We live in a country with equality!". This is a direct example of how group rights can limit the personal autonomy of group members.

An example of the imbalance that exists between rights and duties is how institutional Islam imposes new duties on those who belong to the Muslim culture, compared with the rest of the Norwegian population. Another misunderstanding of rights can be seen in connection with some Muslims' requests to be released from work in order to pray. This is an example of how Muslims may have a desire to obtain more rights from society, which they do not demand in their country of origin. People have their rights, but do not know how to practice these rights, and therefore such requests arise. From 2010, this request has been regulated in a handbook from the Equality and Anti-Discrimination Ombud[34].

Rights and Power Structures

In a multiculturalist society with an excessive focus on culture, religion and ethnicity, people are losing their individuality. The individual disappears behind a group identity with associated group rights. This is not unique to Norway but in fact a global phenomenon. Research from Canada[35] shows that the group rights granted to minority groups (e.g., the right to practice one's own religion) can, paradoxically, lead to the establishment of an independent power structure within the individual groups. Here, religious and ethnic leaders' function as part of the governing power of society with rules that are often in conflict with state law. Among other things, we could see examples of this while the Covid-19 pandemic ravaged countries such as Afghanistan. Despite the authorities' ban on gathering in large groups, people came together because some of their religious leaders asked them to show up for prayer. This highlights how leaders of religious and ethnic minority groups gain authority through speaking on behalf of "a higher power" (such as God and religious books). As a result, the individual loses freedom and has to follow the orders given by "the Almighty", and not the state. In this way, also the state loses its authority. Another example we could see here in Norway is how health care supervisors recommended individuals who were fasting to drink water in order to be resistant to Covid-19 infection. The religious leaders, on the other hand, discourage people from any drinking during fasting. However, there are different interpretations of the Islamic rules. In 1975, when I was a teenager, my aunt told me that I could fast for my father and mother's soul. I remember her saying, "You go to school and play basketball, so you can also drink water." This was a tolerant form of Islam, without a political agenda, which was practiced when I was young.

Minorities suffer under the exclusion originating from the Norwegian ethnic description of the nation, from not having the same opportunities as most in the majority do, and from being cut off from the resources needed for a meaningful life quality. This is a health problem (cf. Baer, Singer & Johnsen 1986: 95) that inflicts pain on my respondents. Twelve years after the release of *Silent Screams*, the dimension of pain and multiculturalism has created several barriers for women. My question is why so often parts of the minority women cannot exercise the same rights and freedoms as the majority women. What is it that restricts minority women's opportunity to make use of the same freedom? In the book "Gender and Culture" (1999), Nina Karin Monsen points out that power relations in connection with minority women must be studied within the Norwegian society.

Nina Monsen and the five power structures

Nina Karin Monsen points to five power structures that show how minority women experience pressure from several layers of power structures. The unofficial multiculturalism is integrated into these.

1. The Norwegian authorities' power over immigrants in various institutions and contexts.
2. The power of the dominant Norwegian culture
3. Men's power over their wives and female relatives according to religious and cultural dogmas.
4. Patriarchal power
5. The power of the masses or the power of the group over the individual.

This is an expression of what Gullestad calls the hegemonic majority perspective in Norway. This multiculturalist way of thinking is dominant not only among politicians, but also in other institutions in Norway, and in politics. I think this reflects an unofficial multiculturalist way of thinking in Norwegian politics, a way of thinking that is similar to what Unni Wikan calls "a conspiracy of silence that (...) has been wreaking havoc with the lives of many immigrants and their children" (2002: 2). This way of thinking creates an asymmetry between the majority and the minority, so that immigrants practically do not receive the same opportunities as most in the majority do. Here lies one of the many causes of pain for many minorities.

Langvasbråten[36] found in her study of Scandinavian discourse on multiculturalism, that the Norwegian government omitted minority women's challenges in legislation regarding gender equality until 2008. In addition, challenges considered specific to minority women, such as forced marriage, have been mentioned entirely separate from action plans on gender equality. This shows how strong multiculturalism is, and that Norwegian politics does not take the many complex issues related to gender and multiculturalism into account.

Hannah Arendt and political rights

We can view multiculturalism in the light of Hannah Arendt's[37] political rights theory. She criticized the paradoxical rights and opposites in society, originating from the political ideals of freedom and equality on one side, and on the other side existing sociocultural, ethnic and religious differences. For Arendt it was important that political rights should not anchor in the exclusion of certain groups. Many Christian, Muslim and Jewish institutions exclude their members from the general community which exists among the rest of the citizens. Arendt warns against that this kind of anchoring can lead to a totalitarian way of thinking. What happens with multiculturalism is that it prevents the building of an inclusive community of rights because some are receiving additional rights based on ethnic, religious and cultural affiliation. When society bases itself on multiculturalism as political strategy, it fails the community between citizens, it misses a community of rights when every group has a set of differing rights. The differing rights do not lead to a political community. For the rest of society, it can also be unclear what minority rights contain, this may lead to misunderstandings. When one person, as part of a group, does something criminal, many are making demands on the group as a whole, and not on the individual who actually performed the action alone. Every single individual who is part of this specific group will be punished with having to show responsibility for the other ones' action. This becomes a great burden on each individual who must be ready to defend his or her religion, believes, or culture. We have witnessed this dynamic through countless incidents in which individuals are pressured because of their perceived affiliation with a particular group. We thus see how group rights can contribute to increasing conflict, on grounds of lacking clarification about rights and duties. As Arendt points out, political rights should not lead to exclusion from the community.

In several chapters of this book, we can see many examples of how part of the majority suspects the Muslim population in the country, and views them as terrorists, without being able to recognize each individual. In chapter seven we will read about the history of Shogofa and the political assassination of the filmmaker van Gogh in the Netherlands. In this example we can notice the imbalance between rights and duties. How is it that a single Muslim individual in Norway is convicted of the actions of one Muslim terrorist in the Netherlands? We see that parts of the majority disregard the individual and generalize the actions of one terrorist to all Muslims. This contributes to create mistrust and conflict in society.

Shazia Majid and the invisibility of minority women

I see a positive development because now there are more books written by people with a minority background, who have a critical outlook on power structures which are often challenging to notice for the majority population. In *Out of the Shadows*, Shazia Majid writes about structural vulnerabilities in society, something that I call *unofficial multiculturalism*. An example of unofficial multiculturalism, pointed out by Majid in her book, is the establishment of segregated girls' classes at Sagene School back in the 80s. This refers to how the Norwegian authorities have contributed to allow gender segregation on cultural/ religious premises, and thus have bowed to the traditional patriarchal system.

Minority women are made invisible through the five power structures, as Monsen suggests. Ignorance is part of multiculturalism as a political strategy. This can be noticed through the power structures which oppress minority women. There are many examples from my own studies of how immigrant women are ignored and made invisible. Yasmin, who had higher education and wished to do research and work within academia, told me that she simply had to forget about it. It was rare to see a minority student receiving an A-level on their thesis so they could continue in academia. In this way minority women are excluded from an important area in society which assists in building our knowledge base.

Shazia Majid's empiricism refers to other examples of such invisibility when the efforts of minority women were ignored, for example while working with the 'konferanseavisen' (Conference Newspaper) Forum 88. "The bitterness over what happened in the 1980s still lingers around and colors the women's struggle even today." Majority and minority feminists often lack a common frame of reference.

The split she is talking about between majority and minority feminists is part of the unofficial multiculturalism. Minority women are seen as a group and therefore there is a struggle between the two groups. The majority does not take the fight for the minority out of respect for their religion and does not realize that the fight against ethnic discrimination is also a women's fight (you can read about a similar example in Arezo's story under "The Power of the Collective over the Individual").

In my fieldwork I found, among other things, that it was very difficult for minority women to have divorces granted and completed. My own experience with the legislation resonates with this. When I was about to divorce my ex-husband in the 90's, I got a divorce decision from the Norwegian state by which they pointed out that my divorce was not final. They expected my ex-husband and me to have our divorce approved by an Islamic authority (mullah), according to my so-called group affiliation. There are very different requirements for women and men to be granted a final divorce in accordance with Islam. It appears that women who want a divorce must go through processes over several years resulting in many giving up. For many, the social control from the surrounding society is also too much to deal with, because women who are seeking divorce often feel punished by God and therefore live with guilt and fear of ending up in hell. This is not written down in any law, but indoctrinated through those in power. The feeling of being punished and fearing the flames of hell creates a pain that controls them. While facing these practices, many minority women are powerless and alone, and can therefore not demand the same rights as majority women in practice. Devaux argues that practices limiting women's autonomy should be avoided or banned, and that states must respect, support and protect women's procedural autonomy. This means the ability to negotiate, reconstruct and resist practices they perceive as oppressive. Traditional societies and groups should be held accountable for respecting this autonomy and the state should have systems in place to support those women.

Shazia Majid, in her fight against the patriarchal system, has a good recommendation on how women's education can contribute to break down the established patriarchal power structures: "This is our educational revolution, and it eats up the patriarchy from within". We can consider women's use of the right to take education as a way to fight against both patriarchy and multiculturalism.

Women establish ways to integrate themselves and their children into the new environment in which they find themselves and negotiate the content and practices within their everyday lives.

Many Muslim mothers I interviewed said, in connection with swimming lessons at school, that swimming is part of the learning process in Norway that gives children necessary knowledge and skills. Therefore, Muslim children must be able to participate on an equal footing with Norwegian children. These mothers considered swimming as part of the knowledge their children needed to learn in school, and as a skill related to everyday life. The women were solution oriented. The emotional relationship or love between mother and child is the first link in recognition. This gives women the ability to listen to their children's desires.

Children themselves are preoccupied with being like other Norwegian children. Therefore, their mothers have to find solutions in everyday life to create joy and a sense of equality for their children. Through participation in swimming lessons, they also free themselves from an anxiety of drowning. This love for children is more important than the fear of hell, religious power structures and the ban on swimming for women. These mothers and my aunt orientated themselves in the reality in which they lived, just as the Prophet once told.

Through the interviews and conversations, I had with the Muslim women, it became clear that their interpretation of Islam is different from institutionalized state-funded Islam which speaks on behalf of the group. The tolerant interpretation of Islam that my own aunt and these mothers had is not based on anxiety, fear and prohibition. It is to a greater extent based on a desire to unite Islamic faith with the new everyday life in Norway. The Islamic Council and other Islamic institutions, on the other hand, have a number of prohibitions and create anxiety among the people.

In my fieldwork, I saw how the encounter with the established power structure, which many minorities did not experience in their countries of origin, as well as the imbalance between rights and duties created family conflicts in Norway. There is often a power competition which results in the woman's loss to the man who defends the established power structure. Many divorces are an outcome of this. It also becomes a great challenge for the children to follow the established power structure and its commands. For example, when children are not allowed to participate in swimming lessons, they also lose the right to enjoy the same freedom as other Norwegian children. The state, through the funding of religious institutions, establishes power structures which inflict pain and isolation on Muslim families, women, children and not at least men. After divorce, women and children have the opportunity to find new paths while men are often left with a persistent pain, isolation and distrust of the state. This persistent pain can lead to misogyny and violent solutions.

The religious scriptures and commands that the imams preach to people are presented as the word of God and not as messages that come from people. In the established Islam, there is no room for saying that God can make mistakes. Therefore, it is also "the higher power" you obey when you follow the group's rules. In reality, it is the religious leaders who are in power while the individual is undermined, since he or she does not have the authority to speak against God. In Norway, this problem is concealed (underlying) and invisible.

Another challenge with group rights arises when individuals lose loyalty to the state and its legislation, while the group's rules gain more meaning and authority in their lives. We can see that in an attempt to protect minority group rights, through state funding among other things, the state supports loyalty changes. Through funding and support for ethnic and religious groups, the state participates in strengthening power inequalities and cultural constraints within minority groups. This can lead to further marginalization and undermining of deeper pre-existing problems. Several researchers in the field argue that a commitment to human rights across religious and ethnic groups in society is important to protect individuals from self-governing minority institutions which restrict individual rights in the name of God, religion or culture.

Aunt Ulrikke's way

An example of the positive development I observe in society is that many immigrants begin to write about the reality in Norway.

In *Aunt Ulrikke's Way*, Zeshan Shakar gives many examples of painful experiences that illuminate the dark side of the misunderstood multiculturalist strategy. Professor of literature, Jeanette Winterson, points out that one must read novels to understand reality. For us anthropologists, novels can be a good source for understanding the time we live in. This is because one is freer to describe within a novel as opposed to non-fiction. The novel becomes a living source for people's everyday lives. Being an author with immigrant background is of great value to Norwegian society, and especially to the majority, as it helps to provide knowledge and understanding of societal structures and institutions. Shakar describes vividly the pain and reality of young people, the mosques' relationship to England and the distribution of money to young people. I call this phenomenon *globalized multiculturalism*, which has a history dating back to the development of political Islam in the 1980s. I want the authorities to take such descriptions seriously.

We can see that the introduction of sharia (Islamic criminal law) was established in 1980 - the time when multiculturalism was institutionalized in Pakistan. It was also the time of the Soviet occupation in Afganistan. The Americans also wanted to Islamize the region and profit from this.

Globalized multiculturalism

In the 1970s, Turkey, Pakistan, Iran, Iraq, and the United Kingdom had a military and economic alliance known as the CENTO (Central Treaty Organization), or Baghdad Pact. Many workers who came to Europe were part of an invisible contract in connection with this alliance. As an example, no Afghans were coming to Norway as foreign workers at that time, because Afghanistan was not part of CENTO. But an Afghan mullah, Sibghatullah Mojaddedi[38], who had a long tradition with the British kingdom, came to Denmark and worked as an imam there. Later he also established mosques in several countries in Scandinavia[39].

The Soviet occupation of Afghanistan lead to a legitimation of Islamic institutions and also enabled the mosques to raise funds to support their resistance against the Soviet Union. Now in a globalized world, this type of institutional Islam spreads to many other countries, including several countries in Africa. In Pakistan, this type of Islam also arrived with the Soviet occupation in the 80s. Under the Pakistani President Muhammad Zia-ul-Haq, Islam became institutionalized in the school system within the same ten-year period. In Afghanistan, it has been strengthened over the last 20 years, while NATO and other Western countries have been present. Mojaddedi was president of the Afghan parliament during parts of this period. He became president of Afghanistan in 1992 and a total of 70,000 people were killed in Kabul that year. From 2003, he served as chairman of several Afghan assemblies before founding his own political party in 2011.

In the period of Soviet occupation (1979-1989) the transfer of identity from an individual perspective to major political arenas is visible, as Bauman has referred to. That period shows how religion was forced onto people with weapons to administer fundamentalist politics. Conventional identity and democratic elements were totally banned. Multiculturalism as a misinterpreted political strategy was also established globally during this period. This institutionalization in Afghanistan took place while the United States and several Western countries were involved in Afghanistan. Now there are many institutionalized religious organizations with money, weapons and power in Afghanistan. They are trying to enforce their version of Islam as the only truth. They want to dominate as an authoritarian religious power without room for individuality. Research which is unable to incorporate global structures has lost value. When talking about Islam, it is very important to include an analysis of political structures and the arms industry as well.

"Administration of hatred" in Europe

On 16 September 2020, the President of the European Commission, Ursula von der Leyen, delivered a speech[40] on solidarity, and the importance of European values and humanist understanding in the times we live in. Her job includes promoting the rule of law and implementing new bills. In today's climate, it is more important than ever to pay attention to the legal security of human beings in order to protect individuals from power abuses. She criticized the lack of solidarity with Greece and the refugees in Lesvos, where the "burden" has been distributed unequally between states. Von der Leyen is a lady with a principle that every human being has an inherent and irrevocable dignity and sovereignty, regardless of origin. In her speech, she redirects attention to right-wing extremists in parliament by saying that right-wing extremists are following a different perception of human value in comparison to herself. They divide people into two categories: "us" and "them". It is they, meaning the others, who are confronted with hatred, but "hatred has never given any good advice". Von der Leyen points out that politicians have different approaches to migration. Thus, right-wing extremists promote hatred, but her approach instead is to find constructive solutions for the challenges Europe is facing.

In the book *The Management of Hate*, Nitzhan Shoshan shares his research of right-wing extremism in Europe and points out that violent and populist forms of nationalism are not a particular exception, but rather an inherent tendency within modernity. Expressions of anti-immigration are not just expressed by the right wing, but across the political spectrum. Von der Leyen therefore has a great responsibility to defend the rule of law as well as the dignity and sovereignty of human beings. This is an everyday struggle in a globalized world where change happens at lightning speed. We must all share this heavy responsibility to be able to live in a harmonious society with less pain and hatred (See Multiculturalism as Political Strategy).

In *the Management of Hate*, Shoshan points out that in Berlin there were 120 mosques for the estimated 200,000 Muslims in the western part of the city (as of 2016). According to the findings of Shoshan, mosques among other things, are considered something out of place and foreign that does not belong in a modern city. In 2006, when a new mosque was to be built in the eastern part of Berlin, the right-wing extremists and the so-called "mainstream" conservative wing merged. These political directions were sharing the same line of thought but expressed themselves in different ways. The far-right wanted immediate deportation of all foreigners while the conservatives, who aimed to increase their political respect, stepped in more cautiously. Their intentions, however, came to light when the leader of the protest against the mosque construction shared his views in a far-right newspaper. He had expressed himself as a very tolerant man but did not want a mosque in his neighborhood because no Muslims had ever lived in his part of town. The same mechanisms have reached Norwegian society after 14 years through the organization SIAN[41]. This has created debate and demonstrations. The findings of Shohan and also my own interviews with people living in Berlin, indicate how religion and mosques are used to separate and spark hatred between people. Religion divides citizens and cultivates hatred between them. We have had similar debates in Norway. Despite the fact that no mosques have public calls to prayers, FrP nevertheless proposed to ban this[42]. It signifies how religion contributes to increasing conflict also in this country.

Our Minister of Culture and "us and them" in Norway

Norway has developed in a positive direction in many ways since *Silent Screams* was first published 12 years ago. These positive changes are plentiful. However, my cause is not to talk about all these positive trends, but rather to highlight the aspects of society which place an excessive focus on differences among people, which create pain and inflict harm. I would still like to point out that the positive trends I have observed are that we have a committed Minister of Culture Abid Raja with parents from Pakistan. I watched the program *Id-Feiring* (Eid celebration) on

NRK in which the Minister of Culture participated together with his family. When he spoke about our society, he expressed that he dared to call it "our country". He pointed out that it is difficult to be accepted in Norwegian society, but it is important to call it "our country" to feel included. When I saw the anxiety in his eyes, I felt a lot of sympathy for him. There are many minorities who have the same feeling. I urge our Minister of Culture to consider that, when society finances and creates institutions which create a distinction between "us" and "them", it becomes more difficult to create a we-feeling. When I captured this anxiety, I felt it was my civic duty to write about why it is so difficult to call it "our country" and be a part of the community. I do not criticize you as a person, but you speak for institutions (mosques and associations) which are worthy of criticism because I see elements of unofficial multiculturalism in these institutions.

Dear Minister of Culture, I have read your books and see that you rose upwards in the political system. We live in a globalized world where characteristic cultural, religious and ethnic identities intensify. Every day, more and more institutions come to work with and focus on cultivating these characteristics. This is the driving force that makes people increasingly different from each other and more nationalistic. It also leads to the establishment of parallel societies. This driving force becomes stronger when it is financed, as we can see in French society, despite a commitment to secularism. Recently (in October 2020), this problem became apparent in France's secular state. We see that religious organizations are in a critical condition. The challenge with parallel societies, which increase nationalism, is that they help to threaten some of the core values of a secular society. As of 2024, following four years of intense French debate, it has found its place in the daily news 18 on Norway's NRK television.

For a society to function, each individual's actions and institutions must create the structures of society. We see that new mosques and different directions of Islam are emerging while society is paying to keep these institutions alive. Many people work through institutions based on religion, culture and ethnicity that are part of modern society. The Pakistani Workers' Union, which used to be located in Maridalsveien 3 in Oslo, now only exists as a name. I have asked several questions about what happened to the union but received no answer. The labor union was not developed and instead mosques and religious organizations in all forms emerged and grew. The authorities want immigrants to become members of various religious congregations, whether they are Muslim, Catholic or similar, and the state finances these. I refer to an example for this in Chapter 11. According to your book *Spokesman*, there were many young women on the board of the Muslim Student Union. They have no common platform with Norwegians and therefore move towards characteristically distinctive associations.

After reading *The Management of Hate*, I wish to have a serious dialogue with you through this book. As Minister of Culture, you have the power to change the structural barriers that exist. This is a lot of responsibility for you, especially when you have been a spokesman for the World Islamic Nation Mosque and the Muslim Student Union in the past. In any society, individuals and institutions create the structural aspects of society. According to your own book, the mosque had 6,000 members and was founded in 1984 in Grønland, a part of Oslo. In 1996, after the mosque was completed with beautiful tiles, it received an extraordinary amount of attention from public administrations and schools who wanted a tour to learn more. I wonder if this attention was coincidental, or if it was part of the unofficial governance policy that schools should visit the mosque? After my own son visited this mosque, he was asked if he was a Muslim. When before there had been no question of religion, the children suddenly began to categorize each other. My own research on multiculturalism began after this had happened. This visit to the mosque led the children to become over-focused on differences, which disturbed the community among them. To me, this is an example of multiculturalism in practice, when individuals disappear behind categories such as religion. Here you have contributed to making discrimination invisible and barriers stronger. The division of citizens into "us and them" is something very unfortunate. This creates a mental barrier which implicitly leads to hatred. This is part of structural racism.

The homosexuality debate became highly topical after an imam from Pakistan was invited to give a lecture here in Norway. He talked about homosexuality and the death penalty, among other things. The consequence of this lecture was that many Muslims experienced being asked for their personal opinion on the death penalty. Here we can see an imbalance between rights and duties. Each individual Muslim is seen in the light of a group identity with specific rights in Norwegian society. The problem is that the duties are not defined; what do you do with the group rights you have, and what kind of duty does each individual have? A large part of the majority and the media allow themselves to ask individual Muslims, who have nothing to do with homosexuality and the death penalty, about their thoughts and attitudes. Every single Muslim does not see themselves necessarily as part of the group that the majority and media assume them to belong with, and therefore it is perceived as inappropriate for them to answer on behalf of this group, while imams sit at the top, holding the power. Every Muslim loses her or his individuality and wonders why they are obliged to answer questions about homosexuality and the death penalty. Each individual becomes vulnerable and ends up in a defenseless situation, when they have to respond on behalf of a group into which they are forced. Here lies the core of my critique of multiculturalism because each individual, and especially women, is squeezed into the five power structures that Nina Monsen points out. This creates pain and is something we in Women and Human Rights want to avoid. While I was the leader of Women Against Fundamentalism, we received no funding. We used the child benefit which we received from the state for our children to organize debates. Later we changed our name to Women and Human Rights in the hope of getting support. Still, we received none. Our goal was to find a common frame of reference with women in Norway and in other European countries, and to fight for democratic values together.

The homosexuality debate constructed a presumed conflict of values that many Muslims have no connection with, but which led to a hatred against Muslims. I shared my experiences growing up in Afghanistan where nobody was punished for homosexuality. The interpretation of Islam depends on the context, the country and the agenda in which it is used. Colonial Islam, for example, was banned in Afghanistan. This was a form of Islam that used religion to exercise power through forcing citizens to obey an almighty god, without questioning. The authorities legitimized their actions in the name of God and religion and did not allow any space for criticism of those in power and God. The British used religion to cultivate hatred between Muslims and Hindus. To control the people, the colonial power (Colonial Islam) used anxiety, piety and threats of punishment. As a result, after Afghanistan's independence, this type of Islam was banned, and mullahs were banned from studying Islam outside Afghanistan. This type of Islam creates a totalitarian form of government, which according to Hanna Arendt destroys the human community and separates citizens in a society. In this context, we can see how this type of Islam creates separation between Norwegian citizens and constructs groupings in the form of who are Muslims and who are not. Finally, the term "colorful community" loses meaning in practice.

In 2008, both, your book *Spokesman* and my book *Silent Screams* were published. These books received two very different reactions. Your wonderful story of your marriage and love that flourished, created a lot of attention and gained wide readership in comparison to my own publication. In addition to advocating for the World Islamic Nation Mosque and the Pakistani Union, your book also supported the "us" and "them" categories. Your book won the competition, *Silent Screams*, which criticized the categorization of people in "us" and "them" remained silent. However, through your two books *Spokesman* and *Dialogue*, you contribute to strengthen the invisible mental wall - to create "us" and "them". Back to your interview during *Id-feiringen* (Eid Celebration) on NRK, I understand your tears related to not being accepted by Norwegian culture. I want to give an explanation of why it is perceived as difficult to be accepted by Norwegian culture while contributing to manifesting the categories "us" and "them". Nevertheless, today we must stand together against the growing hatred in Norwegian society, which we are part of. You, as Minister of Culture, have the power to change things which individuals cannot. You also have a responsibility to change structural vulnerabilities.

4. Life in a Ghetto

When I came to Norway 16 years ago, I lived in a ghetto in the outskirts of Oslo called Angarudd[1]. Most of Angarudd's inhabitants were from minority backgrounds. Except for a few poor people and drug addicts, the Norwegian population of Angarudd had moved away bit by bit over the years as the number of immigrants increased. Everybody noticed this migration out of the area by those who could afford it. Every month, new notices appeared informing residents of the people who had left.

Angarudd's tall buildings looked like factories; they were colorless and 13 stories high. One of my neighbors, Elisabeth from Chile, told me they reminded her of the weapon factories she knew from her past. The corridors of the buildings were dirty. There was garbage thrown on the floor in the elevators that were in constant use up and down the 13 stories. Dirt on the floor made it difficult to find a place to put your feet, the color on the elevator button was worn off, and the scratched, dirty mirror made it hard to even see your reflection. The caretaker of the building could not cope with the filth. Too many adults and children were cramped together in one place. He was tired of cleaning up, he told me; he already worked more than most caretakers. In the corridors, there were lots of shoes, strollers and bicycles, in spite of the fact that the caretaker, on several occasions, had explained to people that they were not allowed to place things in the corridors because of the fire hazard. The air was stale because the windows were not opened, and the smell of food mixed with the dirty air created an uncomfortable atmosphere. To save money, the housing cooperative had distributed boxes of paint to the residents so that they could paint the walls in the corridors. The result was sloppy and unsightly. There were no flowers or other kinds of decoration in the hallways either. I remember the miserable impression these corridors made on me every time I came home after having visited my sister who lived in one of the nicer, Western parts of Oslo. The contrast was depressing.

Many of the inhabitants were jobless, and even if unemployment affected the whole family, it was the women who had to take on most of the burden; they often took the whole load on their shoulders. Like Ezat, a neighbor, said: "I suffer because Norway is not my country. In my country we were poorer than we are now, but I had less pain." The rest of her family lived in France and was in the same situation, she told me. Many of the other women I met in Angarudd also told me that they did not feel good. They had many children and hectic days divided between doing laundry, caring for children and preparing meals. Some of them had a job in addition to this. Because they could not afford it, they could not send their children to an after-school program or to kindergarten.

Angarudd lies five minutes from Marka, a popular outdoor area of Oslo. In Marka, there are lakes to swim in, paths for walking in the woods and lots of other activities. Immigrant families seldom used these fantastic facilities. Instead, they gathered together in groups: Pakistani women on one side, Arabic women on the other. The children, on the contrary, played and quarreled with each other because there were not enough playing apparatuses for all. There was always a line behind the slide and the playground was worn down and in bad condition. In several places, the lawn lacked grass, so that dust filled the air when the children played. One inhabitant, who had a child with asthma, dis- cussed the problem with the caretaker, but he told him that the housing cooperative did not have resources to repair it.

Elisabeth – A Unique Story

One informant living in Angarudd was Elisabeth. She was from Chile, divorced and had lived in Angarudd for more than ten years. Elisabeth invested a lot into her apartment. To have a nice home was important to her after many years in exile. She was an intellectual woman, with a special interest in art. She struggled with getting a home that satisfied her intellectual taste. She had placed books of the Chilean poet Pablo Neruda in the bookshelf and had pictures of him and other well-known authors on the walls, and here and there, sculptures and other art pieces were displayed.

Once, she told me how all the mess, garbage and bad smell in the corridors in Angarudd and the discussions and worries she took home from work made her tired and sad. She told me that she used Friday evenings to relax. She tried to find peace and quiet by lighting candles, pouring herself a glass of wine, and sitting down and reading a good poem. There were elements of nostalgia in this ritual. It brought her back to her childhood, family and home country, to a better time. She could then escape from all the stress and troubles of her daily life, away from the conflicts at work. One thing she suffered from was the feeling of not being accepted in Norway, of not belonging to a community. "How long must I live in Norway to not be considered a foreigner?" she said. "What is the threshold of acceptance? I have a home, I have nature around me, and my children are completely Norwegian!"

But even if she has made herself a nice home, liked nature and appreciated her Friday nights, it was not enough; she did not feel comfortable in Angarudd. The dirty elevator and the depressing surroundings be- came too much. In addition, there was too much quarreling and conflict among the neighbors, especially in the shared laundry room, which was also dirty. She was particularly annoyed at one of the neighbors who used the common washing machine to wash dirty kitchen cloths from the restaurant where he worked, so that it got clogged up with dirt and became unusable. In the end, she bought her own washing machine to solve the problem. The only thing she appreciated about Angarudd was that it is situated close to Marka so that she had the opportunity to take her walks there. She was also very concerned that the Norwegians would move away from Angarudd, and that the area, which was already a ghetto, would become even worse.

Elisabeth had two children who were both born in Norway. The boy

was a member of the local football team and her daughter took dancing lessons. But since Elisabeth did not have a car, she had problems organizing transport for her son to attend his football matches. She was concerned that her children might become isolated from their Norwegian schoolmates who all lived in "Maezon"[2] or in other "good" neighborhoods. She also struggled to network with the Norwegian parents of her son's classmates. She felt that this was the only way for her children to be integrated into Norwegian society. But these parents did not al- low their children to visit Angarudd because it was considered a "bad" environment and they did not want their children to be negatively influenced by this. All these problems led to her eventually giving up and migrating to Spain, where she opened her own shop. Her problem was that she had to escape all the time, and she and her children were facing an uncertain future.

Ezat: Imprisoned by Thoughts about Cultural Difference

Ezat is a Muslim woman from Morocco. She has no education. She too lived in one of the apartment blocks in Angarudd. She used to work at a post office but stopped after the Norwegian conservative government passed a law offering a cash-for-care benefit to mothers who did not send their children to kindergarten. She lived on the benefit combined with child support. She was a mother of five, of which two were under three years of age, while the oldest was in the fifth grade.

The air in her home was so heavy and thick that it was difficult to breath. She did not open any windows because she was concerned that cold air might give her children "lung cancer", an illness she believed to be contagious. Despite this, her children suffered from colds almost all winter and were often absent from school. There was not much light in the apartment because the curtains were always closed. On the walls, one could see pictures of Mecca, the mosque in Jerusalem and other holy places.

Ezat herself was constantly tired from all the work that had to be done in taking care of the children. She was known among her neighbors for trying to negotiate for extra time to use the washing machine in the common laundry room. The allotted time for each family was too short for her to do all the washing she needed. The laundry room was therefore a place that she visited every day. There she met other women, most of whom were unemployed like her. In the laundry room, the women, some of them pregnant, would talk about the government the cash-for-care benefit and other financial support available to mothers. They talked about having more children to gain a higher income for their poor families. They encouraged each other and discussed the pros and cons of having more children. In addition, they thought that God would be pleased if there were more children around who could pray to him in this country. They found a meaning in having more children and legitimized it through religious ideas.

Children were, among other things, considered a source of income, but many of them experienced that the money was insufficient to support the needs of their children. They were used on utility bills and other necessary expenses. Having more children did not improve their financial standing. On the contrary, it worsened. And this lack of money in turn impacted negatively on the children, their rights and future opportunities in Norwegian society.[3] Consequently, poverty was replicated in the next generation, a vicious circle many minority families are unable to escape from.

Nevertheless, Ezat thought of her children's rights in her own way. She was very concerned that they would lose their Muslim faith and traditions, so she tried to make sure that they studied the Quran. On Sundays, she took them to a local center where Quran studies were offered so that they could learn more about Islam, their own culture and Arabic.[4] This center was one of the few she knew about and the only place she could go to when she wanted to get out of the house. She had heard about the center at the mosque.

Ezat was so afraid that her children would lose their belief and culture that she moved to England after being encouraged to do so by a religious organization, so that her children could go to a "real" Muslim school. After a while, she came back to Norway because she felt the welfare system was too weak in England. Ezat placed herself culturally outside Norwegian norms and what she thought as Norwegian culture. She was particularly strict against her daughter and wanted her to listen to her older brothers, an attitude that reflects how daughters in particular are exposed to control in the name of culture from their own parents.

Ezat's husband was unemployed, but he was taking driving lessons in the hope that it'll be easier to get a job after getting a driving license. Ezat protested in vain when her husband used the child support money to pay for his driving lessons. "The destiny of women is like this," Ezat said in a sad voice. "When the husband is pleased, God is pleased. We are Muslims, we have to take care of our family or we will end up like the Norwegians."

Ezat viewed almost everything in Norwegian society as negative, except for the welfare system which she benefited from herself. She was a good example of how minorities themselves form their ideas about Norwegians in terms of cultural and religious differences. Misconceptions and generalized ideas about Norwegian culture are combined with elevated ideas about the most conservative elements in their own religion and cultural background. The consequence is the propagation of divides that are impossible to cross and unavoidable conflicts.

Generally speaking, social control was strong in Angarudd, and it appeared to increase. Women and their daughters were forced to wear the hijab to signal that they were decent people. Non-religious neighbors were bullied by the religious ones, who constituted the dominant group. Divorced women and women who lived alone were considered abnormal and thought to be prostitutes. Some of them wrote an extra name on their door signs to conceal the fact that they lived alone. The social control was also apparent among children. For example, children who ate pork were bullied. People meant that they should be ashamed of themselves.

It is a fact that the dominant leisure activity among minority children is organized by religious societies: 56 percent of Pakistani parents have children who are involved in this kind of activity.[5] Probably this is also true for minority children in Angarudd.

The dynamics are simple. Due to financial standing and Norwegian housing policy – or rather a lack of Norwegian social housing policy – many minority women are gathered in one place. They are all not financially well off. They have taken upon themselves all the responsibility of cooking food, cleaning clothes and everything else their children might need. Very few of them have a job outside their homes. Because of this, they live rather isolated from the Norwegian majority society. The feeling of being excluded and the lack of contact with the majority society increase their own focus on religion.

Due to her environment, Ezat nourishes her rather simplistic beliefs and negative attitude toward Norwegians. Quite a few of those with an ethnic Norwegian background in Ezat's immediate environment are unemployed, drug addicts or in bad health, and therefore on social security. She is seldom in direct contact with the Norwegian majority population, except when she goes to the social welfare office or to her doctor. And because of this, her prejudices are not disproved. Her negative ideas are further confirmed through religious activities.

Norwegian housing policy increases the divide between the majority and the minority, especially in Oslo. This policy leads to a living environment that becomes so alien to Norwegians that they do not want to live there; neither do they want their children to play there. The very real social needs and distress that actually exist in Angarudd are simply perceived as mess and dirt by Norwegians who see it from the outside. I will further claim that this environment encourages social control over women and their daughters.

Social Control in Ghetto Areas

Social control in Angarudd can be illustrated with a woman I will call Jasmin, who is a political refugee. She tried actively to fight against and change the situation in Angarudd. Jasmin was a political idealist, tired of religion and war. She was also tired of how people were labeled based on ethnicity, culture and religion. She listened to John Lennon's Imagine while she looked at the women who sat in groups on the benches and the lawn outside. Jasmin wondered why these women, who had so much pain, never made use of the forest close by. She became sad when she saw how miserable the conditions were in Angarudd and wanted to do something about it. Sometimes she gathered some of the children in Angarudd to take them on walks in the forest, and she encouraged their mothers to come along. The mothers always had something they had to do and could not go, but they were glad she took the children.

Jasmin wanted to do something to improve the situation for these women and their children, and she organized activities for them. Among other things, she mobilized both men and women to establish the organization Women in Angarudd, which was supposed to organize things in the community so that the women would have more spare time for themselves. Some of the initiatives concerned making women more aware of their situation so that they could do something about it. She was also very critical of the influence of religious groups in Angarudd and hoped that Women in Angarudd would become a genuine alternative. As a result of this work, her life was threatened: If she did not stop, she was told, she would be killed. Many women were disappointed and those who had worked with her became isolated. Jasmin reported the threat to the police, but in the end, she had to move from Angarudd, fearing for the safety of her children.

Social control takes many forms in ghetto areas. This social control often contributes toward making some social areas agonizing, especially for women. But there are also other aspects that have a negative influence on people living in areas similar to ghettos. People who live there have not chosen to do so based on genuine opportunities. They live there because it is cheap. Consequently, the poorest segment of the population is gathered together in one place. The main factors for this are financial circumstances, future opportunities, and class.

Class can be defined in terms of distance and closeness to what is necessary. What are necessary are food, clothes and a place to live.[6] One has to earn a living. Many minority families do that first and foremost. For example, they do not have any opportunity to "buy themselves out of" bad living conditions. In Norwegian society, education is available to an absolute majority of the population who can then buy themselves out of many kinds of risks – risks related to health, residence, food, work and old age.[7] Nevertheless, there are some who cannot do this. Minority women, just as the lower rungs of societies in countries around the world, are exposed to risk when it comes to injuries from overwork, unemployment, poor living conditions, and poor diet.

In the Norwegian media today, there is a lot of focus on the upward social mobility of the minority youth. But some are left behind. Among the minority population, there are many who are left behind. In her work about social mobility, Kari Sveen warned against looking blindly at opportunities for individual social mobility because it detracts from the fact that there are still social conditions worthy of criticism: "Anyway, the attention paid to social mobility, diverts attention from the social structures that make this mobility possible for some, but not all."[8]

Class perspectives are completely absent from the debate about minorities in Norway. But in reality, class has a far greater significance than culture in, for example, most of the difficult cases the media focuses on: violence against women, social control and crime. Class also plays a decisive role when it comes to non-Western minorities' physical as well as psychic health, and it is often a decisive factor in what the media call "honor killings".

The Ghetto as a Painful Social Field

That living under impoverished circumstances entails a lot of strain is a fact documented through a long history of research.[9] Impoverished areas have been aptly called "a manifestation of problems."[10] When impoverished areas are populated almost exclusively by minorities, they are called "ghettos". Often a stigma is attached to such areas; the majority population worries both about living there and about allowing their children to visit these areas. Ghettos exist in all Western countries, albeit in varying degrees. The Norwegian situation is bad, but better than many other places, for example, England, France, Germany and the United States.[11] In all these countries, ghettos are the manifestations of complicated socioeconomic problems.[12]

Ghettos statistically end up worse on all indicators of quality of life. This is also true for Norwegian ghettos: Those who live there are poorer, more often unemployed and more frequently suffer health problems compared to that of the majority population.[13] Most of the inhabitants in Oslo with minority background live in ghettos. These immigrants live in one of the richest countries in the world, and still, they experience profound inequality. In reality, the multicultural Norwegian society is segregated. Why is it like this? Is it because people with the same culture want to live in the same area? Isn't this a much too simple explanation? In ghettos in Norway, people from very different cultures live together. What they have in common is that they are not ethnically Norwegian and, not least, that they have a far lower financial standing than most representatives of the majority population.

For years research has shown that it is likely that economic relations play a decisive part in establishing such ethnic concentrations of people: With a lower income and less wealth than the majority population, non-Western immigrants have to live in the least expensive areas out of necessity. Close to 40 percent of the ethnic segregation in 1998 can be "explained" as a result of economic differences. This is a bigger portion than what is found in other large cities in the Western world, and it is increasing over time. But a wish to be close to family and friends, discrimination in the housing market, and the tendencies toward an official administration of immigrant settlements, has also influenced the concentration of the immigrant population.[14]

Segregation has not decreased in the ten years that has passed. As the situation in Norway is today, a very big part of the people with the lowest incomes are from ethnic minorities. It is an illusion to believe that they can choose which part of the city to live in and in which place.

The historian Knut Kjeldstadli has studied the historical development of Oslo.[15] He describes a society segregated by class, which has grown from the 1870s, where government housing policies have done their part in creating and maintaining a form of segregation. Kjeldstadli shows how what earlier was a working-class area has, today, become a residential area with a large majority of non-Western immigrants. The economy and living conditions of the ethnic Norwegian working class in the area has improved and the residents have moved out, while im- migrants have moved in.

Moreover, other scientists have shown interest in the phenomenon. Several years ago, Leif Ahnstrøm, in his research on differentiated city development in Norway, referred to the high concentration of non-Western immigrants in the parts of the city called Gamle Oslo, Grünerløkka, Sofienberg, Søndre Nordstrand, and Romsås.

He noted that the high percentage of non-Western immigrants who lived in these areas cannot be a product of chance.[16] Some of these areas have changed considerably since then. Minorities have moved out, and people from the majority population have moved in. Not surprisingly, this development has occurred in parallel with the areas being upgraded. This is true for, among other areas, Grunerløkka and Sofienberg, and the same thing is now happening in Gamle Oslo. Property prices in these areas have increased steeply, and the minority population is now being pushed out of the central parts of the city. Still, what Ahnstrøm observed earlier concerning ghettos in the inner city of Oslo, continues to be valid: "the geographic distribution of ethnic minority groups in a city influence the understanding of the majority groups concerning the place and role of minorities in their society."[17]

Architect and professor Halina Dunin-Woyseth has also been interested in how segregation has a discriminating and stigmatizing character.[18] This is particularly true for a society like that of Norway, which is characterized by ideas of equality. Ideas of equality elsewhere in society make the ghettos even more negatively charged in the majority's perception. Dunin-Woyseth points to international research that confirms the fact that socioeconomic mechanisms play a vital part in the creation of ghettos.[19]

As indicated above, many scientific studies show that the main rea- son why non-Western immigrants become congregated in segregated housing areas is economic. They live in the worst areas of the city. They often live close to noisy roads. They do not have enough space and the standard of their apartments is lower than that of the majority population. Their neighborhood is often marked by what the majority population considers a congregation of social problems.

As Thomas Hylland Eriksen notes, a concentration of ethnic minorities is not necessarily a problem as long as the social conditions are acceptable.[20] As the situation is today in, among other places, Angarudd, social and economic conditions are at a level that the majority population would consider unacceptable. If Angarudd had less unemployment, more education in parts of the population, better economic conditions and better health, the multicultural environment there would be a genuine resource for Norway. Instead, the area is on its way to become segregated as "a society within a society", and as a very religious one to boot.[21]

Housing conditions are related to health, among other things because health is connected to wellbeing. In connection with The Health Impact Report in 2006, Øyvind Larsen, chairman of The Norwegian Medical Society, summed up the relation between housing conditions and health thus:

In Norwegian society, one has, for the most part, gotten rid of harmful dwellings, among other reasons because of 150 years of work with dwelling hygiene. However, new dwellings also create questions concerning dwelling hygiene, not least because the concept of health has become extended and is now an integral part of wellbeing. For the individuals, the hunt for a dwelling is ruled by need, preferences and opportunity. While, for example, in the period between the two world wars in the first part of the 20th century, it often was conscious planning by the authorities with health as a premise, we see little of this in a free market, where the needs, preferences and opportunities of those looking for dwellings are under pressure from other forces. The health aspect is not prioritized. Because much of the structure in a society is tied to the construction of dwellings, it is important to use the opportunities the society then has for controlling and determining the development of health services and social conditions. This work must take place across the board, from the practical implementation of regulations to political planning.[22]

Elisabeth and Ezat: On Human Potential

Elisabeth and Ezat had totally different opportunities when it came to making their lives better. In her liberal theory about justice, the philosopher and feminist, Martha Nussbaum, studied the possibility of each individual to flourish and live a good and dignified life.

We all have a set of basic qualities and abilities as humans. To develop our basic potential, we need the right conditions, for example, through socialization, formal or informal education, or practice. After socialization in a particular social environment, we end up, for example, with practical competence that in turn constitute important parts of our personal qualities. We all have the ability, the basic opportunity to learn a language. But to really do it and actually speak one or more languages, the ability has to be developed. This is the case for most human abilities.

To attain substantial freedom, the circumstances must be favorable so that we can activate and use our abilities. Only then can we attain the kind of freedom that makes a higher quality of life a real possibility.[23]

It is far to go from the silent needs of a reality where the circumstances do not support the development of potential abilities and ideas to actually possessing the ability and surplus energy to change one's life.

Many of the women I met lacked the necessary abilities to develop and attain substantial freedom. Consequently, they did not achieve real rights either. Many of them lived in silent oppression.

Elisabeth was a highly educated woman, socially well-adjusted to an environment in Chile that had given her the possibility to develop her abilities and potential. Elisabeth was a free woman and had substantial freedom in the sense that she did not choose passive coping strategies. On the contrary, she chose necessary, real and useful strategies to change her life. She managed to utilize her resources and make the radical choice of moving from Norway. However, she did not succeed in being integrated into Norwegian society. Furthermore, she did not manage to use her abilities and potential in Norway as her living circumstances were too difficult. She moved to Spain to build a new life for herself and succeeded in doing so.

I talked to Elisabeth when she was back in Norway on vacation. She seemed pleased then and also said that her health had improved. She was especially happy about getting rid of the suffering associated with exclusion. With a totally different background from Ezat's, she was not only able to change her life, but also to reduce her pain.

Ezat is a woman without education who is trapped in attitudes and opinions that can never improve her situation, and which she was introduced to through the Norwegians' weird opinions about what she needed - it was a Norwegian organization that offered her a course in Arabic and the Quran. There, she was introduced to Norwegian Muslim organizations as well as international ones. One of these organizations convinced her to move to England. Both in Norway and England she was in contact with Muslim organizations that made explicit distinctions between "Us Muslims" and "The West". Ezat came back to Norway disappointed. Here, she still lacks the circumstances that are needed to grow, use her abilities and potential, and to attain substantial freedom so that she can make genuinely free choices in order to really improve her life situation.

5. Women, War, Pain and Intimacy

"This is my grave, my bed." -Belquis

War is incompatible with recognition of the basic needs of people. Many of the women I met have experienced war. The experiences and memories of war have left strong, painful traces in their bodies.

War is the loss of the right to a good life. In the globalized reality of today, women suffer all over the world in countries ravaged by war. On all levels, war destroys the right of the individual to flourish in his/her society; political organizations don't work, legal rights disintegrate, social relations and the possibility of living a peaceful life where you can go to school and work, evaporate. Furthermore, the right to flourish in intimate relations is lost. Various forms of abuse against women are widespread in most societies in the throes of war. For women, war therefore often leads to the devastation of their intimate spheres.

As previously mentioned, the German philosopher, Axel Honneth, defines three spheres of recognition, and claims that an individual must experience all three forms of recognition to feel like a full human being. One has to be able to relate to and have the opportunity to attain various legal rights. One has to be able to experience recognition for ex- pressing opinions and needs within political and cultural communities, and not least, in the workplace. But first, one has to experience recognition and confirmation in one's own private sphere. All individuals need to be recognized for what they are, among friends and in their own family. Love and friendship are basic needs in our life. In relations be- tween mother, father and child, between spouses and between friends, we all need to develop symmetric relations – i.e., equal and trusting relationships where we can express our qualities and values and have them recognized as parts of ourselves.

If an individual does not experience emotional support, understanding and respect, he or she risks the loss of self-respect, which is crucial for personal development. In short, the experience of recognition is a prerequisite for a good life and for what we call happiness.

Violation is the opposite of recognition. Many of the women I met have experienced violations generally and in their intimate spheres.

A Woman's Bed

It occurred to me that the deepest intimacy is linked to the concept of the bed when I once asked several of my respondents what the word "bed" meant to them. Everyone I asked had painful associations linked to the word.

The painful associations were often caused by experiences in their country of origin. But they were also connected with the immigration situation. To many of them, to be an immigrant implies a lack of intimacy in their private lives. The personal intimacy, connected with friendly relations, family and partner, as well as a normal, intimate and safe sexuality, is difficult to experience and to maintain. This is a topic people don't talk about. First of all, the situation of an immigrant in itself demands a lot of focus on other basic needs such as housing, getting a job, acquiring a new language and adapting to a new situation. Secondly, it is taboo to talk about sexuality and intimacy, and the longing for friendship and love in research environments.

Paradoxically, it is the religious groups that are allowed to comment on issues related to the female body, sexuality and intimacy in Norway. In the media, minority women read on the front page about their private parts. Their most intimate body parts are being discussed in a way most people would consider bizarre. The women are against female circumcision. Still, they experience the public debate concerning this issue as very unpleasant.

Psychiatrist Solveig Dahl, who formerly worked at the now closed Psychosocial Centre for Refugees, has met many women who have experienced war. I asked her what she could tell me about the concept of 'bed', and got the following answer:

'Bed is, as you can read in the dictionary, first and foremost used for a place to sleep. But there are also other meanings associated with bed, for example, sexuality. To go to bed with someone can mean to have sexual relations with this person. "Being bedridden" or staying in bed is also connected with illness. A disease can also lead to a long period in bed. A bed in the garden is a place to sow seeds or plant flowers or vegetables, hence, a place where something grows. Bed can also be connected to death and the grave for "eternal rest". There are many associations and meanings linked to the concept that are connected with what one is doing in bed. I have met women who don't want to lie in a bed at all because of bad memories from what had happened in bed. They prefer the floor. And I have met women who, after being raped, feel helpless when they lie down, and who, for example, sleep sitting in a chair. Bed will always have different meanings for different people, depending on what they have experienced in connection with the bed.'

The negative associations of bed that Solveig Dahl refers to, and which I also encountered, indicate a lack of recognition in the intimate sphere. For some, this has to do with actual violations in the past. For others, it has to do with not experiencing love in the life they now live.

Shogofa and the Bed of Love

For Shogofa, the bed was a place for love. "Love is the most important element in life," she told me enthusiastically. She told me about an incident between herself and her husband in Kabul: "I was tired after coming home from work. When I changed clothes, I saw that my beloved husband had placed a picture of the Afghan president Babrak Karmal by our bed. I got angry and said to my husband: "If you don't get rid of the picture, I will put up a picture of Gulbuddin, the enemy of the president there as well. Remember that our bed is for love. Do not contaminate it with politics!"[1] Shogofa said to me: "Remember Farida, we can create peace in the world with love."

Shogofa went on: "Today I am married to the soul of my beloved husband. I live with his name and his memories. He comes to me in my dreams and helps me with everyday problems." Shogofa becomes nostalgic and remembers the happy days with her husband when she made her own decisions. Each time she tells me something intimate, she moves towards me and takes hold of my shoulders. "When I came to Norway, I received a double bed from the social office. I couldn't find any rest in that bed. It reminded me of the empty space left by my beloved husband."

In the end, Shogofa decided to donate the bed to a flea market. "Love is still an important element in life to me as an adult woman. Each night, I look at the photo from our wedding and pray in the final prayer of the day that my beloved husband is all right if he is still alive. Then I read my Quranic quotes to avoid sinful acts so that I can become a decent Muslim and have a place in paradise. Afterwards, I try to sleep and dream about my beloved husband who helps me with difficulties in daily life." When she finished talking, she clenched her fists. After that, she put her left hand on top of the right one in an attempt to curb her swelling veins that bothered her. Her eyes filled with tears. Life as a single mother in Norway is difficult for her. She tells me that she now gives all her love to her children. But she remembers an adult life filled with love and respect. She remembers her lost, happy life in Afghanistan.

Shogofa's Life before the War

As a schoolchild, Shogofa was awakened each morning by her mother, who patted her head and said with an encouraging voice: "Dear child. The sun is up. Be quick and go to school. Look to the west and be quick. We must hurry to be a part of this development."

Shogofa told me of a childhood filled with love, happiness and optimism for the future. As an adult she educated herself to be a teacher in Afghanistan and worked in schools before the Soviet occupation. She had what she describes as an ordinary life, like others around her. She was an active woman, and her education created the basis for financial independence.

Shogofa married for love. She kept in contact with both her male and female friends after being married. She took an independent decision to fight against the Soviet occupation. Neither she nor other women had to use veils or cover their bodies. She, like most women, did not pray five times a day like what is usual now in Afghanistan. Shogofa told me she could go to a café or cinema with friends without anybody asking questions.

During this time, religion was not an articulated part of Shogofa's identity. Islam as a religion existed side by side with development in many areas in society. And there were women in many powerful positions, among others, as ministers, MPs and lawyers in Afghanistan.

Shogofa was what spokesmen in the West today call an urban and modern woman. On the contrary, the poor part of the population in Afghanistan, especially in the rural areas, had neither economic nor practical opportunities to behave particularly "modern". For example, they did not use doctors or modern medicine, even if they wanted to. Instead, they used traditional herbal medicine. At the same time, it was customary to go to a mullah to get protection against diseases and "accidents". People then often received a tavis. A tavis is some sort of religious verse that a mullah or other spiritual leaders have written down. People carry it like an amulet. In actual fact, this may, in the best cases, have a certain placebo effect among religious people.

As I see it, a tavis is an example of a passive coping strategy linked to poverty, lack of knowledge and an underdeveloped health care system. This is also how Shogofa saw it when she lived in Afghanistan. Like many people with an education, Shogofa tried to tell people who lacked her knowledge that this did not work. "I tore the tavis off family members. To those who used tavis to protect their children against disease, I said: Go to a doctor and vaccinate your child! This does not work. Do not play with the health of your own child. Tavis is a false hope!"

War Changes People

Today, Shogofa looks back nostalgically to her past, and tries to understand how and why she has changed: "Even I ended up in a situation where I wanted to take refuge in false hopes when I knew better. This I did out of desperation and powerlessness, to find my beloved husband who had disappeared. All means had to be used."

Shogofa tells a painful story, of how she started to search for her husband after his disappearance. "I traveled to horrible prisons in various villages and saw, up close, what they did to people. In the village of Charasia, close to Kabul, there were drawers with corpses treated with tjuna, a corrosive chemical that was used to destroy evidence and make the body unrecognizable." While she is talking to me about this, she shows how the veins on her hands are swelling again. She is unable to go on for a while. In the end, she said: "Look, Farida. My throat is swelling. What is happening to my body?!" She tried to hold her hands around her throat as hard as she could so that I could see the imprints of her hands afterwards. She said with a voice filled with sorrow: "This is my life and my body today."

After a long search both in official and unofficial prisons, she tried tavis herself. She saw no other alternative. The process was difficult for her. "The queue was long, and it cost an enormous amount of money to visit the mullah who could help." The mullah she sought out used to write religious texts on women's thighs! Shogofa didn't want to show her thighs. She was firm and said: "I cannot show my thighs to a strange man, even if you are a mullah." The mullah put his arms around her and said confidently: "Not everybody gets the same treatment. Your case is unique. It demands other measures." Shogofa continued: "I'll never forget my meeting with this mullah in Teimani. In total, I spent more than 50000 kaldar on him and others engaged in the same type of activity."

There is a huge market for the sale of false hope to desperate people among the refugees from the war in Afghanistan. Many, especially women, have done the same thing as Shogofa.

Shogofa reflects over how her thoughts and actions have changed, and she links them to her deepest sorrow: "I cannot understand how a teacher like me before the war could be changed into a superstitious and powerless woman!"

She tells me about the last "prescription" she received. The mullah said she had to find clothes her husband had once used. Shogofa took out the most beautiful of his clothes. She could smell him, and this made her happy. The mullah wrote down formulas with names and various geometric signs in Arabic letters on the clothes. Afterwards, he asked her to tear the clothes into small pieces and burn them. "This was very difficult for me, because I was afraid that my in-laws might consider me a Jadoogar woman (a witch). I sat and cried and thought about the matter. In the end my brother-in-law came to help me. He said: 'Actually you are stupid! How can you tear apart a memento you have left of your husband?' He took the clothes and said I was not allowed to tear them apart."

The point of the mullah was that Shogofa should burn the clothes and follow the smoke to find her husband. She found some less nice clothes and burnt them. "But the smoke just disappeared up into the air without giving me any direction. Look what absurd actions I performed to try to find my beloved husband. I have become a crazy woman."

A Female "Kafthærbaz" and the Hope found in a Precious Stone

"Farida, listen to the story of Kaftære-e Safied (the white pigeon)," Shogofa said while she laid her arm on my shoulder one day when I visited her at home. "I was told that white pigeons have the ability to find the direction of a missing man. I had to find a pigeon with a totally white breast." I asked her more about the procedure. "The pigeon had to stay with me for one evening. After that, I release it and see the direction that it flies in."

In Afghanistan, rearing pigeons is a common hobby, especially among unemployed men. They are called Kafthærbaz, an expression meaning one who plays with pigeons, and is a degrading term when used on a woman. Shogofa kept the white pigeon together with other pigeons they had at home, for one whole evening. Afterwards, she released it. When she tells me about this, she clasps her hands together and asks engaging: "Do you know what happened to the white pigeon?" "Did it find the direction?" I asked. We both laughed at the situation. "My heart was crushed when the pigeon returned to our dovecote. I had thousands of unanswered questions in my head. Why on earth did the pigeon return? I cried and cried and found no answer. It didn't show me any direction," Shogofa told me.

The mullah comforted Shogofa with an explanation: "It is quite natural that the pigeon returns. It has found its love, its mate, among your other pigeons. It returns to stay with them. Stop crying. The pigeon finds the way for its own love. It doesn't think about finding the direction of your love." He explained to Shogofa that the pigeon had to be kept away from other pigeons, and that she had to keep it for a whole night. Only then will the method work.

Shogofa bought a new pigeon with a white breast: "It was a horrible night. I had the pigeon in my room. I couldn't sleep. All the time, the desperate pigeon flapped its wings and made an infernal noise. While I tried to sleep, I saw the silhouettes of wings on the walls around me. The pigeon was never still. I just wanted the long night to turn into day, so that I could release it and find my destiny and my direction." Finally, at daybreak, she released the pigeon. It flew in the direction of Hezb-i-Islami's terrible prison in Charasia. Only then did she finally try to accept that her husband was no longer among the living.

Shogofa didn't just try strategies linked to beliefs and the supernatural to find her husband. After she had escaped to Pakistan, she contacted Western organizations, among others, the Red Cross. "Do you think anybody listened to protests against the Mujahedin at that time? I tried everything. I contacted all organizations and media." She told me about the disappointment she felt over the Western institutions and media ignoring her. "I wasn't even allowed to come into an office to speak about the disappearance of my beloved husband. I who was in this desperate situation went to all the offices and told my story and cried to the guards to let me pass, but they answered that I should be glad I was alive myself." They said: "Go away and save your own life!"

After this total rejection by the Western organizations in Pakistan, Shog- ofa went back to another impossible strategy to solve her problem. "In the office of Hezb-i-Islami there was a nice man who let me borrow a precious stone that, supposedly, could help me find my husband." He didn't want any money for the stone right away. He said: "If you find your husband, you can give me 1500 kaldar. If it doesn't work, just give the stone back to me." She held her hands around my shoulders and laughed at herself while she told me about how she let the irrational dominate in a desperate situation. "I was very skeptical about the stone being of any help, but I had to try anyway, for maybe I could get my beloved husband back. I held the stone and read verses from the Quran just as recommended, but it didn't work." In the end, she said: "Look

Farida, this was the same Shogofa who once tore away tavis from family members, who now used the same things. What happened to me and many other educated women in my situation? I don't understand. I was a teacher. I cannot understand how I became like this."

The attraction of religious and "supernatural" passive coping strategies is not a unique development for this woman alone. It is a general trend among Afghans, Pakistanis and people in the Middle East in general, in recent years.

Ayaan Hirsi Ali describes a similar development among Somalis in Kenya. She observes a strong growth in the market for magic and superstition: "Modest churches pop up in streets where there used to be grocery stores. People from the Jehovah's Witnesses go from door to door. And of course, there are traditional soothsayers and sorcerers from various tribes at every street corner. Even in my class at Muslim Girls Secondary, some of the pupils bought love potions made from crushed fingernails and animal skin or amulets that could help them with their exams."[2]

The transition from a rational thinking woman to a woman occupied with beliefs and superstition becomes totally paradoxical when one sees this in terms of the multiculturalism that minorities encounter in a country like Norway. What does understanding and preservation of culture and religion mean in such a situation? Which "culture" does Shogofa belong to? What kind of "culture" can be attributed to women from Afghanistan? And what happens if they are attributed a religious identity? Women from several countries, among them, Afghanistan, Somalia and Iran, have experienced being looked upon as women coming from traditional cultures best compared with the European Middle Ages and to an ultramodern society.[3] Thus, they are attributed a culture they themselves have only experienced late in life, and fought against earlier. The historical line that is drawn by the West, from the Western point of view, legitimizes all this.

Memories of Sexuality and Protest against Female Circumcision

"Listen, Farida. It is not always we women who are victims. We had a fantastic existence before the war. The time when I was a teacher was the happiest in my life." Shogofa had felt like a free woman. And she had a good sexual life. She knew that many other women around her were likewise.

Shogofa told me a lot about the good life she and other Afghan women had before the war. She thought many had a good, open and exciting intimate life with their husbands. She told me that the clitoris is called senjed in Persian. It is also the name of a fruit used in a beverage that is commonly drunk when celebrating the new year. The fruit cooks in boiling water for a few days together with other ingredients and turns into a tasty juice named aftmeva, meaning seven fruits. The beverage is associated with love of nature, the new year and sexuality. She tells me nostalgically of the time she drank aftmeva together with her husband. They discussed the taste of senjed, which was stronger after having been in water for days. The beverage and the associations between nature and the female genitalia offered new impetus and enjoyment. To her, this was the good life. She sighed and said: "The war takes our men. I am not alone; there are thousands of Afghan women with memories locked in their sandoque-sine." Sandoque-sine is a Persian expression for a "coffin" within which the memories carried in the heart are locked.[4] Shogofa reacts strongly to Somali women being circumcised. When she compares herself with Somali women, she sees mostly differences. "Somalis cut off their senjed, but we celebrate it!"

Circumcision is probably just as alien to Shogofa as it is to most Norwegian women. But like many other women from the non-Western world, Shogofa has received numerous questions on whether she is circumcised or not. In the eyes of the Norwegians, they are "Muslim women". It means that they are attributed many common qualities, founded in strong notions about religious and cultural oppression. Even if Shogofa does not identify herself with women from Somalia, she does understand that women in Afghanistan today have difficulties. She sees that even if women are not circumcised, their sexuality is more suppressed than ever.

I have met many Somali women who never would consider circumcising their children, even if they had stayed in Somalia. When I spoke to a Somali woman who was a strong believer in Islam about this issue at the Jacob Center, she suddenly closed her eyes and started singing a poem. She sang about how we should not harm anything of creation, how we should not cut our body parts because the prophet Mohammed wanted us to remain as we were created.

Shogofa escaped to Norway. Now she lives in Paris where she works together with her sister in the latter's shop. She still lives a difficult life and suppresses her needs for intimacy. Thousands of women like her live in Afghanistan today - women who have had their intimate spheres destroyed but have memories and longings.

Shogofa also saw oppression of women in the West: "Here in the West it is worse. Did you see in those movies how many men and women lie with each other like animals? Luckily, we were not like that. We were better. There were no pornos, no pornographic books, but women learned from each other."

Shogofa tried to distance herself from both Norwegians and other minority groups, especially Somalis. The only exception was her own group. She tried to elevate her own culture by looking down on others. Many minority groups are exposed to such prejudices. In the hierarchy of minorities in Norway, Somalis are often at the bottom. This form of generalization, hyperbole and misunderstanding of cultural differences, in the end, becomes racism. The unintended downside of multiculturalism is clearly expressed in Shogofa's perception of Western sexuality. She doesn't understand that porn is an industry that most people in the West distance themselves from. She sees it as a part of general Western culture. She interprets what she sees through her own cultural lens. At the same time, she uses what she sees to legitimize her own way of life and considers her own attitudes as culturally superior to that of the West. In this way, Shogofa does to others what she doesn't like others to do to her. Shogofa turns her multicultural gaze on the West in the same way that the majority turns their multicultural gaze on her.

Above all, they make her into an oppressed Muslim woman that is a victim of a culture and a religion that becomes a part of her being. She ends up in a big and imprecise category.

The attitude towards females, sexuality and liberty is a combustible topic that affects non-Western minority women. Here, we won't progress any further if we don't dare to fight against prejudices among all parties in this conflicted landscape. And most important of all, we have to make the right to recognition of women in their own intimate sphere into a premise for the debate. Actually, we have quite much psychological knowledge on what happens when the intimate sphere of a person is violated by violence, oppression and notions of shame and impurity. We must not ignore this knowledge and justify violations of women's private spheres in the name of culture. And then we have to look at the complexity of the matter. For example, Shogofa had had a good and safe love life, but lost it. For her there was no original culture standing in the way for an equal and loving relationship. The loss of this good life, and the sorrow over having lost the life as an independent and respected woman she once had, made her vulnerable and extremely sensitive to new violations. But it seemed that this also nourished her prejudices against others.

Shaeen's Lack of Intimacy

Shaeen is highly educated and is socially well-adjusted in a culture with an almost positivistic way of thinking. The world consists of causal relationships and can be explained. Shaeen is silent about her life. She trusts nobody, and consequently, never speaks to anybody about what happened to her. Even her psychiatrist is viewed as a spy who is reporting on her. She doesn't want me to write what country she comes from. Pain has totally taken over the life of Shaeen. She herself claims that everything bad in the world is the doing of imperialists. Shaeen is a communist, and in the political landscape she previously belonged to, she was "raised" to be an example to a population that still had many traditional Muslim values.

There are mostly men on the committees of communist organizations, and especially in the last 30 years, when religion and culture has developed into important identity markers, it has been important for these organizations to unite with the Islamists. The Iranian revolution, where Khomeini appeared as an anti-imperialist, linked Marxism in the Muslim world to progressive Islam. But the female dimension on the left became silent in this situation. Women who protested against the mandatory use of veils were dismissed as bourgeois. Many organizations, Western ones as well, have supported everything anti-American without looking at what consequences this would have for the women if the movements they supported came to power.

Within this political culture, it has been difficult for Shaeen to fulfill her individual needs. It is taboo for her to talk about her intimacy and private needs. "When it comes to love, I have actually never experienced it." She doesn't want to talk any more about it.

On one hand, Shaeen hates her bed because she is unable to sleep. At the same time, the bed is a place of nostalgia of the short time she spent with her husband, and it is full of books. For she is proud of her past, and over the key role she played in the Marxist-Leninist movement she belonged to, and which she thinks history should remember. But maybe she is too oriented towards the past. She has huge problems relating to her situation in Norway. Both politically and personally, she is neither able to forge any alliance nor participate in an arena. Pain, memories of war, exclusion and isolation, dominates her daily life. She has given up the struggle to find a job. She receives social security benefits and lives, compared to the rest of the population, in poverty.

When she talks about how she is now, actually, she is almost completely occupied with her own illness. The only thing that gives her life meaning is to be together with her grandchildren. Her present is occupied with nostalgia and repetitive stories about the past. The future only brings her closer to death. When she compares herself with her comrades who live in other Western countries, she sees that their des- tinies are similar to her own. This causes her sorrow. Shaeen has never been allowed to fulfill her needs as a woman in a good and safe sphere of intimacy. This marks her. Today, she has the possibility of receiving and giving love to her children and grandchildren. But to a large extent, she is overcome by sorrow, pain and memories.

Belquis: A Lonely Woman

We have heard the story of Belquis, who was first on sick leave from her cleaning job and then became incapacitated and unable to work. One day, when I visited her, she sighed deeply. She bustled around while she gave me a false smile: "Look at the children's room, how beautiful it is! This is important to me. The children must have a nice place to rest and enjoy themselves in their own room." Then she showed me a messy room with only a foam mattress on the floor. She said: "Look Farida, this is my grave, my bed."

Belquis' comparison of her bed to a grave has haunted me ever since and dominates my thoughts when I write about this. To me, this says a lot about the condition of immigrant women. It relates to the condition of illness that Abdelmalek Sayed wrote about when she studied how Algerian immigrants perceived their situation in France.

Belquis is chronically ill. She is marked by the past from her country of origin, but most of all she is lonely, isolated and frustrated in her new homeland. Most of all, it is the lack of opportunities to improve her situation in Norway that defines her hopeless condition. I think both the individual and the structures in society create this condition. In Norway, the individual has many statutory rights that can turn a condition of illness into a life of value and quality. But it is not easy, and for a woman like Belquis, there are many obstacles – both visible as well as invisible.

Belquis told me about an imam she saw on TV. He said that a Muslim woman could well live as a cohabitant, just like Norwegian women do. She finds it difficult to understand that an imam can say this on TV when she knows she cannot do this. According to Belquis, there are mostly unwritten laws and rules that govern the daily life of Muslims in Norway. The focus on these unwritten rules and laws become even more important for many when they live in the west than in, for example, Sudan, where Belquis comes from. But she wonders: "Do Norwegian women, who live with a man without being married, go to a priest to ask permission? Or do priests comment on this issue on Norwegian TV?"

The combination of restrictions founded on religion that affects women's private and intimate lives and their actual experiences with violations is, by itself, difficult to live with. When "representatives" of their own culture in addition can come forward publicly and present lies concerning what they actually allow women to do, the situation becomes even more hopeless.

Baarin: A Woman with Hope

Baarin is, in many ways, the opposite of Shaeen. She has a critical and reflected perspective on her past with an authoritarian family. She went through a divorce that was painful for her. She has left the limitations on her intimacy and freedom behind. Baarin has a poetic and beautiful description of the importance of love:

A life without love loses its meaning. Love is the locomotive that gives you the strength to overcome the difficulties of daily life. It is the premise for becoming a whole human being and something fundamental in the life of a woman that takes into account her own needs. Human history started with a longing for love when Adam and Eve were banished from paradise. This is the meaning of humanity and it gives us the opportunity for happiness. This incident is the start of human civilization, poetry, music and art, which is the basis for human happiness.

Baarin also had a beautiful description of what a bed should represent. She said to me: "The bed is a place, a garden of silence, where you can feel that you exist, and you can find peace and quiet. I think of the present. I live here and now. To sleep well in the garden of silence, you have to have an active day, and a love life."

Baarin has had experiences that have been imprinted into her body, but she focuses on the present. That way, she can control her pain and have a meaningful life – a life in which she herself recognizes her own needs as an adult woman.

To Baarin, to be a refugee is a "gift" from the war. War, with all its misery, destruction and unforgettable memories of executions, creates collective memories that are imprinted into the mind of the individual and society as a whole. All these memories are so embedded that you cannot completely get rid of them. It is not possible to forget. Baarin thinks immigrant women have an especially great need for recognition, love, inclusion and solidarity just because they have experienced so much of the opposite. She emphasizes peace, quiet and safety as pre- conditions for establishing a good life in her new homeland.

Baarin's divorce made her ill for a period. It was not possible for her to make the doctor understand what a strain this was, and why it emerged as bodily pain. An additional difficulty was that she had been taught to understand that the man is "the shadow of God". She was taught to respect her father and her adult sons. But this notion of male authority created a distance and a lack of intimacy and closeness to the men in her life. It was very conflicting for her to decide to get a divorce and rebel against her family and traditions. An honorable woman should endure misery and obey her husband and father. She loved her father and her husband, even if they, in reality, made her life miserable. She could not resolve the conflicting issues where she, on one side, loved her father and her husband and sought respect as an honorable woman, and, on the other side, saw that her daily life was marked by pain and suffering because of her extremely controlling husband who had to be loved.

Baarin has lived in several countries before she came to Norway. Even if her immigration experiences have been marked by many difficulties, and she, in periods, felt that she was drowning in responsibility for her children and family, she still thinks living in Norway gives her new possibilities. She looks at Norwegian women who see themselves as individuals and thinks this gives her the opportunity to look critically at the society she comes from. And it gives her the opportunity to live alone as an independent woman. After the divorce, she attained the peace and quiet she needed to reflect over her own past - a past that is not unique, but on the contrary, is similar to that of many, many other women.

In hindsight, Baarin looks at this as a victory: She got the opportunity to come to Norway and experience a society where women and men are relatively equal. She has no fear in talking about the past. She remembers very well her own actions and accepts them. She looks at them as a natural part of being a woman in the society her family came from. Baarin looks at herself as a pioneering woman who wants to share her experiences, and to encourage women to reflect over their situation and recognize their needs. She also thinks the balance she has gained gives her an opportunity to be a better mother to her children.

Pierre Bourdieu makes a distinction between a doxic and a reflective habitus. The doxic is what is taken for granted, what is obvious, just lying in the subconscious, but which, to a great extent, defines our reality. Between the doxic and the reflective habitus, I see what I will call "the doxic wall". It consists of conservative traditions, religious conventions and metaphysical methods and models of explanation that together create the dominant understanding of the culture all Arab and Muslim immigrants are placed into. The multicultural attitude that now pervades Norwegian society endorses such an understanding of culture. And with this, the road from a doxic habitus to a reflected habitus is made even longer and more difficult. The road to change becomes nearly impossible because people are given an identity that further amplifies what they want to escape from.

Baarin has gone through a personal change and has become a woman who decides over her own life. But if she puts on her tight veil, most people will see her as something completely different.

Global Conscience and Recognition of the Need for Love

Those who come from and live in Afghanistan and Somalia suffer from problems that can be traced back to the Cold War. The war created institutionalized fundamentalism in these areas. During the Soviet occupation of Afghanistan, Islam was also institutionalized in Pakistan. In this period, only religious forces received military and financial support from the West. Western media, with their ability to create opinions, played a key role in this. Moreover, Western aid organizations bonded strongly with religious institutions at the grassroots level. The most conservative religious forces were given the opportunity to grow, and after a while, they created impossible demands and false hopes, especially for women.

"False hopes are the prison of the individual. They just prolong suffering and pain," Shogofa said. She herself was imprisoned by passive coping strategies linked to religious and cultural traditions. Furthermore, Belquis was imprisoned in the combination of impossible demands and false hopes for the future. She was desperate in her belief that reading Quranic verses 30 times each evening before she lay down to sleep would help her daily life. In this way, she lost her actual ability to act, and eventually became even more powerless.

When they come to Norway, they are attributed a religious identity they did not have in their homeland. And they develop and enhance this new identity to a great extent because of the political circumstances in the West. In addition, they are, by virtue of their immigrant condition, vulnerable and not necessarily able to speak out and emphasize their individuality. As a result, they are imprisoned in inaccurate cultural and religious concepts of who they are and what needs they have.

When female victims of war come as refugees, they are classified according to nationality, culture and ethnicity instead of as individuals. The institutions they come in contact with are mainly interested in their rights as members of a group, not as female individuals. Here the recognition of each woman's individual identity is buried. For each individual woman, a national, religious and cultural identity is constructed that is difficult to break free from. The woman is placed in a large and imprecise catch-all category. She then becomes part of a collective group which she is also attributed a collective responsibility for. But her individual immigration story – one that often deals with many forms of violations - is ignored.

For immigrant women, life in Norway often has a difficult starting point. But the possibility for positive change is greater if they are more readily looked upon as individuals – i.e., to be looked upon as a woman with an individual history and individual needs and to be recognized as such. To handle the pain of non-Western minority women better than what is done today, we must understand this reality.

Psychiatrist and psychoanalyst Sverre Varvin, who for many years worked at the Psychosocial Centre for Refugees in Oslo, believes refugees and asylum seekers get their old traumas intensified just by the lack of recognition. "The threshold for feeling being trampled upon may be lower for a person who has already been violated in the most serious way," Varvin points out. At the same time, he thinks that just the way a person is treated in his or her new homeland is crucial for a good and dignified life: "These are vulnerable individuals who are also 'survivors', who have achieved much and have much strength - if only they get recognition."[4]

The need for and right to receive recognition for immigrant women in their private and intimate sphere in their new Norwegian home is constantly being precluded. Among other women in the country, this is an obvious right. It is not always fulfilled, but just the same, most of them consider it an obvious right. For minority women however, it is a silent right - and in this area, we find much sorrow. With their multicultural ideas, the majority population considers the private life of the minority as a private domain.

Maryam Azimis´ book "Det brente hjertet, سوخته دل (1999 ، Aschehoug). In the end of this chapter, I chose some poems from Maryam Azimi (an afghan poet), which are relevant to this chapter. In these poems, Azimi shows us another version of the thoughts of an immigrated woman concerning about homeland and optimism which is visualized in the word bed (bestar/ بستر).

Refuge[5]

Aachen, October 1983

Along the edge of hope I walked, muddy of sorrow,

and believed I could reach the cleanest bed you can think of.

I walked and believed I could dress off my days,

And lie down in the cleanest bed you can think of.

I stood up

and went to the small window that shined red in the morning light.

The morning light spread out over the road outside,

and on this one road out there I could see myself

walk fast and quiet away from myself,

and seek refuge

in the burning hill that I came from.

Awake[6] Oslo, 2003

Alone I sat in the bed of night's with open eyes

I discovered my heart

That lit up my house

In the bed of night's

In the black bed of the night, I couldn't sleep

In the bed of night's can anybody

In peace and quiet keep on making love?

This is female contemporary history. The bed can be an image, like a metaphor for the darkest of the dark and a dream of the lightest and the best.

We have to fight for the right to recognition for these women at the intimate level as well.[7] The starting point cannot be that "they" are so different from "us" that doubt exists whether they really need such recognition. Likewise, we cannot put these women within a cultural or religious context where such needs, supposedly, do not exist.

6. Male Dominance and Social Control

Oppression of women cannot be linked to any particular religion or culture. It appears in all religions and cultures, including that of Norway. However, when minority women are being submitted to oppression and violence, this becomes exclusively linked to Islam and non-West- ern cultural traditions. Oppression of and violence against women exist in all cultures and should be opposed in all cultures!

It is a fact that many minority women in Norway today arrived as part of family reunion programs and were financially dependent on their husbands, or as new wives brought over after the husband has established himself in Norway.[1] They often do not learn Norwegian, and their freedom is, in many cases, limited. This is a situation where the women do not have equal opportunities to develop or establish themselves as independent women. Many of them also live under constant psychic pressure from their husbands. As a result, they often experience a total paralysis concerning what to do. This is a form of invisible but complete male dominance that is ignored by the media.

Violence is only given attention in extreme cases, as when a murder is committed. In recent years, there have been many such murders, not only in Norway but in several of the suburbs and ghettos of Europe. Honor killing is an extreme form of violence against women, and is an expression not only of male dominance, but general social control. Another extreme expression of oppression is some suicides among minority women. These are often passed over in silence. The forms of oppression discussed by the Norwegian public, in addition to honor killings, are forced marriages and circumcision. Honor killing, forced marriages and female genital mutilation are portrayed as expressions of non-Western and Muslim culture to such an extent that all non-Western minorities and all Muslims feel it concerns them, and what is just the view of a small part of this huge group is also assigned to them all.

Stories about Violence and Control

I met Naima in a Quran Group at the Jacob Center. Naima had chosen to go there in the hope that God would punish her husband. She showed me the bruises all over her body after he had been at her place and beaten her to get money. He had not just beaten her, but also pressured her by threatening to tell her parents that they were now divorced. This would have put Naima in a very bad light because according to the ideas in her family, it is the woman who is suspected of having failed when it comes to divorce. Naima is not just dominated by her ex-husband, but also by the social control exerted by her family, acquaintances and the religious environment.

Arezo, the second wife of her husband, also suffers under this form of social control. She is a representative for thousands of immigrant women who experience being dominated both by their husband and relatives. Crying, she told me: "I have been married to my husband for more than 21 years. A few days after the wedding, my miserable life began." When Arezo was still working in her husband's shop, she told me that she had to work in the stockroom. She became tired of carrying the heavy banana crates and wanted to sit at the checkout counter and relax but was not allowed because her husband was ashamed of her. "We women must hide, we are creatures of shame," she says.

It was not only in the shop that her husband forbade her to do the things she wanted. She was also not allowed to learn Norwegian even if she wanted to, and she was not allowed to have as much contact with her family as she wanted. Consequently, she lost her whole social network when she married.

Arezo does not recognize herself in the way Pakistani family culture is being described: a culture where women want to stay at home to take care of the old. "It is the Pakistani men who think of this as a duty and who look at not fulfilling this duty as a shame". She herself misses her own family. "The duty of a woman is to take care of her husband and his family," she says. She does not feel free in her own home. Her doctor had advised her to sunbathe because she lacked vitamin D. Fortunately, her husband and parents-in-law were in Pakistan for a few months so she could sunbathe on the balcony. When her husband was away, she felt free, but still worried because he might be looking for a new wife - the third one. After she became ill, she was worried this was the cause.

That was what happened to Baarin from Iran. Her husband went away for a few months and left her with their three children and a child from his previous marriage. When he came back, he was married again, with wife number three. He was earlier convicted of rape in Iran, and when they came to Norway, he banned her from talking with the others at the Norwegian language course, while he, who took the same course, flirted openly with other women. He didn't even allow her to listen to music. "Why do you listen to those love songs?!" he said. "Are you in love with somebody?" He told her that she was his holy property, and that if he saw her sitting absently looking into space, he would immediately know what she was thinking about. Baarin acquiesced and put up with her husband's attempt to control her - where she went, what she did, how she thought and felt - because she believed it was the will of God that she should please her husband. Yet, after a while, she realized that she had to get out of the relationship and away from oppression, jealousy and control. Today, as mentioned previously, she is divorced.

The Power of the Collective over the Individual

It is not only male dominance which lies behind the total control these women are subjected to and suffer from. There is also a more general social control where group pressure, rumors and collective sanctions come into play when someone breaks with what is considered morally acceptable behavior. Often, male dominance and social control work together, but just as often, I believe, men are pressured by social control in an area dominated exclusively by the minority population.

As mentioned earlier, Arezo was advised to exercise when she consulted her doctor for help against her pains. It is also documented that exercise is effective in alleviating pain. And when Arezo lived in another municipality where there were fewer Pakistanis, she did exercise like the doctor said, and she felt much better. But after moving to Grønland in Oslo, she lost her opportunity to do physical exercise. When she tells me this, she cries and wipes her tears away with the veil: "Here, people go more to the mosque than to the gym. If I tell you more the veil will be completely wet." Her body language told me that she had problems responding, and again, she comes back to the link between women and shame. "Oh, Farida, have you forgotten that we Pakistani women are *sjærm* creatures (creatures of shame). If I go to the gym my husband will be embarrassed, and it will be a shame for the whole family. People will say: 'Look, the wife of Ahmad goes to the gym', and the rumors will be spread in the mosque. The shame around this will create more pain. It is worse than in Pakistan. There, people are not that strict. Why is this? I cannot stand to have a conflict with the family and the neighbors. People will say that I am not an honorable woman."

What Arezo describes is a very complex area of dominance. A man with the same background as Arezo's husband told me that he wanted to take care of the children while his wife went to the gym, like the doctor had recommended because she had diabetes. But in Grønland in Oslo this was not possible, he said. "People were not that strict in Paki- stan. I do not understand what has happened to Pakistanis in Grønland. There, they gather at the mosque and have nothing else to talk about than others and how good they are at watching over their women. The mullahs only talk about how important it is for us to keep our Muslim values and our traditions when we are in Norway."

In Norwegian public debate, this form of oppression is often seen as something culturally imbued. But both what this man told me about Grønland compared to his homeland, and Arezo's description of what she could do when she lived in a Norwegian suburb, show us how dynamic culture really is. Culture and religion have become universal explanations for why these groups and these men do like they do. But we cannot discuss whether and how they are ruled by their culture. Whose culture are they talking about then? We must look, rather, at oppression in itself, and admit that it is real.

Arezo elaborated on her feeling of being controlled in this way:

When I go out, it is a huge burden for me. First and foremost, I must explain to my mother-in-law and father-in-law why I'm going out. I must even think of what to say if I meet the neighbor on the second floor. I must be careful of where I walk so that I do not meet certain persons. I must even be careful to wear Pakistani clothes, or else there will be rumors that I have become Norwegian.

Why is it accepted among men that they do not need Pakistani clothes while we women must have them?

Grønland and similar ghetto areas have ended up almost like rural landscapes – right in the middle of the city - where the social control for some is even stronger than it was in the village in Pakistan. But just a small part of the reason why such oppression can continue may be ascribed to the culture of their original homeland.

It is true that many of the minorities in Norway come from traditional and patriarchal villages in Pakistan, Afghanistan, Turkey, Morocco, Ethiopia and Somalia, places where the honor and shame codex that the social control in Grønland and other places are ruled by, has a strong foothold. For example, most of the Pakistanis in Norway come from Punjab province, where, according to Unni Wikan, more than 500 honor killings are committed per year, and where fundamentalist parties like the Deobandi movement have a great influence.[2] Patriarchal, traditional and religious values have a strong footing and are very politicized in Afghanistan, Somalia, Iran, Turkey, Algeria and Morocco. And this is linked to the historic influence that militant fundamentalist movements have had in those countries.[3]

But here, it is important to be unwavering when assessing this and not define it as absolute cultural differences.[4] Firstly, the culture the immigrants bring with them is a result of a process of socialization that, in itself, is a product of certain social and historic preconditions, such as colonialism, the Cold War and globalization processes, and the link between Islam and politics. Secondly, this "culture" they bring is only a part of what leads to social control. The supposed "culture" is diverse. It has often changed radically just in the last decades, and it also has a great future potential for change. I will claim that factors in Norwegian society are actually quite crucial in relation to the content that the so-called Muslim culture gets, and which direction it takes.

As we have seen, non-Western minorities, especially in Oslo, live segregated from the majority in a "society within a society"[5]. The causes are, as shown, mainly economic. This is a situation that has been constructed over a relatively short time, and it is a phenomenon that we know also applies to all of Europe, North America and Canada. Such places are characterized by the fact that "everyone knows everyone". Persons and families know each other in the context of various roles that may not be so obvious to the outsider. Some ghetto-like areas, like, for example, Grønland in Oslo and Angarudd, are characterized by close family relationships in addition to new close bonds that arise in Norway.[6] This small society creates its own structures. The starting point is economy, not culture.

It is also important to be aware of social control in relation to how the immigrants encounter Norway. When the first Pakistani labor migrants came to Norway in the 1970s, they actually had jobs, but still had great problems establishing themselves. Most of them settled in Grønland, at that time a stigmatized area, where they lived among economically disadvantaged Norwegians and drug addicts. Often, they did not know the language and had no family. Consequently, they had a difficult life and few preconditions for coming into contact with and establishing relations with ethnic Norwegians. Even if they, in the beginning, organized themselves in worker unions, after a while, they started organizing themselves in mosques and used those places to hold meetings. The lack of recognition is one side of modern society that is particularly problematic for immigrants. In this connection, mosques can function as an alternative. They can provide a feeling of belonging and a basis for creating a new identity. In this way, the mosque became an important meeting place in Oslo.

Even if the first immigrants in Norway came as labor immigrants, the

unemployment rate is far higher among immigrants than for the majority. Work can be a crucial factor for the identity of a person to take root.[7] Belquis, whom we have met earlier, said to me: "Work creates a human being". She told me how proud she had been about fending for herself. She felt good because she was not a welfare client but earned her own money, and even managed to find her own apartment, and could send her children to participate in leisure activities. As we saw, it was her situation of being unemployed and in despair that brought about the fact that religion completely took over her life.

Already in 1986, Khalid Hussain wrote in *Pakkis* about how his father began to frequent the mosque after losing his job. He started to dress in traditional clothes and also forced his children to go to the mosque. The increasing influence of the mosques and religious organizations must be seen in the context of such circumstances that are, first and foremost, social.[8] It is not a coincidence that Islamic faith communities in Nor- way have increased their membership numbers from around 1000 in 1980 to 73000 in 2003.[9] The growth is of course partially due to there being more immigrants, but that is not the only reason. We can see a connection between unemployment and religious revitalization. In the meantime, someone discovered that mosques received funding from the state that is proportional to the number of members in the organization, which also must have contributed to increasing recruitment efforts.

The social control, that is so linked to religion, must at least partially be understood in connection to the question of identity and social belonging, as these two factors have been problematized everywhere in our globalized world.[10] Groups who experience that their identity and moral and symbolic order is threatened, have a tendency to strengthen the divisions between themselves and others.[11]

Norwegian policy and the ideas of Norwegians on minorities have, to a large extent, played a part in shaping small societies within the society where social control is strong. And one has, to a continually greater extent, attributed the female oppression this leads to, to the non-Western values this male dominated society, as a whole, is supposed to value. Consequently, the discussions have often been about whether one can take in more immigrants with such attitudes, and whether they can adapt to good Norwegian values after settling here.

But male dominance and female oppression cannot simply be caused by non-Western culture and beliefs, as, among others, the Progress Party, Hege Storhaug and Ayaan Hirsi Ali claim, and like many in the majority believe. It is not that the minorities bring a cultural baggage with them that hardens and cannot be changed when they arrive in a Western country. Like me, many immigrants have, in periods of their lives, experienced a great degree of freedom in their non-Western country of origin. In addition, most immigrants live a life, in common with Norwegians, in which culture and religion do not govern and control all their thoughts and actions! Such a view of non-Western culture in which it is considered undemocratic, static and unchangeable, and one that is totally different from the Western model, is built on stereotypical views of both religion and culture and forms the basis for racism. Based on a failed aspect of multicultural thinking in Norway, it contributes toward culture being exaggerated and turning into an excuse for not intervening.

We must therefore not be content with using men or culture as good causal explanations. We must look at the complexity in the causes. But first and foremost, we must look at what effects the ruling attitudes have for women. Only then can we do something about it.

In the beginning, when I started my fieldwork and interviews with minority women, I was very angry at the husbands of these women because they did not help them, for example, by participating in parent-teacher conferences at school, helping with housework or assuming responsibility for some of the daily chores. Closer to the end of the fieldwork, I had to conclude that it was not only male dominance that was the cause of the difficult lives of the women. Male dominance is the closest and most intimate of many social fields. In addition, to be dominated by their husbands is the first link in a more extensive social control. But this social control has causes, I think, that cannot be ascribed to the men only. We must look at male attitudes, the current sanctioning from the Norwegian cultural sphere, and, not least, how current religious practice impacts the women's lives.

Religious Dominance

The power religious organizations have acquired, contribute, to a large extent, toward the maintenance of the social control that characterizes some minority environments. This is an area that requires more research. My respondents often mentioned mosques when they were ex- plaining the social control they were exposed to. There have also been statements from imams that indicate that they support a form of social control over minorities, like when an imam stated that it was legitimate for a man to beat his wife.[12] However, this generated strong reactions, first and foremost, from minorities who requested that the influence of imams be limited.

Today, imams express themselves in the media concerning many issues about minorities, and they have acquired more power here in Norway than they had in their country of origin.[13]

If these organizations are as central in the maintenance of social control as it seems, it is worth asking some critical questions, both about the influence they have in the Norwegian public, and the funding they receive from the state. It is not enough to note that these religious organizations have a lot of power. We must investigate why and under what circumstances they have acquired such a strong influence.[14] And we must dare to discuss whether the Norwegian state contributes to this influence.

The social anthropologist, Marianne Gullestad, was quite explicit. She wrote that multiculturalism leads to "people being tied to sharply limited and mutually exclusive groups, a danger that is enhanced through a statistically based and rule-oriented administration interacting with the wish of ethnic and religious leaders to consolidate their authority".[15] Thomas Hylland Eriksen, in several places in his publications, questions the idea that religion is a private matter in Norway. Religion, he says, has public influence. Also, Oddbjørn Leirvik points out that religion is a public concern.[16] One aspect of moving this into the public sphere is how the state has actually chosen to respect the autonomy of faith communities in spite of the law of equality of 1978 that forbids gender discrimination. But when freedom of religion violates the rights of women, one must, in a democratic society, intervene. Religious leaders cannot be allowed to act in public as a representative of whole cultural groups, when what they say in reality, has a suppressive effect.

Why Women are Hit Harder by Social Control

Women who don't work, have little opportunity to come into contact with others outside the environment that controls them. The lack of social networks where representatives of the majority population reside is lacking in the lives of many minority women.

A part of being able to function in Norwegian society is to have relations outside one's own family and the homogenous environment one often lives in. This applies to both children and adults. The mothers try to make sure that their children have contact with Norwegian friends, as was the case with Elisabeth at Angarudd. To make contact with and find friends among Norwegians is one of the biggest problems facing many immigrants. Such networks are not only valuable for creating a feeling of belonging and meaning, but also to satisfy a basic need for closeness and intimacy. And there are also practical factors as well, such as finding a job, learning the language, and learning more about the society they live in. But many fail to do so. The distance between the life of minorities and that of majorities is often wide. Isolated, without contact with the majority community, minority people are also far more susceptible to social control.

Both men and women suffer under the social control that applies in

areas with large immigrant density in Norway today. But still, women suffer most. When Arezo points out the reactions that will come if "the wife of Ahmad goes to the gym", and says that this will be a shame, she shows us how social control is aimed particularly at women. Shame is a central concept that underlies social control. The Danish politician, Naser Khader, is among those who have been concerned with honor and shame, and he has, among other things, described how unwritten rules govern daily life for many Muslims.[17] In the same way as the Norwegian anthropologist, Marit Melhuus, describes how honor and shame is linked to gender and demands different behavior for men and women, Khader says that the honor of women is solely linked to her sexual behavior.[18] While male honor is linked to many factors, for example their ability to support their family, it is also linked to their ability to gain respect for the family and to protect the sexual behavior and virtue of their women. Male honor requires that they look after and control the sexuality of women, both sisters and wives.[19] Within this socially controlled sphere, the woman, as an individual, has a small role to play; she is a mother, a wife, a daughter.

In order to do something about the male dominance and social control these women are subjected to, we have to acknowledge that for them, as for women in the majority, social recognition at an individual level is important and absolutely necessary. At the same time, we must not think that the solution lies at the individual level, but that structures, i.e., how society is put together and functions, has an inhibitory effect on these women. Consequently, the solution to the problems lies both in the individual and in the structural sphere.

Neither violence nor social control of women should be accepted, no matter what religion or culture they belong to. Women, who are exposed to strong social control and a lot of restrictions in the way they live, seldom have a choice in deciding to live in other ways. We must therefore do more research and try to identify the many and complex causes for why so many minority women in Norway still have a life dominated by their men, religious leaders and conservative local communities.

Toril Moi defines a social field as an arena of competing relations. The most important and most fatal for these women is that of the private sphere. Here, they are the losers in a power relationship where the man is totally dominant. In addition, they are losers in the social field as well. In minority communities, it is difficult to fulfill all the demands of being an honorable woman. In the minority population, most of those whom I met believed that it is impossible to establish friendship on an equal footing with ethnic Norwegians. They often felt like losers in the society they lived in. They do not understand it, and it doesn't work for them. The doctor's office is just one of many institutions where there are great conflicts between minorities and the majority. There are structural causes we must look closer into if we are to understand what minorities in Norway are actually experiencing. But we must also look closer into the encounters with institutions. It is the particular combination of the lack of recognition in the private sphere as well as the official sphere that burdens these women.

7. Life in the Media vs. Minority Women's Everyday Life

Once, when Shogofa was on her way back from work, an elderly lady came into the bus she was riding on. The old lady almost fell when the bus started to move, and Shogofa hurried to help and offered her seat to her. She noticed that the woman looked at her with hateful eyes and said something Shogofa did not quite understand. "Sorry?" Shogofa asked, and the old lady repeated her words, but it was still not possible to understand quite what she said, just something about "van Gogh". "No," Shogofa said, "the next stop is John Collett Square!" The old lady repeated herself again, and now Shogofa understood that she said something about "you killed van Gogh". Shogofa had no idea what the lady was talking about, but thought the incident was rather unpleasant.

When she came home, she told her children about the incident. "Haven't you seen the news the last couple of days?" they answered. "A Muslim fundamentalist has killed a film director named van Gogh in the Netherlands!" The children had received unpleasant questions about this at school. The media creates conflict, and imams and other religious authorities present themselves as representatives in the debate concerning incidents like the murder of van Gogh and exacerbate the situation.

The lack of recognition of the minority population as equals is enshrined in the Norwegian media. In various ways, the journalists write about the minority population as something different from themselves. Minorities are perceived as fundamentally different from the ethnic Norwegian, and cultural expressions that can be connected to the minority population are generally twisted so that it appears as antagonistic to the democratic and open Norwegian society.

To identify what characterizes "someone", and then refer to them as basically different from oneself, indicates a prevailing power of definition. Do journalists in Norway possess enough self-reflection with regard to this? Do they know what it really means?

In Norwegian media, representatives of the majority population are constantly heard, and they talk about the minority as if it is something people can "choose" to include and accept or not. Such an attitude is one of many indications of who has the power to define, and who can allow themselves to define how a large part of the Norwegian population is to be perceived.

It is unthinkable that the opposite could happen in the Norwegian media: that the minority came forth and reflected over whether one should accept various habits the ethnic Norwegian population had. This is barely acceptable when someone is respected as a "national" comedian to begin with. The majority has opinions about the minority. These opinions are often about being for or against but are still presented as balanced views. Minorities cannot mean anything about the majority - unless they want to be splashed across the front page as someone with extremist views.

Elisabeth Eide and Anne Hege Simonsen show in their book, *Suspicious Foreigners*, how just such a dichotomy between "us" and "them" has been enshrined in the Norwegian media for more than a century. They show how Norwegian media, from the time of the union with Sweden, has portrayed minorities as "others", non-belonging, not-normal citizens of the nation. They also note how this is an expression of the balance of power. They find throughout that "a normative center uses its privileges to define some people as others (often marginalized), usually without having to take responsibility for this. In this way also, the identity of the majority as normal is strengthened".[1]

Eide and Simonsen also placed the classification between "us" and "them" historically together with the growth of nationalism, and points to this by referring to what many studies on nationalism have shown: "how the idea of a national state has a strongly organizing character. It systemizes the difference between us and them and leads to discrimination in institutions and the bureaucracy".[2]

Newspapers and other media have had great importance and power and have shaped and maintained the idea of a large national community in Norway, i.e., a large Norwegian "we".

Multiculturalism and the Media: A Dangerous Combination

I think this dichotomy between "us" and "the others" which, as Eide and Simonsen show, has been present in Norwegian media for more than a century, now has gained a new and dangerous justification – namely multiculturalism.

Multiculturalist thinking focuses on differences, on understanding others first and foremost from the standpoint of religious and cultural differences.

Norwegian media, to a large extent, confirm the multicultural thinking existing in other parts of Norwegian society, while at the same time, both newspapers and TV channels practice just such a way of thinking. "The Norwegians", whom the Norwegian media are made for, are a large and respected community, as well as a seemingly homogenous one. "The others" are different, either in the meaning of being exceptional in a positive sense (skiers, finally having a job, good at school in spite of their minority background) or in the negative sense such as criminals. The media coverage is often a combination of stigmatization and exotification, where immigrants are not considered as individuals.

To obtain statements from religious leaders and present these as representatives for a large group with the common feature of "not ethnic Norwegian" is, as mentioned, yet another way to ignore the individual.

Sharam Alghasi studied how immigration was presented in talk shows and current affairs programs on TV in NRK (the Norwegian Broadcasting Corporation) and in TV2 between 1989 and 1997.[3] He thinks that the content of these programs typically presents the relation between immigrants and the majority as characterized by struggle and conflict. Culture was used as an explanation for this conflict, and the concepts of foreign culture was the basis for the discriminatory attitudes among Norwegians. These programs, Alghasi thinks, contributed to the propagation of existing conflicts. Ten years after this study, Eide and Simonsen find signs of improvement. But there is still a long way to go.

Eide and Simonsen also show how much of the media coverage of minorities in Norway has been oriented towards conflict. The repertoire of roles that the representatives for the minority population take in Norwegian media has been, and still is, limited. Eide and Simonsen identify four different discourses in the media today: The majority as a problem, where the majority society is presented as a hindrance for the minorities, either in the form of a strict immigration policy, racism and discrimination, or in the form of a lack of respect for the culture and values of "the others". This discourse appears most often in connection to "the other" in the role of the victim. Another discourse they identify is "the others" as a threat and/or a problem. Criminality, provoking cultural expressions and the large number of immigrants and Muslims who have come to Norway, are often included in these cases. Within this practice, we also find "the other" as a victim, but then of their own backward culture, like female genital mutilation, forced marriages and other forms of oppression. The third and fourth discourses they identify are the colorful community and "the others" as a resource. Here, the emphasis is on the positive, often the exotic, and that they, in spite of their cultural and religious differences, are equal. In the daily news, the first two discourses are dominant.[4]

The Power of the Media over People's Lives

The media is of great importance in creating attitudes and ideas among both minorities and the majority, particularly because these two groups have little contact. The perceptions we have of each other therefore, to a large extent, come from the TV and newspapers. Elisabeth Eide considers mass media as the main arbiter of power after the economy.[5] The media hence have both great power and a huge responsibility.[6]

It is unfortunately so that the conflict-oriented media coverage, where both the majority and minorities are being portrayed as antagonistic, is what lays the foundation for the social fields in which people from minorities and the majority come in contact with each other. The attitudes created by the media are therefore present at school, in the neighborhood, on the tram and at work. Everybody belonging to a visibly identifiable minority in Norway knows this.

As carriers of a stigmatized negative identity, immigrants have to be extra careful. They have to be impeccable models of good behavior when they interact with the majority in order to be accepted and integrated. In this way, the media contribute toward making the social field difficult for immigrants. Arezo says what many feel; "Norwegians don't like us". She experiences the stigma, and thinks the cause, to a large extent, is that newspapers write negatively about immigrants.

Minorities are often passive receivers of the picture the media present; they do not participate in debates, and consequently lack the opportunity to defend themselves and present a picture that is different from that of the media. Those who are heard in a conflict-oriented media reality are, among others, religious representatives from various organizations that confirm the ideas of "differentness" in the religion and culture of the "others". These are the extreme voices. Others, who are heard and become visible, are those who speak against their own culture – i.e., people who are more Norwegian than the Norwegians, and of course, those who represent a threat.

The women I met suffered under the stereotypical presentation of the Norwegian media. The same goes for their children.

Shaeen and Mullah Krekar, Belquis and Osama bin Laden

Shaeen has a tertiary education. She is self-conscious and engaged in global politics. Yet she feels like a stranger in the political landscape of Norway. She cannot stand to see mullah Krekar in the media. Her own painful memories and experiences with fundamentalists are revived. "Is this freedom of speech?" she asks, "when a criminal appears on TV as if he is an authority, in debate with others? Every time mullah Krekar appears on TV, opinion polls show more hate towards immigrants. Carl I. Hagen, a Progress Party politician considered a right-wing populist by many, gains support, and this creates hate and distance between us and the Norwegians." Shaeen gets a "stiff neck" and a headache when she sees mullah Krekar on TV: "Norwegian society presents my enemy as my representative!" she says, feeling powerless.

Shaeen is concerned with how the media presents minorities and is particularly worried about the populist attitudes that contribute to the

Progress Party becoming one of the biggest parties. Tabloidization and populism weaken the level of knowledge among both the majority and the minorities. The attention that has been directed at extreme and religious views among Muslims has created fear in the majority towards Muslims. This affects every single Muslim - even those who have no connection whatsoever with mullah Krekar or those who didn't even care about the Mohammed caricatures. This puts an extra burden on each immigrant who has to be careful to "behave properly", in order to avoid being subjected to prejudice. The media coverage makes integration on the local plane more difficult. People come to a place already characterized by attitudes from the news. This is true whether it is people moving into a new condominium or going to lunch at the office.

The world of the media affects the life of Shaeen directly, and also causes pain. She not only says that she becomes physically ill when she sees images of mullah Krekar, but also that she becomes depressed and feels powerless when she sees reports of prisoners in Iraq, and extensive violations and oppression in a part of the world she knows intimately. International tragedies are a part of her life, and they also become a part of her depression and illness. She says that she is "dying slowly". However, while he was initially in Norway, he was transferred to Italy during the pandemic in march 2020.

Belquis struggled with her life when she was unemployed, and her worst fear was that she would turn into a social welfare client. She had been proud of not being a part of the picture the media painted of im- migrants in Norway. She had a job, her own apartment, earned her own money and managed as a single parent. It was this life and this self-image that fell apart when she became ill and too incapacitated to work.

Not long after she took her first sick leave, I sat and watched TV together with her. They were showing a program about an Arabian king who handed out soup to the poor, a display of his and his state's charity and kindness to the people. "Why doesn't he give them a job instead so they can choose what to eat themselves?" Belquis commented indignantly. While this program was on the screen, the telephone rang. Belquis answered. It was the doctor's office calling to tell her that her sick leave had been extended by another 15 days. She said "Thank you very much", seemingly satisfied, but after hanging up, she turns to me and says: "Look here, this sick leave is like the soup of the king that they distribute to the poor! When I had a job, I looked forward to getting my salary, and thought that I could buy the same furniture that's in the king's palace." The job gave her hope for a better life, of improving her home, of creating a future. The money she earned gave her an opportunity to do this. She was something other than just an "immigrant".

Belquis was injured in an accident not long after this, and she lost all hope of going back to a full-time job. Because the sick leave had lasted so long, she also lost her sick pay and had to be rehabilitated. This put her in an even more precarious financial situation, which made her take it as a personal loss.

Without a job and having trouble moving her body, she watched TV a lot, but only the Arabic channels. There, she heard the statements of bin Laden and she saw reports from the war in Iraq and other places. Belquis identified herself and her life in Norway with the conflict in the Middle East and the situation of the Muslims and Palestinians there. Muslims are oppressed everywhere, she thought. As mentioned, she drew a comparison between her own relation to her boss in Norway and the Palestinians under Israeli occupation, and she insisted that her previous boss had a hateful glance like that of Sharon's.

"There is hope," Belquis said one day when we were watching TV. "There is a man who weighs less than 25 kg (she believed he had supernatural powers) - bin Laden - who fights against the unbeliever Bush. One day, the world will become more just, and all people will become Muslim."[7]

It was through the TV screen in her own living room in a suburb in Norway that Belquis got acquainted with bin Laden. She looked at him as a champion for justice, against an injustice she herself felt inflicted by. She knew nothing about his past, and she was shocked when I told her about the history of fundamentalism, and of how women were killed and raped by fundamentalists in Afghanistan. Belquis is an example of the power of the media, and how conflicts in daily life find parallels in global conflicts as they are presented in the media – i.e., critical and insurmountable.

Local consciousness blends together with global events for individuals who are already vulnerable. The mechanism for this we find, first and foremost, in the total life situations the individuals are in, and in this case, of each single immigrant.

When the social field and daily life is filled with problems and people are unable to find the correct cause of the pain and powerlessness they feel, it becomes hard for them to understand their own lives. The problem is put into a context that already exists, and where the conflicts are already defined. But by doing this, the solutions to the problems become just as elusive as the causes.

A Blending of the Local, the National and the Global

In the lives of Shaeen and Belquis, local experiences from their countries of origin, global conflicts as they are presented in the media, and local experiences in Norway are intermingled in their view of the world. The mass media, to a large extent, play a part in linking together the local and the global. Anthony Giddens says that the media of today contribute to an "intrusion of distanced events into everyday consciousness, which is in some substantial part organized in terms of awareness of them".[8] My respondents have in common that they come from areas in the world where experiences of suffering are common, and their own suffering was an important reason for their emigration to Norway. In addition, the migration process in itself implies a great burden. Immigrants who come to Norway or other countries in the West, experience a new condition, namely immigrant life. According to Sayed, this in itself can be experienced as an illness.[9] Global conflicts and suffering from other places blend together with what they experience in their new home. They think of and "suffer with" others in the global world who have similar experiences as they themselves have. And they also see a larger picture – that of oppression. This type of experience is part and parcel of a modern society.

Among my respondents, global events and local daily problems were often physically embodied. Their own experiences and the consciousness of the experiences of others lay layer upon layer in the body of these women. Shaeen and Belquis were just two of many examples of this. This type of incorporation of pain, which is like a new disorder, I call the globalization of pain. The media are an important factor in this understanding of the many causes of the problems of minority women.

Women's Traumas: Beyond the Story in the Media

Traumas of war and memories of war are a part of life for many of my respondents. The memories have left their mark. Shaeen, Belquis, Shogofa, Baarin and Tajeba are just a small sample of those I met, who had memories of executions and mass murder. These are people who have lost close family, and who have experienced war directly. The wars and conflicts have created personal as well as collective memories of pain.

As part of my fieldwork, I once joined the "Knowledge Center" for a visit at the Ethnographic Museum. Many women from countries ravaged by war - Ethiopia, Somalia, Palestine, Algeria and Iran - also came. At the museum, there were photos of men with guns. The women couldn't stand to look at these pictures. Two Somali girls sat and talked with each other in Somali while they cried. These girls live with experiences and memories of the past that are a central part of their consciousness.

The girls also told me that they felt their future was uncertain. The combination of bad memories and countless problems in their new life, made it difficult for them to cope. Past and present reinforced each other as negative experiences. They still live with the impressions that experience with war has given them. In addition, they experience a lot of difficulties in Norway.

Shaeen always discusses with her psychiatrist about how she can gain control over her nightmares so that her daily life may be free of pain. Shaeen tells me she has nightmares every night. She sees herself back in jail witnessing the execution of her comrades. To watch the news just makes it worse. Jasmin also has nightmares, even if she is not from Iraq. Her dreams are filled with visions of pyramids made out of prisoners, something she has seen on TV. She dreamt that all these prisoners spoke Urdu and cried "Madji" (mother). This is a blending of past and present pains. The death threat she got because of the strong social control at Angarudd, made the nightmares more severe. Also, the stress she experiences in her daily life affects the frequency of her dreams, but the content is TV images from Iraq.

Shogofa also told me about excruciating real experiences. It was the 28th of April 1991 in Kabul, the capital of Afghanistan, and it was *samanakk*. *Samanakk* is a traditional ritual in connection with the celebration of spring. This is an opportunity for women to gather once every year to sing all through the night. The songs are composed by them and are about the spring, nature and the kinds of love that are usually taboo to talk about in public for a woman. While the women sing, they stir the cauldron where the dish, *samanakk*, is made. In the poorer areas like those where Shogofa comes from, it is extremely difficult to make it through the winter, and the spring celebration is therefore a celebration of an easier life.

This was just after the Soviet Union had withdrawn their troops from Afghanistan, and rival groups came to the capital, Kabul, to gain control. This night, Hezb-i-Islami, Dostum and Ahmadsha Moshod arrived, and they started to do battle. Missiles were shot toward the city, and people had to escape. The missiles hit a residential area at "Balla-hesar", a central military base in Afghanistan and a symbol of Afghan resistance during three bloody wars over an 80-year period: against the British, who never succeeded in occupying Afghanistan, and against the Soviet occupation force. Shogofa lived in "Balla-hesar" and was occupied with the *samanakk* celebration when the missiles hit. In just a moment, the celebration was turned into a nightmare.

Shogofa tells me how panic broke out, of screams from people and of children crying. She tells me how she saw a woman being killed, and of how she was unable to help her; she had to escape and protect her children. Houses and buildings were reduced to rubble. People ran willy-nilly in the chaos without really knowing where it was safe. "Imagine, Farida," Shogofa said, "how 'mahshar' (the Day of Judgment) is. It was like that."[10]

So, she escaped to Dhemazang, further into the center of Kabul. She tells me of seeing the soldiers of Dostum plundering the city. Walking among dead people and bodies, Shogofa saw them, happy and laughing, taking telephones and telephone lines, expensive carpets and fancy goods, and everything of value from "Kabul-nendari", the theatre of Kabul. Then the soldiers jumped into their cars and drove off. They also took with them women and young girls whom they raped. The soldiers of Dostum are called "glam jam", that is, those who "take your carpet". Shogofa had been a member of Hezb-i-Islami herself, and active in the fight against the Russians. Among other things, she had transported weapons, but after this attack, she changed her view. She started seeing Hezb-i-Islami, Dostum and other warlords as criminals.

Shogofa arrived at Dhemazang after a few days, but here the attack continued, because both Hezb-i-Islami and Dostum wanted to gain control over the TV and radio towers in the surrounding mountains. For three months, the missile attack continued. Shogofa, her husband and children, therefore, had to be on the move all the time. They lived one week in one place, then one week in another. In Dhemazang, they moved around like this during the first month. In the end, they found a small basement where they thought they were safe because a martyr was buried there. They lived together with 60 other men, women and children, and they had to live squeezed together and couldn't even stretch their legs when they slept. For washing, they only had a common pond. Drinking water was from a pond next to the first one.

The women washed nappies made of cloth for their children in the washing pond so that it was soon filled with human waste and could not be used any more. The pond with drinking water was soon empty, and many of those who went out searching for water never came back. It was also very difficult to find water close by because most of the houses with running water had collapsed during the missile attacks. For two months, the family lived there while the missile attacks continued: "Rockets came like rain," Shogofa says.

After two months, Hezb-i-Islami and Dostum declared a ceasefire for a week. This was the chance that Shogofa made use of. As an earlier member of Hezb-i-Islami, she had many contacts and succeeded in getting out of Kabul to the Pandjshir valley. From there, it was possible to get into Pakistan. On the way there, they drove to the center of Kabul, down to the Plaza hotel. The whole road was covered with corpses and body parts. Nobody was able to go out and move them, so the only thing they could do was to shut their eyes and drive on. It was horrible, Shogofa says.

When they had left Kabul behind, they went out of the car. Shogofa sat by the roadside and looked at the tire. She felt pain in her neck, and for the first time, the words of Sadi made sense to her.[11] The poem is about how humans are parts of the same body, and how pain in one part of the body leads to pain also in another part. Even if she had escaped, the suffering of the dead was also present in her own body. Her neck got stiff and her veins were bulging. "Where are the human rights?" Shogofa now says, when she thinks back on this event. "Where are the people who defend human rights? Those who have their blood on the tires, where are their rights? Bush and the Russians may deny it, but they are responsible. Afghanistan did not have these rockets. They came from outside. And those who came with them must take the responsibility for the people who lost their lives." There are many minority women in Norway today who have experiences similar to those of Shogofa - horrible killing of civilians, rapes, and political decisions with fatal local consequences.

These are the experiences the media do not see. This is the suffering, the majority population does not take into account. And this is the suffering that is awakened by images in the global media and is embedded in the body.

8. Minority Women's Experience: A Guide to Reforming the Content and Organization of Norwegian Institutions

How can we best identify the extent of the lack of recognition the women I met were so concerned with? Why did it constitute such a large part of their daily life? Where did they encounter it?

Norway is a modern society, and in modern societies, institutions play a central role. The Norwegian school, health care system, social security office and the media constitute a large part of our lives. It was these institutions, as well as the social welfare office and religious and voluntary organizations, that were the places where the women felt that they were not being seen, and not being recognized for who they were. Many of the women I met have had a conflicted encounter with the health care system. But unfortunately, it is not only the institutionalized health care system that is perceived as problematic for first generation immigrant women. My respondents had many frustrating, conflicted and negative experiences from encounters with various institutions in Norway. Also, there are many problematic aspects to the organizational structure of the institutions that are supposed to help these women. Why is it like this? What do minority women experience in the institutions of the welfare state? And what do they experience in well-intentioned organizations?

Modern Norwegian institutions are different from the institutions,

in the countries my respondents come from. Norwegian institutions are built in a way to best safeguard the rights of their clients. Both the health care system and the social welfare office are institutions created to help the citizens of the country during illness or when in difficult socioeconomic situations. Why are the encounters with these institutions then so filled with conflict? How can it be that even the social welfare office, the cornerstone of a generous welfare system, is the scene of so many negative experiences? What happens in the interpersonal meetings in the office or front desk of the institution? And what are the dynamics of the institution?

The Norwegian institutions are, to a large extent, governed by an abstract and formal set of rules that both the functionary and the clients have to follow. One problem for many of my respondents is that they are unable to understand this set of rules.

The functionary who works inside the institution often lacks knowledge about immigrants. What then happens is that meetings and relations between lower functionaries and immigrants are characterized by misunderstandings. This often results in immigrants experiencing the institution itself, or the functionaries, as being "racist" or hostile, while the functionaries see the immigrants as being excessively demanding and troublemakers.

The Social welfare office: A Frustrating Institution to Encounter

Several of the women I met had a problematic relation to the social welfare office. Shogofa was one of them. Today, Shogofa has finally got a job and feels much better. But it has been a long road, with frustrations and conflicts along the way.

Shogofa was educated as a teacher with many years of experience from Afghanistan, but in Norway she found herself in a situation where she no longer could take care of her children financially. "I have an uncertain future," she told me when I first met her.

Shogofa, a woman with education and who had fought vigorously against the Soviet occupation in her home country, had an identity as an independent thinking woman. She felt humiliated by the situation she fell into. "Norwegians say 'poor Afghans', they don't see your background. They don't understand that we had a good life, an identity and an education before the war."

Even if she has taught for many years, her work experience is not recognized: "It is my biggest pain," she says, fed up with Norwegians and Norwegian institutions that assume that immigrants are incompetent, just because they have not worked in Norway. "You have to get work experience, you go from one office to another, they do not see that I already have years of experience working with people." She had sent more than 40 job applications - "40 stamps. That is expensive!" For a long while, she didn't even receive any replies. She had already worked in several internships and received good testimonials from all of them. Without a job her only alternative was to go to the social welfare office to receive help, something she definitely didn't like. She told me that her veins were bulging every time her bus passed the social welfare office, and her hands hurt. She held her hands hard against her throat and closed her eyes until the bus had passed two stops: "I call the social welfare office 'the torture chamber', even if some of the people working there are nice."

The social welfare office demanded that she documented having taken a course in Norwegian before they can provide help. So, she went to the school where she took the course to get verification. But when she came back with the documentation, her caseworker, a young girl, asked her how many more hours of the course in Norwegian she was entitled to. The caseworker was following the rules - if one had used up one's quota, one had to register for unemployment benefits, and consequently, were not entitled to support from the social welfare office. For Shogofa, this meant that she had to go back to the school to document that she had not used up all the hours she was entitled to. When she came back to the caseworker, she was asked exactly how many hours Shogofa had been on the course, and so Shogofa had to go back to the school yet again to get more documentation. Naturally, she became very angry that she had to go back and forth in this way. Crying, she told me of the incident:

I tore the paper into pieces and threw it in the face of the caseworker. I cried and said that harassment and humiliation have their limits! And I said: I am not a beggar! I was forced to come to this country, not for bread and money, but to escape the war. I had a high position in Afghanistan. My husband was a general! I escaped from weapons and war. We had no weapons. It was you who sent all the weapons there and disrupted our peaceful lives: The Russians sent arms to their allies and the West to theirs. Now Afghanistan is a depot for arms. There are guns and killings everywhere. All come from the outside! Please, do not send arms to us so that we don't need to stay here! And when we come here, you continue to harass and humiliate us!

She lost her temper completely in that office and wept and cried about the misery of war. Other caseworkers came running to help and comfort her. To me she explained: "I did not accept humiliation and control from the Russians - I resisted. How can I accept humiliation from a young girl who works at the social welfare office?! It is inhumane!"

The young caseworker had been very surprised. It was also obvious that she did not understand what Shogofa was really referring to. According to Shogofa, the caseworker responded to her despair by suggesting that she had a mental problem: "Please Shogofa, I know nothing about this. I have not sent any weapons. Poor Shogofa, you need a psychiatrist." But Shogofa did not consider herself mentally ill to begin with. It was the social welfare office that had pushed her out of balance. The suggestion that she was ill and needed help only made her angrier: "Poor?! Am I pitiful or are you?!" Weeping, she said: "I don't mean that you or your grandfather sent weapons, I mean that Norway and other countries, especially NATO countries, sent weapons. Don't call me poor! Read your history, what you have done to us!"

For the young caseworker in the social welfare office, the history of Afghanistan is abstract, and probably, also alien to her. For Shogofa, the same history is life experience and embodied despair. For her, this is a story that stretches far outside Afghanistan, a story with global causes where capitalism and the relation between East and West are important ones. This history has ruined her life. In Norway, her experience is that few understand or think about this.

Shogofa is a victim of the Cold War. As a member of the resistance, she transported weapons to the Mujahedin in Kabul, hidden under her chadri. She told me that what the Mujahedin really needed was medicine, but nobody sent that - only weapons. At that time, she did not ask questions, but today she asks: "Who sent those weapons?" For her, it is the weapons and the war in this one part of the world that has made her into an immigrant who now sits in another part of the world and faces huge problems.

For Shogofa, this connection is obvious. To the caseworker, it is hard to see these connections. Because of this lack of knowledge, and for Shogofa, the lack of knowledge of how the social welfare office works as a modern institution, the meeting between Shogofa and the caseworker ends in a conflict with mutual accusations and misunderstandings.[1]

In the end, Shogofa managed to get a job with the help of the Norwegian Public Employment Service. Today, she works part-time in a kindergarten.

I am satisfied with this job, even if it does not fit my education and experience. I am happy about not needing to write hopeless job application letters any more or applications to the social welfare office. When I go to work, I feel like I did when I was a student; I feel the fresh air and I feel healthy. I dress nicely, put makeup on, and this gives me a feeling of hope. I feel that life goes on.

Shogofa is committed to her work and works hard, in the hope of, maybe, getting a secure full-time job. She takes off her hijab when she goes to the kindergarten because she is conscious of the prejudices and the anxiety directed at Muslims, and she does not want to scare the children. After work, she puts the hijab back on again.

When Shogofa now reflects over the conflict with the caseworker, she looks at it from another perspective. She regrets her attack on the young girl and acknowledges that it was not her fault. "Poor girl, I was so stupid saying: 'go read your history' to her. What history? But it is important that Norwegians understand why we are here."

Can Institutions Think? Cognitive, Regulative and Normative Tendencies

Like Shogofa, many minority women meet the social welfare office, the social security office, and the doctor's office in a situation when they are especially vulnerable and need some kind of help. Then an individual meets another individual. But women I have talked with, often experience that they are not treated as individuals in this situation. The one they meet is not interested in the background for their need for help.

The women feel they become "the needy one". This becomes their new "identity". With the media tendency to reinforce the idea that immigrants come to Norway to partake in "our" benefits, and hence, the problems that occur are "their" fault, this becomes a burden for the immigrants. It characterizes their attitude toward and encounters with the institutions, for example, the social welfare office.

I believe that minority issues – the place of minorities in society - must be understood in the context of what really constitutes the backbone of the modern society: the institutions. We must take seriously the fact that many are experiencing what they consider violations in their encounters with the doctor's office, the health center and the social welfare office. We must take seriously the conflicted relations between the employees who work at "the front line" and the minority clients. In the late summer of 2007, this form of conflict came to a head and became public knowledge: The Ali Farah case. A man suffering from brain hemorrhage was not helped into the ambulance because the personnel let preconceived attitudes rule their actions. The decision to not help was based on a general idea of what a man with Ali Farah's dark skin represented in his condition.

Both employees in public institutions and minority clients suffer from conflicts, misunderstandings and prejudices about one another. But one of the parties feels violated, and the other has the power to distribute money or provide help in case of illness.

Norwegian legislation prohibits discrimination in all institutions. For example, it is not allowed to treat someone differently because of their ethnicity, culture or religion - in the sense that some could receive more benefits than others. It is also not allowed to use discriminatory terms. In this sense, the regulations are good. What is it then that makes the experience of being violated in the institutionalized system so intense among many? How should we think about this form of discrimination? How can we identify it?

One can distinguish three important characteristics of institutions in modern societies: the regulative, normative and cognitive aspects. The regulative aspects deal with formal rules created by experts. These rules are meant to encourage and control behavior to achieve the express goals of the institution. The rules are impersonal, which means that everybody has to abide by them independent of, for example, status, family background, and so on. The regulative aspects of, for example, the social welfare offices are general and "measure everyone with the same yardstick". They do not take into account the special situation many minorities find themselves in. They often have little room for exercising discretion. The requirement for the specific documents that Shogofa had to submit is an example of how the regulative aspect sometimes works.

The normative aspect of the institutions develops slowly over time. This has to do with values and norms of behavior for the members of the institution that are not found in written rules. This concerns the framework of what is considered morally "right" to do within the current institution. In spite of Norwegians looking at their society as secular, Christian values characterize Norwegian institutions to a large extent. The way illness and death in the health care system are handled is one example - a Lutheran priest is an institutionalized part of the health care system. Another example is the values in the Norwegian school that, in spite of the teaching of other beliefs, still hew closely to Christian traditions and Lutheran values.

The cognitive aspects of the institutions are meanings and symbols that permeate the society as a whole and influence the actions of each player within the institutions. Cognition concerns receiving and processing impressions. Cognitive aspects of the institutions are views that are taken for granted by the players - "it is just the way it is". Cognitive aspects constitute a common map of attitudes and decide what is perceived as acceptable and normal for the players in each situation.

The challenge in easing the encounters of minority women with Norwegian institutions no longer lie in the regulative aspect. Just the same, the execution of the rules is often too rigid and "square". One could, therefore, in many instances, exercise discretion to a large extent. But the bigger challenge lies in the normative aspect, and most of all in the cognitive aspect.

There is also a strange mix of egalitarian and discriminatory thinking in Norway that governs the norms and perceptions of what is right and what is wrong. On the one side, one pretends that all are equal, such as that everybody is able to adjust to the system, fill in the same forms, obtain the same types of documents and reply to the same kinds of questions. One pretends that everybody can choose where they want to live, where to take an education, where they find a job, where to spend a few hours in a gym if they experience pain, and where to participate fully in the society if they want to. One has a false idea that all are equal to begin with. And one has a powerful idea of how, and how equal, full members of Norwegian society should be. At the same time, there is an increasing focus on those who are different; those with a different culture and different religion. The cultural and religious difference becomes the explanation for everything from ignorance to conservative behavior, while at the same time it becomes the key to solutions. Attitudes formed by this map of attitudes are unavoidably enshrined in all Norwegian institutions.

Our maps of attitudes and our view of the world, shape immigration

and integration policy. For example, a restrictive map of attitudes makes one think nationally on all issues concerning welfare. One then accuses both groups and individuals who come to "us" to take from and who threaten the welfare state - "our welfare", as the Progress Party says, "our liberty", as Hege Storhaug says. But the immigrants take part in creating the welfare state in Norway and other Western countries. They take the jobs ethnic Norwegians don't want. Many of the sectors where minorities in Norway work actually make up the mainstay of the Norwegian welfare system. This fact is simply not part of how many ethnic Norwegians view the situation.

In addition to the attitudes people meet, there are complicated practical problems in the encounters with the modern institutionalized society for many of the minority women I have met. There are forms that are difficult to fill out even for ethnic Norwegians, and not knowing the language makes it worse. It is difficult to relate to a system one simply does not understand - and that one does not know what to do with to understand better. It is often the practical things people wish they could get more guidance and help with.

In addition, it is a strain in itself that processes linked to social welfare offices take such a long time. Many feel that days go by in arranging documents while other tasks have to wait. When Shogofa finally got a part-time job, she was relieved that now she did not have to use all day to try to solve urgent problems for herself and her children. To use such a big part of each day to compile documents that may be unnecessarily difficult, is perceived as an expression of an attitude concerning how one really should use one's time each day.

Still, my respondents tell me that the greatest pain lies in being disparaged and humiliated, of not being recognized for who one really is, but just being seen as one of many "clients", or one of many "complaining minority women". Many of these women simply feel that they have lost their identity and their own worth in their encounters with the social welfare office. Both the social distress they are in to begin with, and the encounter with the social welfare office in itself, are causing illness. It is a serious paradox. The social welfare office is an institution built for the purpose of helping those in difficult socioeconomic situations to get a better life.

Many, too many, minority women that I met, experience Norwegian society as racist. This experience is remarkably frequent based on their encounters with various Norwegian institutions. How can we become better at identifying what is going wrong?

Institutional Discrimination: Is it Possible to Detect?

Many claim that discrimination, for the most part, does not occur in Norway today. But here, we are no longer talking about explicit discriminatory laws or explicit racist statements. For this reason, it is very difficult to detect discrimination, and consequently, also makes it complicated to fight against it. We must look in places other than where there are violent actions and direct derogatory statements.

On the basis of numerous stories from women, I am convinced that discrimination can manifest itself in various institutions like the police, the health care system, the welfare system, and both in the private and public sector. This is discrimination that has established itself institutionally but is often unconscious. Among other things, it lies in the way the employees perceive the world. It is indirect rather than direct. And it is usually received without protests. Therefore, I call it silent discrimination. I do not claim that it is discrimination and racism that is the main cause of the pain of my respondents, but it is still a part of their daily life. It is a part of their total situation in life and their experience of Norwegian society.

Many who live in Norway who are not white have experienced that they have to identify themselves when they meet the police. Many have also experienced humiliating treatment when they return from vacation to the country, in spite of the fact that they have been Norwegian citizens for many years.

In the winter of 2007, the Health and Equality Minister, Manuela Ramin-Osmundsen, had to apologize to the customs service because she said something that could be interpreted as if she thought they were racist.[2] But it is racist to suspect immigrants as a group. The customs service performs stricter controls on this group, without this practice being a written rule. Consequently, this is a part of what can be described as structural discrimination, without every customs officer being racist. But for the individual immigrant who experiences this practice, this is clearly felt as discrimination. Often, situations like these are referred to by minorities, as being exposed to, "a hostile glance".

It is important that we take into account documented experiences of violations to understand unconscious structural discrimination. Therefore, one should not force the new minister to withdraw the statement. Such experiences should, instead, be used as a starting point for new forms of discussions about what is racist in Norway today. This is complicated, most of all, because both sides are right. Those working in the customs service do not have conscious racist attitudes. At the same time, the feeling of violation is definitely real for those who are under suspicion all the time, based solely on the color of their skin.

There are two main definitions of discrimination. One is the legal definition. It refers to unfair treatment, directly and indirectly, in a certain situation, in various areas of society. If people, for example, are being denied the right to settle in a certain area because of their skin color, one can, at least in theory, and if it is proven, use Norwegian legislation to fight against it.

The second main definition of discrimination is the one used in the social sciences.[3] It can also include the individual's own experiences of discrimination, and in addition, it often includes a time perspective, for example, structural discrimination over time. It is the definition from the social sciences that most clearly captures the kind of discrimination my respondents experience. And it is research in the social sciences that we need for this.

Ronald Craig is one of the few who has made extensive research in Norway on what institutional ethnic discrimination really is. He lists the following characteristics: It deals with statements or actions that are not exceptions or isolated incidents - they are woven into administrative practice and organizational culture. This form of discrimination is often subtle, unconscious and difficult to perceive. Structural discrimination in, for example, the workplace involves the use of informal and unprofessional routines and practices for hiring. This means practices that lack the right or the necessary guidance or transparency. In addition, structural discrimination implies an unconscious stereotyping that exceeds the awareness of the individual decision maker - but still shows and can predict how he perceives and interprets something, and what he chooses to emphasize. Generally, we may say that structural differences often do not have a clear and identifiable victim, and also not a clear and identifiable "criminal".[4]

Craig is concerned that this kind of discrimination is too subtle and complex to be possible to solve only with a system based on complaints, meaning people who feel discriminated having the opportunity to complain. Other means have to be used. In the workplace, he thinks that, for example, affirmative action is a solution.

The institutional and structural discrimination I observe, particularly toward immigrant women, I believe, may be solved mainly in two ways.

Firstly, their total socioeconomic situation in life must be changed for the better. Secondly, the cognitive map of society must be changed.

These two things are linked. The cognitive map of attitudes contributes towards shaping the preconditions for the socioeconomic situation. At the same time, the attitudes this map is based on, do not contribute towards a real solution.

It is not possible to think that the total situation in life of these women will improve, as long as the focus on culture, religion and ethnicity still is the basis both for the efforts to help and the attitudes they are met with in Norwegian institutions.

We must be willing to see what cognitive map of attitudes we actually are operating with. For example, much of the expertise minorities possess is lost because it is not approved and recognized in Norway. This leads to much frustration among minorities, and consequently, becomes a cost for Norwegian society. Here, both normative and cognitive attitudes must change. It is not necessarily so that "Norwegian expertise" almost always is the best.

The only yardstick for discrimination is documentation of experiences of violations. Then, we can find out what it really consists of, whether it is an isolated incident or something that is repeated over time, and what the person who violates really thinks about the one being violated. The experience of being discriminated is, for me, a simple and good definition of racism. And to understand racism, we must simply be willing to listen to what people want to say.

Again, the Ali Farah case is a good example. It is a well-documented violation. But his partner, Kohinoor Nordberg, had to tell the story again and again, and it was not obvious that she would be heard. In the beginning, the case was dismissed, just by referring to the men operating the ambulance as not having racist attitudes, and that the Ullevål University Hospital had strict formal rules for avoiding discriminatory actions and statements. The regulative aspect and the possible racism of the individual were brought up. But this is not where we should be looking! It would be impossible to understand and, not least, admit, that this was a deeply violating action, without investigating the experience of the one or those being violated.

Absolutely all my respondents talked about experiences of discrimination. That so many, with such a varied background, tell of such experiences in their encounters with public institutions, means that we should be able to find some institutional causes behind this. Their common problems with employment, health and income point to the fact that there are structural causes behind this.

Work Creates Woman

"The pain of unemployment is greater than the pain of circumcision," Tajeba said to me when I, gingerly, tried to ask her about problems linked to being circumcised.

Tajeba is 42 years old. She is a refugee from Somalia and has no education. Ashe has eight children between the ages of seven and twenty, and she is very concerned about her children getting a good education so that they do not end up in the same situation as her. She has lived in Norway for eight years, and four years ago, she was divorced from her husband. Like many minority women, Tajeba is looking for a job.

Unemployment and poverty are two sides of the same coin. This is true both for ethnic Norwegians and immigrants. When people are unemployed, they reside outside Norwegian society, both economically and socially. What Tajeba wanted most of all was a job.

Tajeba had sought out the conversation group for circumcised women to get acquainted with someone: "I need to find a network that can help me find a job." Actually, she was not interested in problems related to circumcision. When I tried to start a conversation on this topic, she just laughed, surprised that I too, also an immigrant, asked about this – a thing that all Norwegians were so occupied with: "It is in fashion now. Everyone talks about circumcision. Norwegians talk about it. It is their country. They decide how they talk about us." Tajeba was not able to see the positive side of the conversation group she was in, how it was a project to protect the health of women, their rights and their sexuality. For her, asking such questions was an indulgence.

Tajeba told me of her difficulties understanding the system, "everything is paperwork and computers". Tajeba asked me what I was doing, and when I told her that I wrote about pain among minority women, she asked me again, urgently, to help her find a job.

Like Shogofa, Tajeba also referred to the social welfare office as an institution that contributed towards worsening her problems rather than solving them: "I don't want to go to the social welfare office. I get a lot of pain from being there."

The social welfare office is a particular Scandinavian institution many immigrants come in contact with. But this institution and the ideas behind such an institution are completely alien for many. The whole social democratic model – the way it is set up for rights and duties, taxes and social benefits - remain unmediated and a vague idea that many minorities do not feel they are a part of. Furthermore, when people meet an institution they do not understand, they experience it as more rigid than it actually may be. Tajeba had a bigger problem understanding the Norwegian system than those born and raised in Norway. But first of all, the solution to her problems is employment - an obvious solution for Norwegian women with similar economic and social problems.

Work is important for people's self-esteem, sense of self-worth and belonging, a feeling of being recognized for who you are, and what you are capable of. Therefore, employment is also important for people's health: to be unemployed can, in itself, trigger illness or aggravate complicated psychosomatic illness. Work often feels filled with meaning. Still, it is not true that all kinds of jobs are filled with meaning for all people. For the majority population, this is an accepted truth. But minorities often have the impression that they should accept whatever job they are given. Paradoxically enough, Tajeba sought out the Jacob Center, a Norwegian institution, to find a network that could contribute towards getting her a job. She needed a network, and she needed practical help with the paperwork. The only thing she was offered was a conversation group on the topic of female circumcision.

Shaeen, who had a university education from her country of origin, had worked many years as a mother tongue language teacher in Norway. But after Oslo municipality discontinued the mother tongue language program, she became unemployed. The Public Employment Service required her to find work placement, but she was not able to do so. She wrote many letters to various places where she thought she could work, but only received negative replies. So, she asked the Public Employment Service to find her an internship. After a while, she received an offer of vocational rehabilitation in the postal service in sorting letters. Shaeen thought that this was not good enough. Norwegian society had to recognize the expertise of people like her, she believed. Still, she accepted the offer of vocational rehabilitation. While she was working in the postal service, she continued writing applications for various jobs she desired but she was rejected for all of them. After six months in the postal service, she was relocated to a kindergarten. A long stay in jail had made her very sensitive to loud noises. Consequently, her workdays in the kindergarten soon became a strain for her. She had great problems enduring the noise from the children.

Shaeen ended up going from doctor to doctor to seek help. The doctors gave her medicines that had side effects for her. She could not concentrate. After a while, she had problems maintaining a normal routine in her life and became unable to work.

Today, Shaeen feels pushed into a role as a person with an illness. She herself thinks this is a result of her being poor. Like Shogofa, Shaeen has a past as a political activist and opponent to religious fundamentalism. She was a woman with a lot of drive and guts. She is still engaged in global politics and is interested in understanding the causes of why she is a refugee, and why she has ended up in the situation she is in. Depressed, she says: "All the ruins from the war will be rebuilt one day, but nobody can rebuild a human destroyed by war." She does not wish to be a burden to society, as she feels is the case when she had to take sick leave.

It is important to understand that as long as Shaeen had her job as a teacher of her mother tongue, she functioned well and felt relatively good. Admittedly, she had problems. She struggled with memories from her past and painful experiences from the war. But she was able to cope with the problems to such an extent that she had a life she felt was good. In addition, she was proud of her job and of the fact that she was not a burden to Norwegian society.

When Shaeen lost her job and was unable to get a new one, her life became very difficult. Today, she has lost all pride, her social network and her feeling of being recognized for what she is, and what she can do. Not having meaningful work that she is good at makes her ill.

Vulnerable Women: Prejudiced World View?

At the doctor's office, the women I met often felt that they came across as demanding, as an "immigrant" among many, as a "foreigner", a non-

Western woman with an alien belief system. They have private lives the majority society do not know or ask about. They have a vague and strange past and background. And they think they are looked upon as one of many non-Western women with problems that are difficult to solve. The same feelings emerge in the social welfare office. The women I have met think they are received with preconceived attitudes and beliefs about belonging to a group that is looking for a way to "exploit" the Norwegian welfare system.

Is this about overwrought emotions, with statements being interpreted in the worst possible light? Or is this about actually not being met with mutual respect and recognition?

Can we say that not being willing to see the individual behind the "client", actually is a violation? Can we say that not seeing the suffering and pain of the individual, behind all concepts we have about one of all the groups an individual may belong to, actually is a violation? I think this is the core of the matter. And we have to start by being willing to listen to what the person feeling violated actually experiences.

It is also true that the immigrant condition in itself is a vulnerable condition - for the individual. Many of these women carry with them embedded memories of injustice. As such, they are extra vulnerable. Like Shogofa, they actually carry our global reality inside themselves, as a part of their history, their experience, their view of the world: war, injustice, migration, the differences between the West and the rest of the world, between poor and rich.

Initially, the encounter between these women and the health services and the social welfare office does not have anything to do with racism. But the result is still individual discrimination, in the sense that the women do not experience being looked upon as an equal individual. They experience that they do not get recognition and understanding for their ailments by the doctor. And they experience that they do not get understanding for their situation or recognition for their knowledge and work experience at the social welfare office.

In addition, a vulnerable group is also a group that reacts strongly. Individuals being violated before are often hypersensitive to new violations. This must also be taken into account when minorities claim they are being discriminated while the majority claims this is an overreaction.

In Norwegian society, there are many individuals who are ignored because they are being considered solely as representatives of their culture or religion. This is also fatal for the community as a whole. For by ignoring individuals, we also ignore potential resources. The individual as a carrier of potential for change is lost.

Institutions with Good Intentions

When I started my studies on the health conditions among minority women, I began my fieldwork at a center in Oslo that works with minority women who feel isolated. It is called the Jacob Center.[5] The center is described as "a place to be" for isolated women to get the opportunity to come out of their homes. Those working at the center say they are working consciously "on the women's terms". The center garners a lot of respect as having expertise on issues concerning minorities and seems like a link between minorities and various organizations. They are also involved in projects outside Norway, among others, in Africa.

What makes this center interesting in particular is that it has a clear objective to help minority women. It receives funding from the Norwegian state. And it is mainly run by representatives from the majority population who shape the ideas and various initiatives of the center.

The center has various groups, among others, a circumcision group, a Quran Group, a cooking group and a forced-marriage group. These are divided along ethnic lines. They work independently of each other. The groups maintain the language of the respective groups, and they are led by persons who are in the same situation and have the same background as the rest of the participants.

At the Jacob Center, I met many women and children of different ages. I had respondents from three generations: children, adult ladies and the elderly. I did not focus on a particular nationality. My respondents had backgrounds from countries like Pakistan, Somalia, Morocco and Algeria. Common for these women were that most of them had little education, many were unemployed, and had many children. In general, their quality of life was poor. They suffered from poverty, isolation and did not feel like citizens of Norwegian society. They received little information about Norwegian society and did not know their own rights. Many were religious. Suffering and pain were part of their daily life.

Tajeba from Somalia was one of the women I met there. She had contacted the center because she wanted a social network and help with some practical problems.

I participated in the Quran Group for Pakistani women and at the weekly internal meetings at the center.[5] I was told by Tajeba that the center had the same program for Somali women the year before. The group was called the Health and Quran Group. The leader of the center told me that the women themselves wanted to learn about the Quran, and that this was one of the reasons for this group. According to him, the Quran Group was an initiative that would give the women insight into their rights and health issues by studying the Quran.[6] The center thought that in this way, they could be integrated into Norwegian society.

This combination of health and religion for Muslim women is symptomatic. Why in the world must the Quran be linked to the health of women? Why would anyone suggest holding a seminar about God, the bible and problems related to pain among ethnic Norwegian women? The name and members of the group reflect a widespread idea in Norway: that women from Somalia, first of all, are religious. From such a starting point, other ideas about their way of thinking are born. Everything from the raising of children to health is seen in a religious context. In this way, their questions related to health are denigrated to something non-scientific, something that is not on par with the modern state of health in Norway, and that doesn't need to be either.

The leader of the Quran Group at the center looked at everything from her religious perspective. Nasrin is in her forties and came to Norway early in the eighties. She has an education from Pakistan and speaks English well, but not Norwegian. When she told me that she did not speak Norwegian, she sighed, looked down and said: "Oh, my husband told me that I should manage just with English." It was clear from her body language that she really wanted to learn Norwegian, but that she had to give it up to fulfill her duties as a housewife.

She did not have a job where she could use her education. And she did not like to stay at home so much. She told me that her daughter says she has sacrificed her best years to take care of the family, and recently she had begun to think about this herself. The only time she gets out of her home, is a few hours a week when she works as a leader for the Quran Group at the Jacob Center.

Nasrin is sad and obviously depressed at times. "Pain and womanhood are two sides of the same coin," she tells me. "This life is short anyway, it is the other life, that comes after death, that is important." Hence, she lives morally right according to the Muslim faith, with Mohammad and the four caliphs as role models. Practical problems related to her daily life as a minority woman in Norway has to be "solved" with the Quran. With this attitude, she "teaches" the other women at the center. Those who run the center look at the initiative as help for isolated minority women. But what thoughts are behind help such as this? Are all participants supposed to think as passively about their situation as Nasrin?

I think the Quran Group at the Jacob Center reproduces problems for the women participants instead of solving them. To me, the Jacob Center represents something worrying in the institutions of Norway. Unfortunately, the attitudes lying behind the "help" they offer, are very common.

The Quran Study Group: Reproduction of Suffering and Inequality

The activities at the Jacob Center are based purely on multicultural thinking. They implement measures for "others". Both the Quran Group and the center for courses in Arabic are aimed at Muslims. The center argues that these women need to know their rights through their own culture and religion first. After that, they can get to know their rights in Norwegian society. But it is not Islam or religion that can contribute towards solving the everyday problems of these women. Their everyday problems lie in a complicated convergence between Norwegian society and its institutions. They are unable to cope in their encounters with Norwegian society, and they are unable to do what they want for their children. The Quran Group is yet another arena where others define what they need. It is also where the ideals for what they are supposed to be and what they are supposed to do are far higher than most of them can attain.

Every meeting in the Quran Group starts with Nasrin reading a series of quotes from the Quran in Arabic, before she translates them to Urdu and gives an interpretation. Afterwards, she taught the Quran in strict fundamentalist terms. Before the group started, everybody checked that their veils were put on properly. Even those who, before the group started, had their veils on their shoulders now put it on their faces out of respect for the Quran. Nasrin wrote on the blackboard: "God is great, and Mohammad is his prophet" and "God created earth and air for us humans". She told us that as Muslims, we must remember that we are created to pray and do what is right. "Muslims must have a soft heart", that is the most important precondition for belief. Infidels, on the contrary, do not have a soft heart. For people to be good, God created punishment. Through punishment we are cleansed and learn to be good. If you do not do what is right, you end up in hell. But God has a plan for how we can avoid ending up in hell. We can read sura Ikhlas and sura Nafel four times, Nasrin told us. We must read every night to avoid punishment.

Nasrin also talked about sura Baqarah. It tells us that what is most

important for women are to be modest and shy. She talks about honor and how important it is that Muslim women cover their body. Punishment and fear of God was a dominant theme for Nasrin. Each time she talked about punishable actions, there was great interest among those present.

To me, the Quran Group at the Jacob Center after a while represented yet another sphere of silent oppression. In spite of the center's intention that these women in the end will liberate themselves from their isolation, the opposite is happening. The women are made passive, and in addition, the moral expectations for their way of life are lifted even higher and become even more unreachable. In this way, the Quran Group contributes towards maintaining the difficult situation of these women and reproducing the painful social fields they already belong in.

The women participating in the Quran Group are the losers in all their relations in modern society. They came there because they were isolated. They had already lost the competition for a job. They all had weak finances and as a consequence, were losers in the housing market. They lived where few Norwegians wanted to live. They talked about their inability to help their children. And in addition, many were losers in the gender relations between man and woman. In other words, they had little power over themselves and their own situations.

Powerlessness leads to inability to act.[7] The way the Jacob Center communicate the message of the Quran, with a focus on guilt, punishment and inadequacy, reinforces the feeling of powerlessness.

One day I discussed what it actually means to work "on women's premise" with the leader of a Somali group: "If you could choose to start a group, what kind of group would that be?" She smiled. And answered: "I would form a group that could learn about democracy. This is the greatest need for Somali women who come from a country ravaged by war. People know nothing about democracy." I believe that this woman pointed at a real need among many of the women who came to the center. To believe that women from the non-Western world are to be integrated into Norwegian society with the help of Quran Groups, testifies to a culture-essentialist way of looking at "women's premise".

The families that come to the Jacob Center during the weekends do not have any alternative activities for their children: they are poor and marginalized. Grete Brochmann writes about nationality, citizenship, and belonging. She says: "Strangers become more like strangers the poorer they are."[8]

To describe the needs of immigrants from their culture, leads to misguided policies. In addition, there is a danger that culture may replace the concept of race. As Wikan points out, the immigrants are themselves a part of the process of reproducing such categories.

This way of thinking overshadows a growing problem in society and is a problem that affects us all. In principle, this is about the rights of the citizens. Like Grete Brochmann says, there is a large gap between formal rights and reality in Western societies. Fortunately, this lack of civil rights and access to basic material and immaterial resources, has met resistance in the form of a new wave of the struggle for civil rights, where immigrants claim their rights. "We wash your cars, build your roads, we are a part of society" is a slogan for this movement, which claims immigrants must be included as full members of the nation.[9]

The Strong Force of Multiculturalism

As shown through the various chapters in this book, the multicultural way of thinking expresses itself in a large array of areas in society. In particular, it is when it expresses itself in institutional Norway and is voiced by politicians with much power that it really becomes a strong and dangerous force that can have serious consequences on the way we organize our society.

All the unuttered preconditions, what we think is common sense and therefore don't question, what actually may be prejudices but that each and every one may still think represents an understanding of how different we are - it is when these thoughts are turned into real policies that they become a powerful force in Norwegian society. One example of this is the way the problem of criminal gangs came under the spotlight in 2001. The then minister of justice, Hanne Harlem, claimed that the imams and the religious communities had to intervene to prevent and stop gang criminality in Pakistani communities. She and the police obviously reasoned this way: Because many Pakistanis are Muslims, gang criminality can and must be defeated by Muslim religious authorities. But why must religious authorities be part of the solution of a social problem just because we deal with Muslims? When was the last time priests and the Norwegian church were appealed to, to fight crime among ethnic Norwegians? Crime must be solved by society and the expertise that exists in this. It is not a religious issue that religious communities can solve. To fight crime is a great responsibility to delegate to religious communities, a responsibility they neither have the knowledge nor capacity to undertake. Not unexpectedly, imams suggested "prison" in the mosque, an arrangement that really would have created Taliban-like conditions in Norwegian society.

One of the most distinct voices in the Norwegian public discourse about Muslims and immigrants is, unfortunately, Hege Storhaug. Her reasoning is also based on multicultural thinking that exclusively constructs immense differences between "the Western" and "the Muslim". According to Storhaug, Muslims are necessarily conservative, hostile to women, undemocratic and supporters of a religious state. When Hege Storhaug writes about how Muslims occupy Oslo, and through arranged marriages with brides from their country of origin threaten our freedom, she subscribes to essentialism. She essentializes the category "Muslim" and uses it politically. And she uses religion and culture as a driving force in her argumentation. Storhaug talks about democracy and human rights, but reasons solely in a way that makes these values the values of the West. She sees a gap of religious and cultural differences and is unable to see structural factors such as poverty, exclusion and isolation. Also, she does not see the dynamics in the socialization of the Muslims into Norwegian society, where they face various obstacles on their way to being fully integrated and experiencing good quality of life.

Both those who fight for the specific rights of Muslims, and those

who fight against them, are grabbing the cultural characteristics and symbols and fight over their power and meaning. In this way the hijab becomes important both for the Islamic Council and Hege Storhaug as a marker for a culture that they, each in their own way, fill with a quite specific and limited content.

We must ask ourselves what we want. Do we want to create a harmonious society, or do we want conflicts? Do we want to fight on for the meaning of excessively narrow categories? Or do we investigate how minorities, for example women, really feel in Norway today?

To think in the categories of culture, religion and ethnicity is not the way to go if we want to help isolated minority women like those at the Jacob Center, or if we want to move further in the Norwegian integration debate. Neither Hege Storhaug and Human Rights Service or the Islamic Council has a real function in relation to the situation of these women. Both the Jacob Center, Human Rights Service and the Islamic Council represent institutionalized multiculturalism. And all these voluntary organizations are funded by the Norwegian state.

The New Society of Organizations: Is the Map Correct?

Organizations are an important arena where we come together to promote our interests. In this way organizations have an important role as "representatives" of various interest groups to the state.

Norway is a world leader when it comes to the establishing of organizations. Each Norwegian is, on average, a member of 5 to 6 organizations, whereof many receive support from the Norwegian state. There also exist many immigrant organizations that get support from the state, based on their country of origin, ethnicity and/or religion. Afghans, Tamils, Turks and many more groups have created their own organizations. In addition, there are many organizations based on and funded by a specific religious group.

Getting support or not, contributes toward the creation of norms and realities and furthermore organizations growth or decline. The economic power of the state is transformed into the power of definition. The state distributes funds according to what policy is wanted and according to what needs they think the various organization cover. The multicultural ideas shape a policy whereby resources and the responsibility for the integration of minorities are being delegated to organizations.

The secular democracy in Norway uses huge economic resources on religious organizations because they think that they can assist in solving an integration problem, and thereby reducing conflicts between the majority and the minority. They support organizations that either protect the culture or religion of their members like the Islamic Council or define their activity according to cultural or religious boundaries like Human Rights Service where Hege Storhaug runs a campaign against "alien" culture and religion.

Organizations that build their activity around these factors create exclusion, racism and discrimination. Poverty, unemployment, exclusion and lack of belonging in Norwegian society are hidden behind ethnic, religious and cultural categories. Only the women this book is about are the ones who come off worst! In the long term I think the consequence is that the active role of the citizen is weakened by this policy. Individuals are pacified. This creates a parallel society and a feeling of being a "guest". The funding is allocated based on statistical categories, and it creates a persistent form of exclusion from the community.

We must change our attitudes. We must let our changed attitudes be enshrined in the institutions of society. And we must change the organizational map!

The institutions are much more closely connected to the state than the organizations. But often, the organizations also implement the political strategies of the state. In today's globalized reality national states are weakened, and many organizations, therefore, have gained a newer and more influential role than a few decades back. They become part of institutionalized Norway. On one hand, the state delegates tasks to local initiatives. On the other hand, it is easier to create global forms of organizations.

In the globalized society of today it is important to admit that we cannot consider the local, national and global as completely separated from each other. All levels in society, the interpersonal, the organizational community of interests, the state institutions and the global organizations, are affected by the local, the national and the global at the same time.

An example of this is when Muslim religious communities engage mullahs from Pakistan with the help of funding from the Norwegian state. Mullahs without knowledge of Norwegian reality, society and language can come to teach and preach. The starting point is a policy to support and preserve a minority culture locally in Oslo. In reality the policy becomes involved in global relations across borders, where religious conservative men have extensive power, and women do not. In this way the state contributes towards creating parallel societies and enhancing the differences that are already problematic. Men who already have power get more power, and women get even less than before. In this way structural differences are fortified even further. In this way today's Norwegian organizational map becomes a source of discrimination instead of a source of egalitarianism, more rights and more equality. To overcome this form of discrimination, the purse strings must be closed and reopened. Financial support ought, to a greater degree, be based on general human rights and less on religion, ethnicity and culture. Gender equality and human rights for all - also children - must be central in our ideas about equality and our policies to gain a measure of recognition for minority women.

Institutions in Norway with the Ability to Change

I see a great potential for change: the institutions are conducive to change and renew themselves constantly. The institutions have their own way of functioning, their special dynamics. But they also have potential for change. They are dynamic. Institutions based on modern democratic ideas have reflexivity as their most important characteristic. This is also the most important feature of the modern society. Reflexivity means that there is room for reflection and exchange of ideas, values and practices. Experts play a central part. Their task is to collect information to design and change the institutions so that they function as well as possible. It is not only experts who decide the process; political control also plays a part in the design of many institutions. In addition, historical and social factors play a part in how institutions in Norway look today. Norway, like the other Nordic countries, has its own history where social democratic values have been strong. These values and mentality are based on Nordic law and institutions. The institutions in the Nordic countries focus on the needs of the individual. At the same time, they are based on ideas about the individual as part of the society they live in, and the structures they live within. In this way all the Nordic countries have "lifted up" a large Nordic working class and given it the opportunity to gain knowledge and to have meaningful and secure employment. In return for these rights, it has certain duties and obligations. Still, the state has not yet managed to integrate a continually growing minority population into its social democratic system. Here lies the great challenge.

9. Globalization and its Abject

The daily life of my respondents is marked by two important processes that also mark the world of today: delocalization and globalization. Our age is "delocalized". The place where you live have lost its central importance. To my respondents this local dimension, their daily life in Oslo, is just a part of their reality. Their lives and pains also have a national and a global dimension.

In the same way that we have a globalized economy, I note that the thoughts and relations of people are globalized. There is a parallel between the earnings of the businessman and the pains of my respondents. Everything can be moved from one corner of the world to another, at the speed of light. This is true also for information from other countries (about realities) that create new pain and remind people of already existing pain. Belquis, Shaeen and Shogofa are among those who were forced to leave their family and friends, their homeland, their language and their culture. As a result of this they have close relations across borders between countries and continents. While a Norwegian businessman delocalizes his company and invests in China, immigrants in Norway think of their loved ones who may be spread all over Europe and the world. It is not only company owners and politicians who are "globalized"; poor immigrants also think globally.

Globalization has two sides: winners and losers. The winners are the rich part of the world; the common man and woman in Norway who enjoy good and cheap imports, exotic food and the possibility to travel all over the world on vacation. The winners have "the world at their feet". They can travel, experience other cultures and gain economically from global relations.

My respondents are globalized losers. People in the same situation exist in many countries. Science shows that in all metropolises we find a lower class, mainly marginalized and poor immigrants, who suffer under socioeconomic and health problems. People like my respondents live in Melbourne, Toronto, Paris, London and Stockholm.

Globalization has created enormous opportunities for women and women's liberation. But just the same, many minority women struggle in big Western cities with poverty, bad health and poor quality of live. Their need for freedom becomes a superfluous objective beyond their reach.

When I look at the pain of Belquis, Shogofa and Shaeen and the rest of the women I have met, it is a pain with three dimensions: global, national and local. The local dimension is the problems of their daily private lives and in the public sphere in their encounters with institutions described earlier in this book. Nationally they see themselves as part of a marginalized group, "immigrants". They feel excluded from the national community. Each and every day they meet attitudes that indicate a lack of recognition that expresses a perception of them as "the others". And they meet a media reality where they feel stigmatized.

But it is mainly global circumstances that have led to their immigration to Norway. They have escaped from societies in Afghanistan, Pakistan, Chile and various countries in Africa. They are victims of unfair relations linked to global insecurity, geopolitics, terrorism and conflicts. My respondents suffer because of events that cannot be linked directly to each individual. The causes of their situation, for example conflict and war, also often lie beyond the borders of their original countries. The consequence is that they move among various countries and parts of the world. They carry with them embedded collective memories and pains. This is their global consciousness.

Globalization of Pain: Examples from Several Countries

In Sweden, already in the 1990s, a comparative study was conducted of immigrants and Swedish-born patients at a series of medical and physiotherapy clinics in southwestern Stockholm.[1]

Demography and socioeconomic status varied systematically between immigrants and the Swedish-born who participated in the study. Immigrants more often lived in segregated and poorer areas than the majority population. They suffered higher unemployment, and more people had been dependent on social welfare initiatives in later years. Compared to the Swedish participants, more of the immigrants were "blue collar workers" (factory workers, manual labor). They reported having been unemployed more often, lived under greater financial pressure and experienced longer periods of sick leave. The study shows that the problems of these immigrants are created in the host country by structural factors. Mainly, they cannot be linked to culture and religion brought from their countries of origin, like it is often portrayed in the official discourse.[2]

Several of the immigrants also reported having experienced violence and/or threats in their host country. Immigrants from Iraq, Chile and Turkey said they did not go out in the evenings because of their fear of violence. Among these, 40-50 percent linked this fear directly to ethnic or religious discrimination.[3] Often they used passive coping strategies to escape from the situation. They prayed.

The data that was collected,[4] show that immigrants were in poorer health than the Swedish patients. They generally had lower mental wellbeing and were more afflicted with serious mental illness than the Swedes (56 percent of the immigrants compared to 33 percent among the Swedes). In total it appeared that patients who were immigrants experienced their situation as more difficult than the Swedes. This was true in financial relations, in relation to mental wellbeing, pain, and the handling of work and employment related strains. In addition, the immigrants felt their pain more often, more intensely, and as a bigger obstacle in their daily life. Feelings of insecurity in daily life, lack of leisure activity, low material wellbeing and unemployment was more common among immigrants than in the Swedish majority population. They also used more medication and found the effects of this as weaker.

The Danish scientist Peter Hervik describes a similar situation for immigrants in Denmark.[5] He shows that they generally have lower-paid jobs than most members of the majority and are more often unemployed. Hervik also shows that the media's depiction of immigrants in Denmark is populist and essentialist. The Majority and the minority understand each other only to a small extent, he says; they have little contact with each other. The media work as a common frame of reference, where the majority and the minority learn about and get an impression of each other. This tendency is amplified by political parties, especially by the way the Dansk Folkeparti speaks about immigration and immigrants. Hervik shows that there is strong social control over immigrant women in Denmark and points out that there exists a veil of silence around this.[6]

Social control and maltreatment of minority women in Muslim communities were considered a cultural phenomenon by the Danish judicial system as well. But after the Mohammed cartoons, the authorities were shocked by how dominating Muslim extremists and organizations are in Denmark. Extreme forms of violence to women are now being prosecuted. After being witness to the global mobilization of Islamic forces in the wake of the Mohammed cartoons, Danish authorities seem to have understood the perils of a multicultural policy that gives both room and power to religious organizations. Religious organizations are even more active in Denmark than in Norway. There has been a tendency of Danish authorities not to listen to moderate Muslims, but now, this is starting to change.

Peter Hervik claims that Denmark has an explicit multicultural policy, and he criticizes how it functions to preserve the difference between the majority and the minorities. Hervik points out that this policy also contributes toward the majority feeling fear and insecurity with regard to "the dangerous Muslims". The analysis of Hervik gives us an understanding of the way the majority is negative towards immigrants, and how the populist picture of immigrants appearing in the media contribute towards maintaining the negative impression the majority has. In this situation the minorities are under stress both from their social and socioeconomic situation, and from the stigmatizing attitudes they are subjected to.

Margaret Lock, in her turn, describes the daily life of a handful of Greek immigrant women in Canada. Their lives are marked by "diffuse" pains and a feeling of frustration described by the Greek word "nevra".[7] Lock describes the life situation of these women with economic exploitation in the work market (they work or have worked in the textile industry), together with limited freedom in their private spheres. Immigrant women often exist in a borderland. Traditional codes that provided pride and honor in their home country can be a hindrance in the adaptation process. To become a Canadian, a Greek woman must continually cross-cultural boundaries that are a part of the essence of female identity and self-esteem in Greece, and many do not get the opportunity to learn the language in their new homeland properly. The men, who also feel exploited in the work market, and also suffer from cultural shock, often show their anxiety by taking an even stronger grip over their wives or resort to verbal or physical abuse. The feeling of loss of control often leads to acute nevra, and when these periods come often, the frustration often becomes chronic.

Multiculturalism is a key concept in Canadian integration policy, which describes the country as a "mosaic" of different cultures. The attitude is that immigrants should adapt to clearly delimited ethnic groups within a largely tolerant host nation. Lock points out that the complex process of migration becomes hidden by the rhetoric of "the mosaic of Canada" because it creates artificial boundaries between ethnic stereotypes. These stereotypes seldom correspond to how the immigrants perceive their own culture, and they do not take into account factors such as class and sex for the identity of a person. They also hide the fact that the immigration situation in itself and the employment situation is part and parcel of the background of a person.

London's Health Commission writes in its "Health in London" report from 2004 that "non-White groups (are) far worse on (…) unemployment, GCSE attainment, unfit housing, domestic burglary, road causalities and self-asserted health status".[8] This is a clear indication that the total life situation among immigrants and minorities in London is far more difficult than among the majority.

Similarly, in France minorities are in a comparable impotent situation, and the same goes for the USA.[9] In his *In Search of Respect*, Philippe Bourgois contributes with an extensive analysis of the total life situation of Puerto Rican immigrants in the ghetto, El Barrio, in New York, based on five years of field work when he was a resident there. Historically, various immigration groups have been living in El Barrio and then moved as they became better off. Just like Rosenborg in Sweden,[10] Angarudd and Grønland, El Barrio is a symptom of a lot of socioeconomic problems. Bourgois shows how the high unemployment and poverty in El Barrio lead the inhabitants into an economic underground based on narcotics and crime. El Barrio had a bad reputation, and the inhabitants were stigmatized. Few had the opportunity to move to a better area, even if most of them wanted to.

In spite of the similarity between ghetto areas in Western countries we must remember that the Nordic countries are marked by social democratic values not found in ghettos in the USA. One example is when the Norwegian ski association in cooperation with Oslo municipality offers free ski education for the children of Angarudd. This is an excellent initiative that the parents of these children do not have the opportunity to provide.[11] There are many examples of how social democratic initiatives relieve social inequality: subsidized kindergartens, free schooling, a strong healthcare system, to mention a few. Still the minority population is not "lifted" from their socioeconomic distress to the extent necessary. One of the causes, I think, is that integration is increasingly left to ethnic, cultural and religious groups.

Globally Institutionalized Religious Organizations are at Work

In Norway and Sweden, we have been shaken by brutal killings perpetrated by immigrants and refugees on their own wives, sisters and daughters in recent years. We must understand that these tragedies involve people who are a part of the Norwegian social structure, instead of "understanding" this as unchangeable culture and religion. Also, the men experience the structural discrimination nobody talks about. These immigrant men are often losers in their social relations, in their struggle to find a job, a home and a dignified life. The only place they can exercise power is, at home, over their women. When Muslim men kill their wives, it is often the same circumstances as when an ethnic Norwegian man does the same: powerlessness, frustration and acute mental instability. But in addition, it often concerns the power that a conservative Islamic society has over its members in Norway, among other things in the form of having an established strong institution in said society. And where this institution is allowed to exercise power, its autonomy and its own rules.

Today religious organizations like mosques have become places where unemployed and discriminated immigrant men congregate. The mosques function as passive coping strategies whereby these people are able to endure and accept their situation. They find what seems like solutions in moral acts and superficial solidarity, but their real problems are not solved. The mosques have no capacity to solve the problems these men endure in their daily lives.

The growing importance of the mosques is a trend in all Western countries. Institutions are created with the objective of promoting religious and ethnic/cultural activities in the big cities, often with an official objective of fostering "integration" that will garner funding from the state. Even if these people create and increase welfare in the big cities, this is not mentioned in the immigrant discourse. In all metropolises we find institutions based on the essentialised categories of religion, culture and ethnicity that are the sources of constant conflicts. These institutions are, in the end, counterproductive when it comes to their intention of integration. Instead of integrating they become part the problem in that they create and support mental ghettoization, which in turn creates even more painful social fields, especially for women.

In all big cities people like my respondents live in ghetto areas, like the ones in Oslo. But both they, and the majority society they live within, are also mentally ghettoized in the categories of religion, culture and ethnicity. The media, political parties and organizations run the discourse concerning immigration and refugees around these categories. This exclusive focus is what I will call a constructed global myth. Particularization linked to culture, religion and ethnicity creates conflicts and has acquired a global dimension. This is a constructed reality that both the majority and immigrants struggle under. An example is the media focus in the aftermath of the Mohammed cartoons where extremists on both the Christian and Muslim sides ended up dominating the debate. When extremists have the opportunity to dominate, the debate turns into entertainment. An image of the enemy as "the dangerous Muslim" is created, something that is fatal for all parties. This one-sided focus makes us blind to other dimensions such as the relation between power and lack of power, and socioeconomic factors. This happens because Western institutions are built on multicultural principles that discriminate. The mental ghettoization is institutionalized, and it works both ways!

Consequently, there is a "revitalization" of religious and ethnic belonging. This is indirectly funded by the Norwegian state. The real cause of this must, to a greater extent, be analyzed in relation to socioeconomic realities and an increasing feeling of violation. Luckily, we have seen a somewhat more balanced discourse in Norway lately. We have a lower level of conflict than in other parts of the world. However, also in Norway heated debates about everything from circumcision to the use of veils are made into entertainment by the media.

New forms of Global Discrimination: A Win-Lose Relation

Lise Widding Isaksen denotes today's situation as a global crisis of care.[12] Immigrant women come to help wealthy people in the West and other rich regions as housemaids, au pairs, nurses and the like. At the same time, they miss the care and closeness of their own family and children. The oftentimes hopeless economic situation in their homeland leads them to suppress their own needs for love in order to give themselves and their families a safer economic future. Consequently, the globalized economic situation creates a new form of immigrant.

Widding Isaksen has studied the migration of female healthcare workers from poor to rich countries. She points out that around 180 million people move from poor to rich countries: from Eastern Europe to Western Europe, from Mexico to the USA, from South Asia to the Arabian Gulf. Most of these immigrants are women. There are more Malawi doctors in Manchester than in Malawi, and also more African nurses prefer to travel to and work in Western countries. She quotes Lewis, who wrote, "people talk about the world having to subsidize Africa, but to me it looks like the opposite is the case. It is Africa that subsidizes the Western work market with healthcare workers".[13] She criticizes the tendency towards commodification[14] and says that macroeconomic processes create new forms of differences between poor and rich countries, while it "on the micro level is (...) about an increased vulnerability for human relations to be made into an ordered product".[15] She interviewed female healthcare workers and their family members, for example Gina, a 31-year-old nurse from Latvia who worked in Norway. She has a hyperactive son she had to leave with her husband at home in Latvia. Gina misses her son, and he misses his mother and is unhappy. He sent her a drawing showing his sad experience of being separated from his mother. In the drawing he had painted himself standing alone in front of their house. His face was colored dark green, which made him look sad.

This study shows how the deregulated market economy, based on profit and money, regulates immigration. That a woman from Latvia has the opportunity to travel to Norway to work as a nurse is a sign that "the market functions". The philosophy behind a liberal economy is that with a free market, it will regulate itself so that employers like Norwegian hospitals that need more workforce, get their needs fulfilled, and the unemployed (or workers earning too little) get theirs. There are still some human costs involved in moving across national borders that are probably larger for the non-Western woman than for the Western one, in addition to needs that have to be suppressed for what they consider the best for themselves and the family, economically speaking. So, who creates welfare and for whom?

As we have seen, there are great economic and health differences when we compare the situation of the majority with the minorities in Norway, Sweden, Denmark, England, France and the USA. Economic and health differences are ignored, while ethnic, religious and cultural differences are emphasized and constructed as steadily greater. But like the situation for immigrant women who come to the West to work, this, more than anything else, concerns people who live at the bottom rung of society, whether it be the national or the global economic system.

The Socioeconomic Perspective and Women's Rights

In a welfare society we must dare to ask: who are benefiting from the welfare system? In Norway we must, to a greater extent, dare to discuss who are allowed to benefit from the social democratic rights that are felt as a given for Norwegian women. The dream of being free, being protected from threats of violence, acquiring knowledge and having an education is not only the dream of Norwegian women. This also goes for the dream of being healthy and experiencing mental and physical wellbeing. And it concerns the dream to have a financial standing that is high enough to provide for themselves and their families.

Professor of social anthropology Unni Wikan is in many ways a pioneer when she points out fundamental imbalances in Norwegian integration policy, and how the right to exercise religion and culture comes into conflict with basic human rights. In the book about Fadime from 2003, she discusses the problematic relation between individual rights and group rights. She describes how the media focuses on ethnicity, culture and religion. "Culture and power go hand in hand," Wikan writes, and quotes the Indian anthropologist Veena Das: "Culture is a way to distribute pain unequally in a population."[16]

Wikan's book about Fadime is also about paradoxical rights promoted by various institutionalized organizations such as freedom of religion contra women's rights. But it lacks an analytical attempt to explain the relation between the paradoxical rights like the rights of the individual, women's rights, group rights, freedom of religion and universal human rights. There is no attempt to analyze and communicate the institutional dynamics leading to this institutionalization of religious and ethnically based forces that we see today in various modern Western societies, such as in Norway. This is the core of what I call unofficial multiculturalism in Norway. I miss a far greater focus on socioeconomic differences in the Norwegian population. And I miss, before all, a discussion of what rights we must put highest.

The women who are the losers of globalization have much in common with the losers in the Norwegian nation like the minority women: Weak health, poor financial standing and a lack of equality and recognition.

10. The Way Out: Minority Women's Hope

It is important to be a good listener to understand how people really feel. It was this that was my goal when I started my study of the health of minority women in Oslo. My starting point was physical pain. But an abyss was opened, of mental, practical, social and economic problems. And at the same time, this strong feeling of lack of belonging is linked to a feeling of lack of recognition, both in their private as well as public lives. And they wanted to belong! They really wanted to create a better life for themselves and their children. Even if the women were born and grew up and were socialized in distant countries, and had different backgrounds, they had hopes and dreams similar to those of other Norwegians. The dreams concern peace and liberty, recognition and equality for themselves and their children. At the same time, they were characterized by an awareness of injustice at the global level.

Belquis' dream was to go to the theater. "I want to go to the theater and watch Karius and Baktus (a play for children) together with my kids like rich people do, instead of going to the Jacob Center." Shogofa formulated her dream in an e-mail from her new home in Paris thus: "I have lived many years in Norway and want to call myself Afghan-Norwegian when Norway starts to build factories and good hospitals in Afghanistan, and export peace and not war to the country. I hate guns (weapons)." Baarin, with her ability to reflect on being a socialist in a male dominated culture, said: "I have attained a lot in Norway. I am able to express my feelings as an independent woman. But my greatest wish is that Norway stops producing imams and religious authorities that claim to be my representatives here. In the Norwegian church there is talk about the possibility of having gay priests. But for the minorities, they support traditional, fundamentalist forces." Elisabeth's wish that was not realized here in Norway was inclusion in the majority community. In an e-mail from Spain, she wrote: "New-Norwegians as a concept, promoted by academics, must be practiced in all parts of society, from the housing market, working life, at the university level." Tajeba, who is a strong Somali woman, still dreams of finding a job. "I hate the social welfare office and papers," she said yet again when I met her once. She looked around to make sure nobody was close by before she said to me while she pointed with a very angry and rigid gesture towards her genitals: "Norwegians only focus on this when they talk about Somalis!" Her wish is that Norwegians understand that Somalis are more than just about female circumcision. Ezat's dream is mainly to escape poverty. She stopped working because of the cash-for-care benefit, and started having children, hoping that it would make her financial situation better. Today she wants, most of all, that her children will get a better life. Nasrin's wish was that Muslim children get the right to learn to swim like all other children. The prophet Mohammad said that you must orient yourself in the reality you are. Nasrin's opinion about Islam is not the same as the one expressed by the Islamic Council. Norwegian society and the Norwegian state must listen to women like her who, in spite of their religiousness, have the ability to orient themselves in a new reality. Arezo has a lot of fighting spirit in her, in spite of all the defeats she has suffered. She wants to understand why Pakistanis in Norway are stricter towards women than in Pakistan. With a serious look while putting her hand on her chest so that the traditional Pakistani bracelets jangled, she said: "In Norway my culture is not considered true Pakistani culture. I am Pakistani and want my parents-in-law to live at a nursing home. Why is this shameful? Who creates this feeling of shame? When the newspapers write about my culture, it is not about me. Luckily, in Norway we have places that can take care of old people." While she talked, she gestured, and the traditional Pakistani bracelets continued to jangle. They created a tune that gave me a feeling of optimism. Shaeen said: "The media worsen conflicts today. Is it possible to reduce this level of conflict?" Her life is characterized by big questions concerning structural injustice. She continued: "I wish for a society and a state that can give people a harmonious life."

The dreams of these women, their reality, and their solutions alternate between a longing for recognition of their own individuality and seeking refuge in religion and rigid ideas about their own cultural belonging and differences from the majority. Many of the women I met expressed explicitly that they wished to be seen as individuals and not as representatives of a culture and a religion that the majority has a lot of problems with and generalized ideas about. Many chose precisely the religious "solutions" to their problems. But many chose conscious strategies to avoid being considered just "Muslim", "Afghan", "Somali", "immigrant" or other all-encompassing terms they felt were a strain. Many, I think, chose to enhance their religious and cultural belonging as a "salvation" because their ties to Norwegian society became too difficult. Many thought they were exposed to prejudices, based on exactly this: ethnicity, culture and religion.

In many ways the women wanted to be full participants in Norwegian society. But they had difficulties finding fruitful strategies. Ideally, they should be strong enough to shake off the prejudices they met and express their individuality. Ideally, they should be able to find practical solutions for attaining a better life. But there are many reasons why they are unable to do this, and we must acknowledge and accept that a big part of the cause of this lies outside of themselves.

What is to be done if the women I met in my fieldwork are able to choose strategies that make them feel better? What is to be done to prevent their cultural and religious attachment from mainly confining them in passive coping strategies, and instead, becoming a strength and pride? How can they ideally balance their need for individuality with religious and cultural attachment? And how can they finally be able to feel a long-awaited belonging to Norwegian society?

Individuality and structure are two sides of the same coin. As individuals we can do much, but not everything! As I have tried to show in this book, there are two factors of importance in this process that society as a whole must do something about: widespread multicultural attitudes and socioeconomic realities. These two factors are linked.

From Unofficial Multiculturalism to Universal Pluralism

Many scientists criticize parts of society and suggest minor changes. But few are talking about what it takes to make more extensive changes, something that also involves questions concerning the kind of state we want. What should the role of the state be? What official strategy should the state actually have concerning integration? And not least: Can the state play a role in changing existing attitudes at so many levels in society?

Grete Brochmann who studied power, has, as mentioned, claimed that the state has the power to ignore, exclude and include citizens in society.[1] Minorities experience that they are being ignored and excluded at an institutional level. Therefore, we must, as Brochmann claims, extend today's concept of nationhood to include many ethnic groups.[2] The state, with its power, must be inclusive all across the board. Knut Kjeldstadli has criticized today's policy because it still may be associated with the concept of "the Norwegian Norwegians". He claims that the nation as a concept has to be studied as a historical process.[3] Kjeldstadli analyzes the future of Norway as a multicultural society where we must try to find a balance between being different and being inclusive.

In my opinion, we must think in a new way about nation and community. Paradoxically, it is just a nationalist ontology that lies behind the idea of the Norwegian man and everything Norwegian, and the new ethnic, cultural and religious delineations of the new groups. Multiculturalism is small-scale nationalism! It is a nationalist ontology that contributes to the classification of people according to what group they belong to, so as to establish simple and clear categories such as Afghan, Pakistani, Muslim and Somali - and Norwegian. Today, in Norwegian multicultural society, we recognize, to a great extent, the dangers of nationalism, but we do not see the dangers of transferring the same basic way of thinking to the new minorities of the country. We must think about community in a new way. Those who live here are to be full participants, independent of ethnicity, religion and culture.

Cultural, religious and ethnic differences cannot be the basis for state policy and allocation of funds. These categories should also not be the basis for deciding who should be integrated. No matter what, this can only be a policy led by vague assumptions of the relation between group identity and individual identity. And such a policy neither solves the problems of the individual nor fulfills their needs. It can neither be inclusive because it does exactly the opposite: It excludes less presumptive communities from the larger community around which the Norwegian state is structured.

A dominant theme in Report to the Storting no. 49 (2003- 2004) is that in Norwegian multicultural society, the inhabitants having multicultural backgrounds can choose their identity.[4] But as long as the media enhance the feeling of the minorities of being stigmatized, and the state does not use its power to include them in an active way, belonging becomes difficult in the Norwegian nation. When you are always stigmatized as "the other", it becomes impossible to "choose" to belong while relating to Norwegian society. The extreme case of Belquis is the result. She looks at Norwegian society and the rest of the Western world as hostile to her and all Muslims. It is "them" against "us". She identifies with Osama bin Laden and all suffering Muslims in the world. Belquis is an extreme example. But as I tried to show, her feelings and that of many minorities of being "the other" is a role that they struggle to relinquish. The state, with the prime minister at the forefront, must use its power of definition and define the new-Norwegians, who are born in and well adapted to Norwegian society, as full members of the nation.

I consider the perspectives of Thomas Hylland Eriksen on universalistic pluralism as the cornerstone for an alternative society. Hylland Eriksen presents the concept of universalistic pluralism in connection with the way the educational system should be in the 21st century, but I think that this perspective should be applied to the entire political land- scape. It may be the key to a society that has a place for all individuals. Universalistic pluralism is a comprehensive knowledge system based on the democratic view that all must take part in establishing the terms for the institutions of our society. But I will add something fundamental to the model of Hylland Eriksen: The philosophy of Axel Honneth about recognition. What is universal must be the fundamental need for recognition in each individual. This means the right to avoid living under oppression and humiliation, access to statutory rights meant for all citizens of a society, and the right to be afforded understanding for the situation individuals actually live in, for example, cases of financial need. The pluralist dimension is that, at the same time, we are all different. We all, ethnic Norwegians included, have a cultural, and in many cases, a religious background that shape us. But this mainly shapes us as individuals. Consequently, there is always a raft of different individuals that must be the basis for finding a way to get society to work, and not assumptions about groups of people who we think of as almost identical. We are different as individuals. It is this that requires a basic pluralist attitude. Religion, culture and ethnicity are far from being alone in shaping our individuality. And we all have an identical need for recognition.

Society, with the state as a driving force, must ensure that this form of individual pluralism permeates the regulative, normative and cognitive aspects of institutions. This means that the consideration for the need of the individual for recognition becomes a basic map of opinion when society includes minorities. When we use the identical need for recognition of the individual as a basis, there is no room for a privileged group to monopolize the definition of reality, such as we see today.

Hence, we also have to include everybody in the social welfare society, including its obligations and rights. My wish is that the idea that "these people take our prosperity" be dropped. "These people" take part in developing Norwegian prosperity. At the same time, more of "these people" need help, because they are ill, or they need jobs.

Attitudes based on research about how reality actually looks and is experienced for each person, should replace the existing multiculturalism and assumptions about how, for example, Muslims actually are and wish to behave. Only with a perspective that puts the individual before the ethnic, religious or cultural group, can we develop attitudes that recognize and include people with minority backgrounds in society.

Global Conscience: A Necessary Basis

To put culture, ethnicity and religion a bit on the sideline does not mean that we avoid gaining knowledge about other cultures, religious traditions or the situations of ethnic groups around the world. We must all continually increase our knowledge about one another. To try to see the wider connections and the global reality is precisely what we must do. For it is a global reality and consciousness that characterize the life of minorities in Norway. When Al Gore received the Nobel Peace Prize, he said the following in his speech:

In every land, the truth – once known – has the power to set us free. Truth also has the power to unite us and bridge the distance between "me" and "we", creating the basis for common effort and shared responsibility. (...) We must abandon the conceit that individual, isolated, private actions are the answer. They can and do help. But they will not take us far enough without collective action. (...) We must understand the connections between the climate crisis and the afflictions of poverty, hunger, HIV-Aids and other pandemics. As these problems are linked, so too must be their solutions.[5]

Local, national and global realities are linked in the world of today. The most basic element in our new map of opinions must therefore be a global conscience. At the same time, it is important that the global conscience does not turn into a question of individual morals. If this happens, the exhortations to make changes in society will become nothing more than religious preaching. Fundamental changes are needed to solve the climate crisis, as well as to stop wars and global injustice. It is only when we start making structural changes that the morals and actions of the individuals become meaningful. We must therefore acquire more scientific knowledge about the actual situations in the societies Belquis, Shogofa, Baarin, Shaeen, Naima, Kamilla, Elisabeth, Tajeba, Ezat, Nasrin and Arezo come from. We must look at the political and global realities and, with this as a basis, develop our global conscience and work towards big structural changes. "Knowledge alone cannot change the structure," Arne J. Vetlesen says.[6] But when knowledge is linked to power, the structure is changed. Hence, the role of the state is of utmost importance.

The Rights of Individuals in Norwegian society: Advice on the Road to Recognition

To put culture, religion and ethnicity on the sideline does not mean that people cannot be proud of their cultural background or be allowed to express their beliefs. It is an asset in today's multicultural society that so many come from other places, have so different experiences, speak so many languages and have so many ways of looking at the world. But for these differences to become a resource, they must not be politicized and made into an arena for struggle and conflict. We must actively use them as a resource ourselves.

When Walid Al-Kubaisi participated in the celebration of the ten most successful immigrants in Norway on January 8, 2007, he formulated ten commandments for immigrants. One of them was this: "Do not put your cultural background in front of you. You will stumble in it, and it will become an obstacle on your way forward. Put it behind you, so that you can drag it where you want, and lead it there, instead of being led by it. If you feel your background is too heavy, throw away the part that slows down your integration."[7] In this way we can both maintain our individuality and cultivate our uniqueness that is linked to our cultural belonging. If the circumstances are favorable for this while we choose this road ourselves, then we who are the minorities in Norwegian society can live a better life, with our cultural, religious and ethnic belonging. Then we may be on our way towards a more harmonious society.

Some of the women in this book "stumble" in their cultural and religious background. It becomes an obstacle to a better life. This is due to both their own way of thinking and the society they encounter. Both prevent them from withdrawing from their cultural and religious context when they need to, to solve practical problems or to acquire more freedom. But the society has also laid out some tripwires. And it is only when society opens the opportunity for substantial freedom that it can be up to the individual to increase its quality of life and become an active part in society. Hence, we must create conditions under which individuals can improve their lives themselves.

The women we have met in this book are in a distinctly difficult situation in life. This is the main cause of their poor health. But both the problems and the solutions must be linked to a bigger picture: a less conflicted and more constructive meeting between the individual and the structural in Norwegian society. As mentioned, in the Report to the Storting no. 49 (2003- 2004), the section on "Political challenges connected to health care" points out that health must be understood in connection with the person's life situation.[8] But who has the responsibility for looking at this connection in the public sector in Norway, and in what way? The report does not specify what the challenges are, or what health clinics must do when they encounter people whose suffering is connected to their whole life situation. In biomedical practice today, doctors are not obliged to have a routine for or to evaluate the patient in relation to their total life situation. The only thing the doctors can do, are to prescribe medication or, in the worst case, write them a sick note. Social problems are turned into medical ones.[9] So, what can we do in concrete terms?

My suggestion is that the tasks of the general practitioner must be

coordinated with that of the psychologist and the social services to a much wider extent. This requires that bureaucratic barriers between the various institutions be lowered. This can lead to more people getting help for what they actually need the most: knowledge and advice about how they can solve practical problems and, in some cases, help to deal with pain that is basically due to mental and social reasons.

I also believe that the total life situation must be a part of the medical consultation, just as blood tests, temperature measurements and X-rays are today. Illness can be due to social and economic factors just as much as bacteria, viruses or other environmental pathogens can.[10] Here, we must increase our research and knowledge. Anthropologists, social workers and psychologists, with a broader perspective on the social aspects of illness can, to a greater extent, play a complementary role to biomedical practice.[11]

The GP's office is a meeting place between the vulnerable individual and one of the institutions of society that, to a far greater extent, must be used as the basis for finding new solutions. My empirical data and the HUBRO study show that there is a link between physical inactivity and gender, low income and education. This again is connected to poor health. The consequence of the individualistic way of thinking that dominates biomedicine is that physical activity becomes the choice of the individual. But when people are poor and lack knowledge, they don't always have the premise to make the right choices for their own health and wellbeing. All municipalities and neighborhoods in larger cities should offer physical activity to residents with low income, particularly the unemployed, single mothers and minorities. This is particularly important for diabetics, where minority women are overrepresented. Existing exercise programs for people with low income should be extended.[12] Every municipality and neighborhood should have an agreement with the local fitness center so that people have the opportunity to exercise where they live, together with others. It is important to avoid a congregation of marginalized groups in one place, because then, many will avoid these exercise programs. This program will give people more energy and better health. The doctors must use their authority and knowledge and pro- vide prescriptions for training when required, instead of sedatives. Better health is the basis for a better life for minority women in Norway.

The preconditions for Norwegian women attaining greater freedom and more opportunities are kindergartens and retirement homes. It is particularly important that we also dare to discuss the opportunities of each minority woman in connection with these important social institutions. I therefore think that the consequences of the cash-for-care benefit for minority women and their children must be analyzed more carefully. According to my study this policy is very unfortunate for minority women with many children. The cash-for-care benefit as a structural factor degrades the premise for opportunities and limits substantial freedom. They lose control over their own body because of poverty, and as a consequence, further propagate poverty. Children become a source of money for these women, as it's a matter of survival. Politicians argue that the cash-for-care benefit provides opportunities for choosing better alternatives. But poverty and lack of knowledge make it impossible for people to make real choices. For minorities it is very important that they send their children to kindergarten so that they can learn the language as early as possible. The best initiative for the integration of minority children is heavily subsidized kindergartens.

Today, minority women carry most of the burden of taking care of their elderly family members. Municipalities and neighborhoods often base their thinking on an essentialized understanding of culture when it comes to how minorities use these services. We remember Arezo, who claimed that she wanted to send her parents-in-law to a nursing home. It is very important that the use of nursing homes is normalized for minorities. Minorities must also try to liberate themselves from the idea of shame regarding this.

Improved quality of life is often about having the energy and the opportunity to do something other than striving to acquire the bare essentials. Access to rich cultural programs is therefore important. Such cultural programs must not be the sole domain of the rich part of the population. It would be constructive to link health and culture. It might be an idea to let the state and municipality enter into agreements with cultural institutions working with theaters, cinemas and music venues to also let low-income groups have the opportunity to enjoy culture. Today, religious institutions often have some sort of monopoly concerning activities for poor and marginalized groups. These activities, all with good intentions, play a part in enhancing the barriers between the marginalized part of the population and the rest of society. The poor must be included in ordinary cultural life, across their various cultural backgrounds, religions and ethnicities.

Contact, relations and friendship between the majority and minorities will make a difference. Today, these relations are often difficult to establish. Arezo told me that she took the initiative to invite her neighbors, but did not feel this was reciprocated and, therefore, became convinced that Norwegians are racist and do not want to have contact with immigrants. For many immigrants it is important to understand that in Norwegian society social relations are, for the most part, not established in the neighborhood, but in the school, workplace and various organizations. In Norway, we primarily need to integrate the minority population in the neutral meeting places that exist.

We must therefore not give up the most important thing of all: to integrate minority women in the most important meeting place in Norwegian society, i.e., the workplace.

This is how society as a whole can start to do something concrete, on the road to a more successful integration that means equality and recognition.

What concrete tasks can we then start ourselves, we who belong to the minority population? It is paramount that we who are minority women realize that receiving social security is a prison without opportunities. It is an opportunity when no other opportunities exist. We must fight to avoid being caught in an everyday life where everything revolves around finding documentation for our own illness and inability to work. If we are able to work at all, we must use our energy to document the expertise we actually have. We must focus on increasing our knowledge and competence.

Knowledge and competence build the core in our modern lives. Minorities, both women and men, must therefore seek knowledge, about the Norwegian language and Norwegian society. The Norwegian language is the gateway to full participation in society. It is difficult to learn a new language when you are an adult, but we must still do all we can and find new arenas to increase our proficiency of the language. If you don't know the language, you won't be able to act. In addition, we must learn how a social democratic society actually works. How do the various institutions function? What are our rights? But also, what are our obligations? Here, we must be willing to learn, and the learning program offered must be as good as possible. This will serve both the minority and majority in the long term.

One last suggestion concerns the school, which initially is a good, neutral sphere for meetings between the various strata of society. As parents, adults can meet with a common interest: a good future for their children. It is a place where the invisible wall of multiculturalism can be torn down. As minority women and men, we must realize the importance of being engaged parents. Go to parent-teacher meetings. If you have a life that makes this difficult, explain to the teacher why you cannot attend. Use your child's link to the school to improve your proficiency of the Norwegian language and to understand one of the most important institutions in Norway. Participate as much as possible. Only then will you have authority as a parent. Teachers must avoid the tendency to consider children as just "immigrant children" and place them in the category of "the other". If we together manage to see these children and bolster their confidence, knowledge and network, we lay the foundation for a generation of great citizens. These children carry with them a transnational knowledge from home that, in the future, can make them into the greatest ambassadors for a global nation of peace such as Norway.

These are the most concrete suggestions, which we all, minorities and the majority can start with. And some of these suggestions can make a difference for the women we have met in this book. But in addition, we must all shift our focus from the religious, cultural and ethnic to socioeconomic measures and universal recognition.

In today's Norwegian society there is a continually greater focus on representatives from the minority population who have done well, who have received an education and have good jobs, and to see them as representatives of "successful" integration. This is an important perspective.

The women we have met in this book are representatives of those who still have such difficult lives that the road to change and a better life remains long and hard. I still think that it has been important to shed light on just their specific situation, and to identify both the structural and the individual changes that are needed so that many more can have a better life in Norway. If we manage to change the structural aspects, the attitudes about "us" and "them" based on cultural, religious and ethnic differences that hide socioeconomic differences and challenges, then we should be able to really open up many opportunities for individual processes of change.

But then, we must also look at our fundamental equality: we are all human beings! A global conscience is a feeling of certainty that humanity is linked together like a body, and this must be the basis for our struggle for social change that can improve the situation of minorities in Norway and the world today. The global conscience enables to recognize the need of the minorities for love, justice and solidarity.

The state, scientists, organizations and individuals must all work together as a team in order to develop this philosophy of recognition in practice. Only then will we have the opportunity to create the world's most inclusive society, just as Prime Minister Jens Stoltenberg intends.

11. Let us rise up for peace and happiness

I'm a follower of James Larkin, who once said: "The great appear great because we are on our knees. Let us rise!"[1]

In this concluding chapter, I will focus on two things. First, I argue that we are in the middle of a Third World War where war has become a driving force that enslaves both those who suffer and those who profit from it. In this case, the globalization of pain and suffering has become part of the war's driving force. Secondly, I argue that those in power do not realize the structural dimension of this world war. Many developed countries profit from the arms industry, but this is all too often overlooked by the media. Influential writers and journalists focus primarily on the details of lives of vulnerable individuals. Journalists establish a disorienting darkness in society that makes us scared and confused. Not everyone who participates and benefits from it, understands the mechanisms of war. This creates a situation where individuals appear as voluntary participants in warfare without basing their choices on underlying factors such as social, political, and military situations. Individuals do not make choices in a vacuum, but based on their environment, the context in which they find themselves, and the substantial freedom[2] each individual has to make their choices.

The first edition of this book was published in 2008. Now, in 2024, the global community has undergone major and comprehensive changes. The global community is marked by a globalization entailing war, suffering and pain to a greater extent than before. We have read about Belquis and how her prayer for Osama bin Laden worked as a passive coping mechanism in connection with her painful encounter with Norwegian society. We have also seen how such strategies prevent individuals from seeing the real cause of their pain. The same strategies also prevent individuals from working to overcome the pain, and instead lead them to acceptance and resignation.

Why do passive coping mechanisms lead to pain? This is because they reproduce suffering and lead to powerlessness in the face of our fate. Religious propaganda leads immigrants like Belquis to view themselves as abnormal. Belquis lost her job and contacted the Jacob Center since she thought it was a mosque. This Christian organization is in contact with several different Muslim groups, and they gave her a brochure explaining how she should cope with losing her job. According to the brochure she was given, praying more often would be of great help. She ended up praying all evening for bin Laden to come to Norway and to do justice by taking up the fight against Bush and Sharon. Belquis interpreted her losing her job as a result of being Muslim. She told me that it looked like the eyes of her boss were glowing with the hatred that exists in people like Sharon and Bush. By reducing Belquis to religion, by encouraging her to pray instead of taking up the fight against the injustice of Norwegian society, she was eventually excluded from the Norwegian community. No one had told her about the rights and protection she is entitled to as an employee in Norway and instead she was manipulated by a religious organization.

Multiculturalism is a governing strategy for states to control immigrants and refugees in many of the world's countries. This feeling of social exclusion makes people like Belquis feel like building a wall between themselves and their peers. This type of differentiation leads to hatred and depression. It is necessary for individuals to feel that they belong, and for Muslims, mosques create this sense of belonging. In a society where they experience exclusion and stigma, the mosque is the only place where they feel at home and accepted. The mosque even gives Afghan Marxists, who do not believe in God, this sense of belonging. Religion establishes a sense of kinship for individuals who need it and has become an influential part of civil society in large parts of the world.

In Norway, Christian Social Democrats have played a defining role in the formulation of Norwegian laws, rules and values. In the 80 years that the Afghans fought against colonialism, they did the same with Islam. People gather in mosques to take up the fight against injustice and colonialism. Totalitarian regimes that profit from war have abused this sense of kinship that the mosques facilitate. Through multiculturalism, totalitarian regimes play an active role in warfare, by manipulating and radicalizing religious societies. Culture, religion, ethnicity and nationalism are used as free advertising for the arms industry, and for justification of war; an advertisement that is hidden and hidden in our daily lives. It is necessary now, to create a neutral meeting place, where the majority and the minority can build trust in each other. We humans are connected to each other similar to how body parts are connected to each other. The problem, however, is that this body is divided and fragmented into several pieces.

A process of radicalization and exclusion?

When you feel that you do not belong, it becomes easy to raise walls around yourself. Mary Douglas gives an example of how many immigrants feel: Hair on the head is natural, but hair on a dinner plate is disgusting. Some populists in the majority associate immigrants with the hair on their dinner plate. This comparison offends many immigrants, and this can lead to hatred. This establishment of hatred does not only come from political parties, but it is also even more dangerous when individuals think that they do not fit into society and thus look for other solutions. When such situations arise, things are going wrong. Mini nationalism is growing in many immigrant societies as a reaction to Norwegian nationalism. This rise of mini nationalism is not an event that has created itself, but instead was accelerated by multicultural politics. The more hatred that arises, the more powerless you feel. Multiculturalism is the spark that makes it burn.

"We are Muslims, and they hate us," says Belquis. She hates the majority in society, the majority who defines her and other Muslims as "the others". This majority has, according to her, caused her to lose her job, and this feels like an attack, as she says. This lack of belonging has its roots in the useless politics of multiculturalism, and it acts as a catalyst for the increasing fragmentation of society.

Earlier in the book, I mentioned the sociologist Benedetto Vecchi[3] who argues that fundamentalists have an appealing and mobilizing power. According to Vecchi, the various religious fundamentalist directions are nothing more than the transfer of identity to the political arena of cynical magician apprentices. If you want to understand this process, you need to reconstruct this transfer mentioned above: from defining the transfer as an individual dimension, to defining it as a social convention. The lack of identity that many Muslims feel is being abused and turned into a political strategy initiated by cynical political parties.

Maja Touzari Greenwood is a researcher at the Danish Institute for International Studies in Denmark (DIIS). Greenwood has conducted extensive research on foreign fighters such as al-Qaeda, al-Nusra and ISIS. In her article "*Islamic State and al-Qaeda's foreign fighters*", she explains in thorough detail how the recruitment process of foreign fighters takes place, their journey, and how they receive support[4]. After the foreign fighters are recruited, or after they have volunteered, they are picked up by, and become part of, an extensive network created for mutual support. They travel to Turkey, and then cross the border into Syria. The foreign fighters are paid compensation for what they have left behind; a compensation for the hassle of leaving the comfort of their old life. The monthly payment of $200 is higher than the $120 that local IS fighters receive. The foreign warriors are housed in villas and luxurious mansions in the richest parts of the cities they are in, up on hilltops, so that they can look down on the locals in the city. Mohamed-Saif Al-Mofty, a writer from Mosul who now lives in Norway, explains what happens when the foreign fighters first arrive in Syria. They are, as told by Greenwood, housed in large luxurious villas. In those villas they are shown propaganda videos that tell the story of how the Prophet has fought for 1400 years, and that now it is their time to fight for the Caliphate. These are incredibly strong videos, which appeal to the passion and empathy of those who watch, according to Al-Mofty. The foreign fighters are then transported to military training camps and taught that violence is necessary and justified as long as the violence is used to protect the Caliphate. In summary, the propaganda videos hit the foreign warriors right in the heart, and they are affected by the message to such an extent that they consider violence, the use of weapons, and war as a necessity.

When I interviewed Afshin Ismaeli, a journalist at the Norwegian newspaper *Aftenposten*, it appeared that it is not only people with religious motives who choose to travel to Syria to fight for the Caliphate. The prisons in Mosul are full of criminals who have left their country to fight for the Caliphate, especially individuals from Western countries. These are opportunistic individuals who want to take advantage of polygamy and sex slaves. A German prostitute converted to Islam on a superficial basis to have the opportunity to engage in sex work in Syria because working conditions and pay were better there than in Germany. Furthermore, more and more young people with dark and violent fantasies are fleeing to Syria for the opportunity to perform horrific and brutal acts that are usually reserved for film and video games. This war is a dirty war, a war that is seen by many simply as pure business and not as a search for justice motivated by religious idealism.

Breivik's manifesto and critique of multiculturalism

On 22 July 2011, Norway witnessed in shock how Anders Behring Breivik attacked the executive government quarter (Regjeringskvartalet) and politically engaged youth on Utøya island with cruelty. This created pain, fear and insecurity among minorities. The pain dimension was high for all, including the majority and minorities. After his motives became clearer, even I felt a shame and pain over being a critic of multiculturalism. The fear of being his ally made me curious. I watched the trial at the courthouse and read what I could find about his attitude towards multiculturalism. Later, I sometimes heard from Norwegians that they do not support his actions or violence as an option in general, but that they understand and support some of his ideas. No matter how little it is, there is some acceptance of his ideas in Norwegian society. The emergence of right-wing radical websites such as *Document* and *Resett* can also be seen as a sign for this.

Analyzing Breivik's manifesto is an outrageous and discouraging reading task. It is commonly known that large parts are not his own writing, but directly copied from the texts of other right-wing extremists (see Breivik, 2011). His idea of *Eurabia*, a Europe invaded by Muslims who have eradicated European cultural heritage and way of life, is well known. Probably it is this perception of immigration as a threat, and what some Norwegians perceive as unreasonable cultural tolerance, which generally legitimates the above. What has been discussed more seldomly from his manifesto in comparison to racism, Muslim hatred, white supremacy and right-wing extremism, is misogyny[5]. As he and his followers see it, equality is to blame for the fact that Europe's men have become feminized and weak. European men therefore have a poorer starting point in the supposedly inevitable, recent and decisive war between Muslims and Christians. A pervasive envy of Islamist and jihadist movements and groups can be traced in the manifesto; in particular, Breivik has a noticeable and unwilling admiration for Osama bin Laden and al-Qaeda. The way they recruited and oppressed through violence, to create a global movement in the service of the 'last struggle', marks the strategy he himself wishes to induce as a European movement. He believes that Muslim men have taken care of their masculinity in a different way than Norwegian men through dominance over women and through unconditional support among each other. Some of these ideas seem to build on experiences from his own youth, when he chose to hang out with boys of the same age with an immigrant background because he felt safer with them. Other scholars have pointed out the ideology between his right-wing extremism and radical jihadism[6]. They identified the totalitarian mentality together with the production of enemy images and doomsday prophecies, as the overarching common denominator.

Without success, I have trawled the manifesto for a definition of multiculturalism, hoping to understand what his critique is aimed at. A check in Adobe Reader shows that the word 'multicultural', 'multiculturalist', 'multiculturalists', 'multiculturalism' and 'multiculturalisms' appear 1164 times within the 1515 pages. Ultimately, it is obvious that he fosters a deep hatred for all forms of *equality*. The manifesto affirms people with an attitude to and understanding of the world similar to a self-righteous form of social Darwinism, meaning the rights of the 'strongest' prevail. Whites should dominate blacks. Men should dominate women. Europeans must dominate the world. Men and women who stand for universal human rights and equality for all, regardless of gender, skin color, origin, orientation, disability or anything else, are traitors and enemies. Institutions that encourage and foster international cooperation, such as the UN and the EU, deserve nothing but despise. Traitors and enemies are divided into types and degrees.

I finally realized that we are very far apart, despite the common criticism of multiculturalism. Where he wants to institutionalize violence against women and children[7], I am fighting with all my might to counteract exactly that. Where he wants one group to dominate others, I want to defend the rights and freedoms of the individual over group rights. This type of totalitarian mindset has little to do with constructive criticism of various forms of multiculturalism.

Polarization of religion

Anne Hege Grung's lecture during a seminar was important to me because it points to the unofficial consequences of multiculturalism in Norway, which in this case is more hate. In recent years, the attitudes of the majority have also become more hateful towards Muslims and Islam. Grung says that after ten years of polarization, she recommends replacing polarizing categories such as "us and them" with a common category: "we". This is a job for religious groups, individuals and states. This point is interesting because she illuminates polarizing categories that are the basis for multiculturalist thinking.

Multiculturalism inflicts pain because it promotes polarization and creates distinctions between us and them. Cathrine Thorleifsson also notices that there is increased polarization, right-wing extremism, fear and hatred in society. She also refrains from talking about multiculturalism directly but points out an important element in polarization. She emphasizes how there is an experience of existential insecurity among those drawn to populism (including the case of Philip Manshaus who killed his stepsister and attacked a mosque). The solution for many becomes the prospect to restore "purity" in society and being able to use violence against opponents. In connection with Anders Behring Breivik and his actions, most people distance themselves from his terrorist acts, but many actually agree with the basic ideas that led to the violence. She points out that right-wing extremists who commit terrorist acts may appear as single actors while in reality they have a community, sharing their perceptions and ideas - communities that often meet on "dark" parts of the internet and create subcultures.

NAV and the abolition of radicalization

The government has produced a new action plan against radicalization and violent extremism through which the municipalities and the Norwegian Labor and Welfare Administration (NAV) will contribute to prevention by following up those who are unemployed. It is known that many right-wing extremists today are adults outside the labor market, which can increase the vulnerability to radicalization[8]. In the radio program *EK* on 17th June 2020 on the same topic, Prime Minister Erna Solberg expressed that she understands the need to have a group identity. It is important to recognize this need among people, but what is painful for minorities is the lack of belonging to Norwegian society. It is even more painful to be pushed to embrace a particular group identity. Seeking a group identity that stands in stark contrast to the values of the larger society is often the last resort when no other integration possibility seems available. Seeking such an identity means that the individual actively constructs a false reality instead of fighting to establish a broader identity and a "we-feeling" with the rest of society.

However, what we see is that people in crisis, or those who fall outside the community, often seek comfort in religious or extreme groups. We have also seen an example of this in Philip Manshaus who carried out a terrorist attack aimed at a mosque in Bærum. It is told that he immersed himself in Christianity and the Bible before the attack took place. Extremism researcher Cathrine Thorleifsson suggests that affiliation with Christianity among right-wing extremists is not necessarily related to faith, but that it is more about identity[9]. Extremists, both within Islam and Christianity, embrace religious symbols and identities to further a specific purpose. Attaching oneself to religious symbols and identities is in itself a way of defining oneself in contrast to others. This creates polarization and justifies hatred and violence against those who do not belong to the same identity. Faith and identity in a globalized world are therefore two sides of the same coin. I agree with Thorleifsson's reasoning, but further question who is misusing religion for their purpose - the individual or the organization? It is also important to clarify that all religions can be misused for political purposes, and we must focus on the institutions and their role within radicalization processes.

n Norway, many religious powers exist which are receiving support for working with social issues. The same year *Silent Screams* was published for the first time (in 2008), the Minister of Labor and Social Inclusion at that time Bjarne Håkon Hanssen provided financial support to the

Catholic Church for the integration of Polish immigrants in Norwegian society[10]. Is the integration of immigrants through religious institutions a good way to go, or does it contribute to further estrange them from the community?

It is positive that NAV is included in the work against radicalization and violent extremism. However, my personal experience has made it clear to me that the administration may indirectly contribute to the problem. I have been to a NAV office myself. They handed out business cards from the Jacob Center, inviting people in need to come to their institution. I have discovered that the center's way of working is characterized by a multiculturalist way of thinking, for example through close cooperation with Muslim and Christian organizations that are not neutral in their way of working with people. They take advantage of people's vulnerabilities and cover their false needs. NAV indirectly contributes by supporting the agenda of such institutions, through allowing people in need to find comfort in constructed group rights within these institutions. I want the country's politicians to understand how religious organizations create an unnatural need for group rights which in the long run can provoke conflict between groups.

I ask the government to see the continuity of world history. Radicalization in society does not come from distant planets, but from our own society and through cooperation with religious and non-religious organizations. The insecurity that people in our society feel is often concealed. I am concerned with the silent, unspoken attitudes that create pain within individuals - pain we often do not want to talk about loudly. The different religious movements create a bubble around themselves and establish a definite separation between "themselves" and "the others". This contributes to hatred, and when the concealed hatred is expressed physically, this feeling of hate becomes even more stimulated.

In the coming years, I would like to see more research on the stimulation of hate and a focus on organizations that generate hate. Research could review hate especially in light of the examples we have of right-wing extremist terror and people who travel from Norway to war zones to participate in terrorist organizations, sometimes together with their children. For me as a researcher on pain, this is the highest degree of the pain dimension. Those who create this pain and hatred, who radicalize people and who send people into war should be brought to justice.

The individual and systematic perspective on radicalization

Public debate, reports and books on radicalization and extremism tend to focus on the individual characteristics of those who become radicalized. By doing this, one loses sight of the systematic perspective in which the religious organizations and institutions radicalizing vulnerable people are in focus. For me, it is very important to emphasis the concealed pain dimension which exists in this debate. Radicalization is not just about individuals, but the people around, the dynamics of society and our experience of peace. Åsne Seierstad's *Two Sisters*, which deals with two young women who went to Syria to join IS, is an impressive example of a book that inspires debate in this thematic. Sven Egil Omdal from the Norwegian newspapers *Bergens Tidene* and *Stavanger Aftenblad* wrote a note on the back of *Two Sisters*: "About the young people who voluntarily choose hatred and darkness. Maybe if they had made a different choice, they would have become a part of us"[11]. This is an important question, and I believe in the compassion that underlies this statement. But is it fair to say that the two sisters voluntarily chose hatred and darkness? According to my research in the field, hatred and darkness are not chosen by the heart, but instead forced by the setting and the factors around us.

This is something Nussbaum calls *substantial freedom*; when the circumstances around a person provide opportunities to develop competence and ability to act. Åsne Seierstad writes in detail about how the two girls were socialized through different religious organizations that created room for action for them. After reading the book *Salafism in Norway*[12], I can see that the substantial freedom to become a foreign warrior or terrorist existed around the girls. The two girls are first and foremost a product of circumstances in Norwegian society and not of the cultural baggage they carried with themselves. Religious organizations manipulating and brainwashing individuals such as the two sisters, through conversations about the Caliphate and Islam, are operating here in Norway and are organizing trips to Syria. This is something that can happen anywhere in the world. The people who brainwashed the two girls and organized the trip for them are still free today. This is why I ask journalists and researchers to reconsider. I would like to see all of us adopting a broader perspective focusing on the system, on the organizations and institutions, on the arms industry and the creators of war, and finally those who benefit from sending people into war.

The question Sven Egil asks whether the girls would have chosen differently if they had been one of us, is very important. What determines how they become 'one of us'? This is the sense of belonging, the feeling of being part of a larger group. Pain and suffering begin with a lack of recognition which further leads to isolation and discrimination. The result is a situation where an individual may experience not belonging to Norwegian society. Institutions such as religious organizations, mosques, schools, and the media are treating people differently, despite the fact that many often-called *immigrants* were born in Norway. Teachers ask, "Where are you from?" and "How is it in Somalia?". These are questions that play a major role in the fragmentation of society by constructing a distinction between "us" and "them". Immigrants experience this gap every day. The mosque tells them that they are real Somalians. They preserve your national and religious values. In itself, there is nothing wrong with this, but it reconfirms the distinction and construction "us" and "them", a difference that the immigrants' children are being confronted with at school. Questions of origin tell you that you do not belong, but that you are welcome to preserve your own culture and religion, something that fosters parallel societies. The fostering of such parallel societies leads to experiences of threat and fear by both the majority and the minority, because the people are limiting themselves to their respective cultural "bubbles" without having contact with those outside of it. The lack of affiliation creates a constant form of pain which doctors cannot prescribe any medication for.

It seems clear to me that the two girls in *Two Sisters* suffered from a lack of belonging in Norwegian society, and a lack of protection of women's rights, even though they were Norwegian women. When your family comes from war-torn countries, such as Afghanistan, Somalia, Palestine, Iraq or Syria, you will always compare the country you live in with the country your parents grew up in. The two sisters compared the countries and began to critically question the injustice that exists in the world.

Two young girls did not have the same passive coping strategy that Belquis chose to process her pain. She read the Qur'an, was patient and waited for God to change the world, as she was recommended by the Jacob Center. The new generation of young people, and the two sisters, have another strategy for processing their pain - active action. Young people are active in the fight for justice, and it is through this form of action that they become vulnerable to the influence of those who use religion to enslave them to participate in acts of violence. Young people are looking for solutions in globalization processes which change the world at a pace making it impossible to stop. Religious organizations are changing so frequently and rapidly that neither the state nor our brains have the opportunity to keep up. When society creates and finances institutions based on religion, ethnicity and culture, it constructs a need which does not necessarily reflect the essential needs of each individual, regardless of culture, religion and ethnicity. This is multiculturalism in practice. In Norway, it functions as unofficial multiculturalism.

The vehicle of globalization runs on two wheels. The first wheel is the well-known concept of homogenization which refers to an inclusivity with those who can afford economic materiality and mobility. The second wheel, which is less well known, is particularization. Particularization includes the "losers" of globalization, individuals such as the two girls in *Two Sisters*. In many countries, particularization deals with the intensification of distinctive characteristics such as locality, own culture, religion, ethnicity, and a declining sense of belonging in combination with increasing racism. In the process of particularization, multiculturalism, with its focus on religion, culture and ethnicity, gains more incentive and acts as a catalyst for conflict in any society. Multicultural institutions strengthen this particularization process which pushes individuals towards exclusivity. Particularization is free advertising for warlords and the arms industry: the war profiteers. However, this field lacks research. My claims are based on my own experience and my research linked to Afghanistan. I have seen the development of political Islam driven by these processes, which were funded by the United States in the 1980s. This was the origin of terrorist organizations and terrorists like bin Laden.

What is not studied thoroughly are the circumstances, institutions and social structures that surround individuals who become radicalized. Why don't journalists, politicians and researchers ask more structured questions about the system that has been built around people like the two sisters? Why does IS exist at all, and how do they operate in Norway? Today's journalism, research and authorship are neither attending to the manipulation and brainwashing that is taking place, nor to the experienced lack of belonging to the Norwegian society. Journalists such as Seierstad and Omdal prefer to go deeper into the world of the individual. They cannot see the forest for the trees. Vulnerable individuals are tricked into becoming part of cynical systems. The people who manipulate and brainwash are never studied thoroughly and made responsible. Thereby the problem is that it is more entertaining and reader-friendly to follow stories about vulnerable individuals and their choices. While politicians and legislators are debating whether the two sisters should be imprisoned, the man who is probably responsible for their radicalization walks free in Norway.

Most politicians and journalists do not see unofficial multiculturalism as a leading political strategy for immigrants - a strategy that limits the individual to the categories of culture, religion and ethnicity. Defining the individual based on these categories causes them to lose their own individual identity while being affected by pain. The result may be sacrificing oneself on behalf of a group, as the two sisters did. Consequently, they were manipulated to adopt a particular group identity, to live and to breathe for it, as well as to suffer for it.

Why are so few journalists talking about this strategy? It is strategic to create the distinction between "us" and "them". Should we talk about the individuals or the system? In my eyes, we should talk about both. The most important thing, however, is that we are talking about the system, the laws and the rules, as they provide guidelines for individuals' actions and create or diminish room for action. If journalists had asked more critical questions and shed light on the people and institutions behind the radicalization, it would have been easier to identify the consequences such processes have for people's lives, and thus prevent similar incidents in the future.

The secret dimensions of war and pain

Linge and Bangstad provide a detailed description of how various Salafist organizations have been institutionalized in Norway and globally. The type of Islam that these organizations stand for is very different from ordinary Muslims' perception of Islam. They point out how theology, politics and identity interact in the rise of global Salafism, and how this has evolved into a modern movement that differs greatly from previous generations. They suggest Saudi Arabia to be the center for this movement and its affiliated organizations. Hegghammer[13] gives a good description of the so-called 'Peshawar kitchen'. Here different interpretations of Islamist mindsets met, they shaped each other and led to a new doctrine of *jihad*. Azzam assisted in reforming Islamism by putting forward a new military strategy and setting martyrdom at the center of Islam. By shifting the focus from fighting inwardly for the 'correct' interpretation of Islam, the new military strategy shifted the gaze outwards towards an external enemy. At the same time, Azzam put the armed jihad at the center of Islam. *Tawhid* is the doctrine that there is only one God, and Azzam actively used this to make jihad the individual duty of every orthodox Muslim. Martyrdom was portrayed as the 'ultimate stage' of jihad, and together this laid the foundation for global jihadism. Azzam was basically a war preacher, a charismatic ideologue. Another one who was also part of the Peshawar kitchen in the early 80's was bin Laden. The two began collaborating on an organization that would help Afghans in the fight against Soviet occupation, called the *Service Agency*. Among other things, the recruitment of volunteer fighters led to seven thousand Arabs traveling to Afghanistan. The cooperation between them fell apart at the end of the Soviet occupation because they pursued different strategies of jihad. Bin Laden started al-Qaida in 1988 as an alternative to the Service Agency.

During the Soviet occupation of Afghanistan, due to poverty, unemployment, and hardship, many were wandering between different religious schools in Saudi Arabia and Qatar, which were funded by Western countries. These served, among other things, as boarding houses. There they became soldiers, brainwashed and armed. What today is called the Taliban is in fact a product of these religious schools. The wars in Bosnia, Chechnya, Jordan and Syria all have in common that these people can be traced back there. They have learned that it is their duty to fight for Allah, and they live of wars. They legitimize their war activities, and they are convinced of following a violent path to please their god, and that they lack alternative paths to a 'normal' life. The Taliban offer higher wages than the state and other regular jobs, and they do not get any other incentives to change course. This is very dangerous. Acts of war transfer the identity from the individual to a larger, public and political arena. These are mechanisms that war profiteers actively use to recruit and appeal to the individual. War becomes part of the social and political identity of entire groups of people.

Those of us who want to try to understand the problematic aspects of society have to look at the relationship between institutions and interest associations for war and the arms industry. You only need to go for a walk at Raufoss ammunition factory to see how many arms are produced in the small country Norway, and where these are going to be used. War is fragmented and complex. It is a battle between different interests and powers, leading to enormous suffering and pain in the world. The stories told about war are tainted by the background of the narrator; whether the person in question has experienced war on their body, or whether the person has a self-interest and gain from war. It is extremely important that we point out all the different facets of war and be critical of the link between war activity and the various organizations that legitimize hatred in the form of religious beliefs, and that promote participation in war as a religious duty.

In December 2019, the *Washington Post* published 2,000 documents, called the *Afghanistan Papers*, providing insight into the thoughts of US authorities, Western allies and high-ranking participants in the war. After three years of fighting in court, these secret documents finally became public knowledge, and shed light on a number of publicly unknown aspects of the war until then. My whole adult life has been marked by fights against war activity. I also encourage journalists, researchers and everyone with an interest in questioning the problematic aspects of society, to go deeper and ask more critical questions. It is our duty to speak out against war and the arms industry, which is in need of continuing war activity, as well as all organizations that are collaborators in war. I further encourage journalists, researchers and authors to write in detail about the link between the arms industry and the losers of globalization. I ask them to use their qualities and skills to see the link between those who have an interest and gain in war and the arms industry and the conflicts we observe in the world today. I am concerned with this because war culture and dynamics are sources of pain and suffering and need further research.

Stories of radicalization that focus only on the individual hide the dynamics of war and the power structures that lead to the continuation of the war. The war industry is enormous, and several countries are active participants in the form of producing war materiel and maintaining war cultures among other things. Ignoring the profitability of war and its central role in the economies of many countries and communities distorts our understanding of war causes and the fighters who participate in it.

For many Norwegians, the fate of the two sisters, and hundreds of adults and their children participating in the war in Syria, is not a big problem. It is a book that lies on the bedside table and is read before going to sleep. The problem is far, far away and not part of their own lives. But I, who experienced the war up close, and who spent large parts of my adult life in prison and in war zones, am living proof that this is not a game, but extremely serious.

The loss of people's lives, as well as the suffering and insecurity that afflict the people of Afghanistan, Palestine, Syria, Iraq and many other places, are caused by war. We have to talk about this. Groupings in religion, nationality, national borders and ethnicity conceal the problems and blind us to the fact that what is happening there is about us and our mistakes – among them, our hidden interests in war and desires to sell war commodities. It is dangerous when journalists and researchers only talk about parts of the truth, but not the full truth. This is leading us down a dead end without understanding reality. If I had not been born in Afghanistan and not seen and felt the war on my own body, I might have been among the journalists and scientists who only scratch the surface. I would have been involved in the creation of a constructed story separate from reality. Sharing a fragmented understanding of a complex reality proves to be more harmful than useful. Individualization of war is an example of a fragmented construction of reality. In comparison, the non-constructed reality can be linked to the war interests of powerful states and global **actors.**

Future research and lack of global understanding

It is our duty as researchers to fight against fragmented knowledge. While I was working on my book From War to Peace Our Global Responsibility, a seminar was arranged in connection with the celebration of the ten-year anniversary of the completed research program *Cultural complexity in the new Norway (Culcom).* During this research project, an interdisciplinary research collaboration could be seen for the first time. Elisabeth Eide, who has worked in Afghanistan for many years, chaired one of the panel discussions where various topics were discussed, including how refugees are creating instability in Europe. In Despite the fact that the researchers and speakers who participated in the seminar discussed cultural complexity, nobody mentioned multiculturalism specifically. Nevertheless, several pointed out some important elements related to this. However, Elisabeth Eide forwards an important issue by highlighting the lack of transnational understanding. My understanding is that refugee instability is intricately tied to powerful states producing and trading arms, fueling wars. Extremist organizations didn't emerge from distant planets such as march or jupiter but implemented in Pakistan through Western financially and military support, for Afghanistan against Russia.

I recommend individuals and institutions who worked in warzones like Afghanistan, whether from the East or West, to write down their memoirs. Understanding the development of institutional extremism during the Soviet occupation is crucial. Lived experiences are wellsprings of knowledge, shaping many into renowned experts on Afghanistan, holding influential positions in various global universities. Extremist organizations also operates in Western countries, utilizing religion as an identity marker to interpreting own way of Islam.

In this way, they justify war activities, intimidation, killing, and the isolation of democratic forces under the guise of God (religion).

Most muslim minorities cannot critizise God, and the most majorities remain silent, exercising self-censorship in the fear of not being labeled as racists. my research question is: *where is the freedom of speech in the western country?*

In my research, multiculturalism functions as a leading strategy, serving as a powerful catalyst in the ongoing complex dynamics of today's pain, suffering and war. In research, it is very important to include the relationship between the local, national and global levels in the analysis. This should be a major focus for the next ten years, spanning from 2020 to 2030.

Professor Thomas Hylland Eriksen said that 'part of the job for us researchers are to highlight what we do not otherwise see and use magnifying glasses where we need them.

Are we in the Third World War?

Professor Steven Colatrella, who works at the University of Maryland Global Campus, wrote in 2015 that the Third World War will occur soon. A world war that will be even more catastrophic than the previous two. In my eyes, however, the Third World War has already begun. There are several conflicts and wars around the world that bear a few similarities with the previous world wars. The conflicts taking place now resemble pre-modern warfare. They are not directly linked to states, but are heavily influenced by the arms industry through warlords, terrorists, militias, and assassins, with the goal of conquering territories to exploit resources and labor.

In his book *The Dirty War on Syria*[14], Tim Anderson, a professor of political economy, removes all myths about Western countries and powerful states as self-righteous interventionists in other countries' internal affairs. The United States in particular has a history of provoking war through pretexts to invade, destabilize, and colonize countries. According to Iraqi authorities, the United States has exported weapons to IS in Syria and Afghanistan; they arm Islamists, and when civilians are attacked, they blame it on Assad's government. The war between the Syrian opposition, backed by the United States, Qatar and

Saudi Arabia, and the Syrian Arab Republic, backed by Russia and Iran, is a prime example of a new type of conflict. This is a war created by superpowers, which ends up destroying Syria. In the Western world, authors are writing books about this reality, such as *The Danish Civil War 2018-2024*[15], written by Kaspar Colling Nielsen. In a book, you have the opportunity to comment on and criticize terrorism and war crime without major consequences. In 2014, Pope Francis addressed the problem of today's wars during a celebration for veterans who lost their lives in the First World War: "Even today, after the catastrophe that was the Second World War, there is talk of a third war. A war fought on different levels and in different parts, with crime, massacres, and destruction."[16]

Belquis lives in Norway, but her pain is not locked to a geographical area, it is globalized and found in several of the world's areas. When she compares her boss with people like Sharon and Bush[17], she links her pain to the pain of thousands of other people. People in Afghanistan, Syria, Iraq, Palestine, Yemen, Nigeria, Niger, Chad, South Sudan, Libya, Congo, Kenya, Myanmar, Colombia, Venezuela, Israel, Pakistan, India, Turkey, Ukraine, Burundi, Philippines, Ethiopia, Mozambique, Peru, and all other war-torn places, are sharing the same pain[18]. This pain is not only found in war zones but can be found all over the world. Through such networks of people and the hegemonies of superpowers, the Third World War is formed. The engine of the war machine is activated.

The difference between the Second and Third World War

The dichotomy "us" and "them" has led again to war, just like it did during the two previous world wars. Nationalism, an essential issue in war, is also present. However, the war we are experiencing now is drastically different from the Second World War. Nationalism is repeatedly increasing but is now driven by a form of particularism resulting from the extensive globalization in today's society. A nation is now understood as a unit based on religion and ethnicity.

Within their nations, people have moved deeper and deeper into their respective domains of ethnicity, belonging and culture. Such domains are getting stronger every day due to the particularism that stems from current globalization. Multinational corporations and far-right populists are on the rise and are becoming increasingly popular in Europe. There is an invisible connection to the increasing power that Muslim extremists gained. Officially, according to the media, these two groups are in conflict with the fundamentalists, but they have covert links to each other. This is the battlefield of the Third World War. The battlefields of the two previous world wars have been easy to define, we know where the front was, and where the armies met. We know where Ypres and Leningrad are, but this is not the case for this war. The Third World War is a series of proxy wars. Multiculturalism as a misguiding political strategy has created a war-like dimension with clear mental fronts. The focus on culture, religion, and ethnicity pours fuel on the fire of this ongoing world war. These are the factors that create the backdrop for this new world war.

I see this world war everywhere. I see it within the pain of mothers who fear for their sons. I see it within the concrete blocks around the Parliament in Oslo. In World War I, soldiers wore uniforms, and their families had legal rights. The ongoing world war is not systematic; soldiers die unregistered, unregulated, and informally within a massive chaos. I see the war within the undocumented Afghan who is being manipulated and sent to the war in Syria by the Iranian military. He sent letters to his family with a copy of the contract he had signed with the Iranian authorities. When he died, the family asked for his pension to be paid, as well as to stay permanently in Iran. Shortly after the man's death, the family's application for residence was rejected. I also see the war within the family who think their son is working in Iraq, while he is actually in Syria and fighting against IS.

I see the world war within Solveig, the Norwegian. Her son Bjørn was sent to Afghanistan together with other Norwegian soldiers, where he works with IT. He was not given the pension that he was promised and therefore quit his job to work for an American company instead. Bjørn's story is an example of the transition from conventional to modern warfare. Now you can simply push a button and kill from a distance. I see the ongoing world war within traumatized computer engineers who press the buttons and feel like murderers without even having looked the enemy in the eye, and without having seen one drop of blood. I see the world war within the eyes of Torill and Samira[19] who lost their children in Syria.

Elements of the Third World War can be witnessed everywhere. The Third World War is taking place in Norway. At the same time, it is ongoing in Afghanistan and in France, when the French do not want to help a young girl who has gone to Iraq and faces execution. I see the war within a mother, who sent 50 Francs to her daughter in Syria to get her home to France and then was accused of supporting terrorism[20]. The Power Axis and the Allies were the participants in the Second World War, but in the Third World War it is not as easy as splitting the participants into fascists and anti-fascists. Participants are more difficult to define now. Who is fighting against whom? 21 terror organizations are currently in Afghanistan, despite NATO and their "peacekeeping forces". Who are they? There are no clear definitions.

I saw the third world war in the eyes of the immigrants that I interviewed in Maximilien Park in Brussels in August 2018 in connection with my fieldwork. People from all war-torn corners of the world are gathered in Maximilien Park to be trafficked further, following promises of a brighter future. Immigrants told me that they cannot work neither in EU countries, nor in Norway without official papers. The traffickers, on the other hand, guarantee the immigrants that they can work in England illegally and without documents. This promise makes many people choosing to wait until the opportunity to travel to England appears. When I went to interview the young refugees, they assumed that I was a trafficker and asked me how much they would have to pay me. Others were too dehydrated to talk. Every migrant will contact different criminal groups based on religion, culture, and ethnic background. I talked to a starved man who appeared to be highly educated. Traffickers take daily payments from migrants with promises to send them to England one day. The starved man said to me: "Do you know why England wants to leave the EU? It is because they want to be free from laws and regulations set by the EU, so that they and the United States can work together in the criminal and unofficial economy that we are in right now. But I, I choose to go to England regardless of this. " Well, does he have a choice? All this takes place openly and almost worry-free, due to a police force doing nothing against human traffickers.

Fortunately, there are some young and hopeful volunteers who have traveled from Australia and New Zealand to Maximilien Park to help, and to make migrants think of something other than the desperate situation they are in. Even in this dark undertone of society's reality, there are people and organizations who do what they can to make people believe and hope for a better everyday life.

I saw The Third World War within the eyes of a young man from Darfur. I see The Third World War within unemployed immigrants who are seeking work in Saudi Arabia and the Arab Gulf states and ending up being sent to the front in Yemen. I see The Third World War within the eyes of crying mothers. I interviewed a Taliban man who told me that the pain which led him to become part of the Taliban was his crying mother. He did not want to see Americans inflicting any more pain on the mothers of the village where he came from. He felt that he was forced to fight. Human traffickers and arms traders belong together like a hand and a glove. We have to talk about human trafficking and about war. When we talk about war, we need to talk about those who profit from war: the arms traders and the arms industry.

In his book *Fred er ei det best*[21] ("Peace is not the best") the brave author Dag Hoel writes "Society needs to take greater responsibility and control over the arms industry [...] The capital claims that we can just as well produce ammunition as food, and we are supported by the media's signal drums warning us of the coming enemies. As long as these conditions are maintained, the dance will continue around the cartridge box at Raufoss [arms factory]". Hoel's book has helped me to reflect on my own experiences in war and has made me see what I, as an individual, can do. In 2008, I interviewed a man who was responsible for Norway's arms exports at that time. At the end of the interview, I asked him to answer a personal question, but of course he declined. I told him that I see people being shot on TV, that I see bullets exiting the arms and penetrating my fellow human beings. I said that I see the blood flowing, and even from my position, watching through the TV, I get a repulsive and uncomfortable feeling, almost as if I feel their pain in my own body. Such scenes make me struggle to sleep at night. I asked what happens to him, based on his role and responsibility in selling arms and ammunition. I asked him how he reacts when he sees people being shot and killed, with the same bullets that he is responsible for selling. Finally, he chose to answer my question. With a calm and relaxed tone, almost with cold blood, he replied to me: "I have a legitimate job like everyone else, just like nurses, doctors, and teachers, and therefore I do not feel guilty. And I have to tell you, I do not have time to watch TV. After I finish work, I am taking my children to a violin course. "

Global conscience and activism

Despite the increasing globalization of pain, war, and suffering during the last ten years, we raised higher awareness for what is going on around us. In 2018, the Nobel Peace Prize was given to the Congolese doctor Denis Mukwege and to the human rights activist Nadia Murad. Their struggle with raising awareness about the use of sexual violence as a weapon of war is now world famous.

In 2018, Professor Nora Sveaas was awarded the University of Oslo's human rights prize for her work with refugees and people who have been subjected to torture and trauma. In her speech during the award ceremony, she said that we live in a time when human rights are under pressure, when international agreements are questioned, and when nations avoid publishing truthful reports of human rights violations within their own borders.

In recent months, a debate regarding Western foreign fighters for IS and their children sparked interest. Many children either left with their parents or were born on foreign soil. The question frequently debated is whether these children should be allowed to return to their home country, and what should happen with their mothers. Politicians from many countries have made strong and harsh comments regarding this issue. Among them is Denmark's Foreign Minister Anders Samuelsen, who has stated that he does not want any of them back in Denmark.

The Norwegian Prime Minister Erna Solberg first stated that the children should not be sent back to Norway but ended up changing her mind. Now the question in Norway is what will happen to the children after their mother's prosecution. Thomas Hegghammer, a researcher at the Norwegian Institute for Defense Research, claims that these repatriated citizens will cost around one million euros per person, since they will not be able to find a job[22]. Hegghammer further suggests that the security risk will be very high, because the terror networks will be extremely interested in contacting these repatriated citizens. I wish to ask Hegghammer, if he would be interested in examining the statistics that exist on how much money has been spent on brainwashing and arming these people, and how much the profiteers have earned from this war, so that we can have a more nuanced picture of The Third World War. These are citizens whom the state is obliged to take care of, citizens for whom the state is responsible, citizens whom the state must protect from being radicalized and thus of becoming potential terrorists. Why was nobody working so they would not leave Norway? Norway, as participant in the NATO agreement, sends soldiers to Afghanistan to fight terrorism, but takes no action against terrorists in their own country. A legitimate state with civil rights as part of a legal system has the ability and the duty to prevent this type of brainwashing and radicalization.

What are Hegghammer's calculations based on? The one million Euros that Hegghammer is talking about reflect the capitalist system which is influenced by multiculturalism. It is a system that creates opportunities, or as Nussbaum calls it 'substantial freedom' – also the opportunity and freedom to become a foreign warrior. All the tools needed to become a terrorist are already within the system. It begins with creating hatred between people. But who controls this hatred? Why is everyone traveling to Syria learning this? Who pays for the flights of the foreign fighters? How much money is spent on war preparations? How much money is spent on the various religious organizations? These are not isolated measures, but symptoms that are related through a faulty system, a system that we find in many Western and developed countries.

The hatred of foreign fighters and the ones traveling to Syria has been fuelled by superpowers. So why do journalists like Åsne Seierstad choose not to talk about this? Many journalists in Western countries choose to focus on stories such as the one about the two sisters from Bærum. The individual side of the case, the personal stories, the unimaginable life they have lived. These are stories that sell books and are lucrative. The war profiteers, arms industry.

The ones traveling to Syria from Europe, whom we choose to distance ourselves from, have been socialized by the superpowers. Media reporting these cases focusses rather on the individual, for example when they are Norwegians who go to Syria to fight for IS. They ask: "How can humans do this? Why are they evil?" This rhetoric is seen a lot in Western countries' journalism. The journalists' attempts to answer such questions are flawed, because they do not see the impacts that institutions have on the individual.

While journalists here in Norway choose to focus on the fates of individuals traveling into warzones, a video from *Deutsche Welle* News shows, a German media outlet, the 70-year-old Niaz Bibi all alone taking care of 40 children in Afghanistan. The children's parents were killed in a conflict between the IS and the Taliban. With a rifle over her shoulder, she walks everywhere with the children, and she looks after each of them[23]. This brave woman and the 40 orphaned children, whom she cares for have not ignited a spark in the media debates. Their parents were killed in the same conflict as the parents of our Western children. They are victims of the same system, but not all children are worth the same in the eyes of the media. 8,000 IS soldiers have been deployed in Afghanistan following their military defeat in Syria. No one knows who caused this defeat, but locals in Syria say it was the Americans. Again, an incident arises that needs to be investigated more deeply. And again, the Americas have a reason to stay in Afghanistan, where they claim the necessity to protect the local civil society. Åsne Seierstad has reported from many different wars, maybe now she could write a thick and comprehensive book about the systematic relations in this unsystematic war?

What can be done?

In the fight against the Third World War and the fight to create global peace, we must take action on three levels. First, each individual must fight against his or her own powerlessness, and we must as James Larkin suggest, "rise up." Secondly, we must fight for peace by supporting institutions that are against war. Today, most of civil society, human rights organizations, peace movements, and other organizations and institutions are split. They are limited to national and individual levels.

Many such organizations are influenced by the particularism of globalization. The result of particularism is that most individuals and organizations become preoccupied with their own specific interests and fight for their own narrow identity, religion, ethnicity, or a combination of all of these. When each institution or organization limits its vision to its own specific needs and goals, they remain blind when it comes to seeing injustice and discrimination at the global level. This type of organization only creates more conflict and suffering. Such specific and self-occupied organizations can easily be exploited by warlords and global powers which benefit from war.

Thirdly and lastly, there is a need for a global institution that I have given the name "global conscience", an institution that is universal for all nations, so that all nations hold including power as well as exclusive power. A global vision is necessary to fight for local communities and national justice, because it is our true reality. We need to create awareness around our real needs.

Therefore, this new institution will work with a new cognitive map, integrated with the pain and suffering of each nation, to fight for global peace, justice, and happiness. An institution for global conscience is a necessity. Regulatory, normative and cognitive aspects are ways to change a society, and global conscience needs to look at these three aspects. These three aspects must also work on three levels: individually, institutionally, and globally.

Powerlessness at the individual, institutional, and global level is currently the greatest vulnerability of our global system. The UN's powerlessness is visible through the UN representative who cries when she sees pictures of dead children in Yemen; she sees the suffering and war, but she is unable to do anything to stop it. We can see the lack of executive power by the UN through the words of Nora Sveeas. She says, as mentioned earlier, that human rights institutions at the global level are under severe pressure. The UN no longer fits into our reality since our societies have undergone drastic changes due to the globalization of suffering and war. Unfortunately, the UN as an institution established after the Second World War and it too old now to go with the current situation of our globalized world.

Modern institutions have three aspects to them. First, the *cognitive* aspect, which is a set of concepts, thoughts, and symbols found in the societal context which influence the actions of individuals. The idea behind the cognitive aspect was established after the Second World War. We need to define a new cognitive aspect for today's institutions. Further, the *normative* aspect is a set of values or criteria that form the legalization of a society. The norms show how a society works. This normative aspect is now outdated and needs to change. We need new norms based on the reality of today's society. We need regulatory aspects that control the laws and rules of a system. The *regulatory* aspect is also outdated and ineffective. We need a new regulatory aspect and a new global system. It is imperative that the UN changes the aspects mentioned above. By global conscience we mean the new regulatory, cognitive, and normative aspects of the UN. Global powers spend money on creating and legitimizing their own actions as well as themselves. We need to be cooperative and dynamic on an individual, institutional, and global level in order to reshape the UN. We must value each other through these three levels, and these three levels should be based on justice and peace, not on the size of financial contributions.

We need a new universal institution based on this global conscience: a new UN with executive power. The UN was created as a result of the Second World War, and all the countries of the world could see the necessity behind such a governing and administrative body. Now that The Third World War is taking place around us, we have an urgent need for new solutions. Globalization is constant, but war is evolving at the speed of light. We do not have time to understand every little detail.

Young activists such as Greta Thunberg have proven that it is possible to mobilize large groups of people for a single cause. There is a strong connection between war and climate changes. The obvious disregard of human life and of the environment stems from the same thoughtless capitalist mentality. Nobel laureates Mukwege and Murad stated that there was no need for sympathy, but instead to act for justice.

Our duty to speak and act

During the 2020 ceremony on the terror attack of 22nd of July in Norway, one of the speakers talked about the fact that we all have a duty to speak.

This term, *duty to speak*, is important. For example, it is important that I am true to my duty to speak and to share what I have found in my research. I have great faith in this quote from Bertolt Brecht: "Those who do not know the truth are just fools, but those who know the truth and call it a lie are criminals" (own translation). Not telling the truth is criminal and serious, but I understand it well. Brecht wrote this while fascism reigned in his home country Germany, and war was underway. I myself used this quote actively when I fought against the Soviet Union in Afghanistan. My resistance there consisted also of the duty to speak. The Russian intervention was portrayed as a struggle for women's liberation and justice but in reality, it meant the occupation of Afghanistan.

That's why I got up and fought. Now it is my duty to express my research, to speak loudly about what is going on within global multiculturalism, its connection to war, how it leads to hatred and creates pain and suffering. Each individual can fight with their heart and their ideals, use their identity and commitment, without understanding that they have been brainwashed to take on a fight that others profit from. This is the basis of the Third World War; a silent war, which is not necessarily understood by those who participate in it. People are participating in wars from which only the arms industry benefits. This war has nothing to do with Islam. These are vulnerable people who give service as soldiers without being aware of their role in the silent Third World War.

Every cell of my body understands this connection as a result of my socialization within the war in Afghanistan. Those who use Islam for extremist purposes have had the same socialization. Forty years of warfare in Afghanistan have given me a basic understanding of war dynamics, radicalization and what goes on beneath the surface. It is my duty to share this understanding with others. In this way, I want to promote the part of Norway that is a peace nation, and not the part that is a war nation. I want to promote a Norway which through its efforts in the UN can be purely a peace nation, and I am happy about being part of this nation.

My duty to speak in light of the Ukraine War

While I'm writing this book, war is raging in Ukraine. Even though it came to its full crescendo in February in 2022, the conflict initiated in 2014. "World War 3" is no longer silent, once again Europe is mobilizing. What really hurts me is the world's superpowers appetite for war mongering, weapon transactions and militarization. Additionally, we observe blatant hypocrisy regarding refugees from western nations.

Afghan citizens and other immigrants that are currently in Ukraine are not receiving the same treatment as Ukrainians; they are not welcomed such as the Ukrainian people. This is clearly a double moral. Is Afghan and other refugees blood not of the same value as Ukrainian blood? It is good to see the solidarity from western governments and people with Ukraine. My question remains, why did the Afghan people not experience the same solidarity when Taliban came to power? After all, it is western superpowers who are responsible for the current situation in Afghanistan. Over the course of 20 years, the Americans established a system that gradually gave power to the Taliban, they have a responsibility. The misery and painful situation in Afghanistan are a result of failed militarism from the global superpowers.

The Ukrainian refugee crisis revitalized my pain and suffering. I feel the pain and suffering in my body and mind; it passes through me as a film. I remember when I witnessed in the "Tribunal de permanent de peuples" the 16th of December 1982. I travelled as part of a delegation to talk about torture, imprisonment, and the war in Afghanistan. During a meeting organizes by French feminists, a woman from Soviet Union posed the question: "How can the Afghan people create peace during the war?" I answered: "The war was not started by the Afghan people; we were forced into it. Peace cannot be achieved, the war was created and manipulated by the global superpowers. It is a global duty to create peace in Afghanistan." At the end of the meeting, she approached me while I was alone, with an important message. Two women, who were officially declared as enemies had a long and friendly discussion a café nearby. She told me that she was a member of a secret organization called "The soldier's mother against war". The war in Afghanistan was a nightmare for Russian mothers; their children were killed or injured for life. She said, "we force our children to get a good education, otherwise they would be sent to the war in Afghanistan." Together, we made a deal that the only solution for peace was international cooperation. She began by emphasizing the need for us to collaborate, holding me close in a shared embrace marked by both tears and a somber yet hopeful smile for peace. We agreed to work with the United Nations, through our organizations: As an individual, she raised awareness to Russian soldiers to not bomb and fire at Afghan farm and people. I had the mission of informing the Afghan resistance to not kill Russian soldiers who did not have the power to solve the issue of war and peace. After our conversation I spoke with Gol Mohammad, a key member of our Paris delegation. He had been a great help during my solo travels, earning him the title of my spiritual father. He, a simple Afghan peasant, carried the weight of painful war experiences, deeply intertwined with fellow Afghans who had resisted the Russian occupation. I emphasized to him the necessity of ending the conflict through peaceful resolutions, steering away from guns and violence.

I wrote a letter to the UN, but sadly the letter never got answered, at this time. Today, as the war is ravaging Ukraine, I think about her and all the Russian and Ukraine mothers against war. I still hope that people mobilize to such organizations to create global peace.

the war is ravaging the people of Ukraine, and both sides are suffering, while western countries send weapons. This is only an extension of war and the people's suffering. No state is listening to the General Secretary of the United Nations, António Guterres.

For 43 years, I, and all Afghan people, have carried pain and suffering from war on our shoulders. Especially, women have an essential burden of war created by the Russians, Americans and their western allies, and the Chinese. War is contempt; it is a violation of our needs such as love, rights, and solidarity. My thought goes to all victims of war, regardless of being Ukrainian, Russian, Afghan or from other warzones our media never talk about.

My goals as a victim of war are to turn globalization of pain and suffering to globalization of peace, happiness, and justice. It is striking that many people want peace, yet nobody is working towards forbidding war. 43 years with war experience gives me an understanding of the dynamics of war, radicalization the consequences of war in every-day life for people. It is my duty to speak openly about this issue. I prefer to be a part of Norway as a peace nation, not a war nation. I would like that Norway with active participation for peace through the UN, to fight for peace.

We live in a globalized world which is dominated by pain and suffering of war. Society is changing at the speed of light, but the United Nations and their laws does not function in this reality, they are outdated. UN as an institution was established after World War II, in which great powers were given veto rights. Today, the veto right is extending war and suffering. We need to create a new UN with executive powers, in which all nations have the same rights. This new institution must create a law to forbid war, and sanction states committing war crimes. The military fabrics must replace its killing machinery with a production of human needs. In this way we can create a world where humans, animals and plants may live with a harmonic ecosystem.

For the sake of our health, and to reduce everyday-life pain and suffering, I encourage my readers to overcome the symptom of our time, being powerless. Remember, as a human, we have immense power to make a change. Our world needs people who think like Mahatma Gandhi. I encourage everyone to pioneers and work for peace and happiness simultaneously in three levels: individual, institutional, and global. A law to forbid war is our global need and our global responsibility.

I, who am a victim of the 40-year long war in Afghanistan, want to fight against the globalization of war, pain, and suffering. I want to fight for the globalization of peace, justice, and happiness. I still believe that people are connected to each other, just as parts of a body, as is written in the poem of Sa'adi[24], which is inscribed on the walls of the UN. I started this book with this Persian poem, and I will end the book with it:

The children of Adam, human beings
are each other's limbs,
created, as they are, from the same core.
When time inflicts pain in one limb
the others can find no rest.
If you do not care about the suffering of others
you do not deserve to be called human.

Terminology

1. **Universalism**

Universalism means that all humans have the same needs regardless of culture, religion or ethnicity. This means that all humans are equal and have the same value.

2. **Relativism**

Relativism is the reduction of universalism. Humans are products of culture, religion and ethnicity, and have differing needs. If you believe in cultural relativism, you do not believe in universal moral stating what is right or wrong. Therefore, any unjust deed can be legitimized. For example, British colonists used cultural relativism to legitimate their practices through using tribal and religious leaders as a link.

3. **Multiculturalism**

Multiculturalism refers to the existence of several distinct cultural or ethnic groups in a society. It is also a governance strategy that controls the relations of immigrants and refugees in many countries. The term "multiculturalism" started with Canadian social democrat Tyler. In the beginning, oppressed groups used it as a rallying cry. But now, it has turned into cultural relativism, producing added pain and suffering for many, especially women. In Persian the effect of multiculturalism is described by the expression: ´to kill with cotton´, and Professor Thomas Hyland Eriksen calls it 'apartheid' with a kind face.

4. **Pain**

Pain is an uncomfortable or unpleasant sensory or emotional experience associated with potential or actual damage of bodily tissue or the psyche. The division into a model "body and soul" is no longer correct. The pain in my book Silent Screams is the total feeling of discomfort and pain, both, in the body and soul of the human. WHO defines health as "a human optimal state". Health is then the absence of discomfort and pain. According to WHO, pain is a subjective feeling, but today we can use technology to objectify subjective feelings.

5. Medicalization of social problems

Immigrants and the weakest in western societies experience that their pain has a different origin and needs other forms of treatments than the doctors suggest. Over-consumption of drugs is mostly to the advantage of the medical industry, but not for the treatment of pain and suffering among immigrants.

6. Psychosomatic Disorder

Pain acts as a barometer in the body. A psychosomatic disorder occurs when mental strain becomes so strong that the body reacts with physical pain. Mental strain affects the body's enzymes and hormones. For example, blood tests from a woman with severe neck pain showed the enzyme troponin in her blood. Based on this, the doctors suspected she had a heart attack, but her heart and blood vessels were normal. Healthcare calls this "undefined pain". One of the reasons is that the male body generally is used as the norm.

7. Andronormativity

Andronormativity means that the male body is used as a norm when doctors examine a body. Nevertheless, physical symptoms, such as heart problems, can differ in both, cause and symptom between male and female bodies.

8. Passive coping strategy

Passive coping strategy is a procedure that does not directly treat the cause of pain. This strategy is widespread among religious organizations and "New Age" movements. Christian and Muslim organizations recommend to members that they pray and read religious quotes to solve problems. In Afghanistan, one strategy is to hang a "tavis" which means 'amulet' around the neck. Today, passive coping strategies are also a "business" strategy that uses wounded and desperate individuals, who are trying to get rid of their pain, as a target.

9. Recognition

Recognition is commonly understood as a confirmation of existence, validity or legality of something. I agree with philosopher Axel Honneth, who says that the meaning of human existence is to fight for recognition; that is love, rights and solidarity. I consider human existence and recognition as related to these three needs.

10. Social Field

Social fields are a set of competing relationships in everyday life. Social fields are an arena of relationships where people compete with each other to meet their needs. Women often lose these competing relationships.

11. Substantial Freedom

Substantial freedom is the complete set of circumstances surrounding a human being with opportunities to develop skills to their potentiality. We all have a set of basic qualities and abilities. To attain substantial freedom, we need the right conditions that allow development of these basic abilities, for example through socialization, education, or practice. This enables us to use our abilities actively. Only then can we attain the kind of freedom that makes a higher quality of life possible.

Socialization entails social life where we meet others and learn. After socialization in a particular social environment, we have developed practical competences that in turn constitute important parts of our personal qualities. For example, we all have the ability, the basic opportunity to learn a language, but to really do it and actually speak one or more languages, but to actually speak one or more languages this ability has to be developed. Minorities and immigrants often do not have the substantial freedom to cope in a new society, especially when their skills and work are not approved.

12. Intimacy

Intimacy is the physical, emotional, mental and spiritual closeness between two or more persons. It can be between familial relations as mother and child, or between two people who have sexual relations.

13. Assimilation

The word assimilation means to totally absorb information and experiences. Assimilation is the first process the nation state uses to adapt minority groups to the dominant culture. The assimilation process creates a lot of suffering for minorities because they are not allowed to speak their own language or have their own culture. Assimilation was so ignorant that newer integration concepts developed.

Assimilation, integration and inclusion are concepts that show the development of society. For example, in Norway the Sami people had to be assimilated into Norwegian culture and for a long time they were forbidden the use of their own language. However, they did preserve their own culture and language, and were Norwegian citizens.

14. Integration

Integration is used in different scholarly subjects, and in Silent Screams integration is a process where the laws and rules of the new society are accepted whilst simultaneously culture, religion and lifestyle is preserved. Integration does not sufficiently explain the needs of society. A newer concept is inclusion.

15. Inclusion:

Inclusion happens when all people have the same opportunity to participate in society. The concept refers to a situation where participation is built on the differences. The essence of 'inclusion' is therefore to increase the individual's participation and furthermore the benefit created through participating individuals who influence the community in effect.

I named my book Silent Screams because refugees do not have the same opportunities as Norwegian born people. For example, immigrant children, especially Muslim children use entertainment organized by religious venues. Many of these children are not becoming included into Norwegian society while they also go to religious schools. Education and youth entertainment facilities must therefore have requirements to be an inclusive arena and build on both, people's distinctive characters and equality. Everybody in a community should be able to participate equally - professionally, socially and culturally.

16. Global Conscience:

Global conscience is an ideal institution with executive power in which global standards are based on human recognition. Globalization and long-standing wars indicate that we have a great need for such an institution. I believe that the UN must have a global institution that caters to people in terms of global laws and regulations regardless of culture, religion, residency or ethnicity.

17. Nation

A nation can be understood as a large group of people who have a shared identity who make up what Benedict Anderson calls an "imagined ethnic community". This identity is often based on shared culture, history, religion, ethnicity or language. Therefore, it is not bound to statehood, although it may claim state-like characteristics. In a modern understanding, the nation is often limited to a certain geographical territory.

18. Nation intimacy

Nation intimacy is a collective memory created between humans and nature. It is the relation and closeness between people and nature, where one feels nature with all one's senses. Through the bodily experiences this relation becomes embodied and creates a stronger collective social memory.

19. Primordialism

In primordialism existential factors like biological roots define individual identification and distinctiveness between communities.

20. Essentialism

In essentialism people or things have fundamental, intrinsic characteristics that are unchangeable. It allows people to categorize and create distinctive groups based on a particular nature or culture of a person or thing.

21. Habitus

Habitus is a system of personified character, which influences individuals' behavior and identification with the social world around them. Habitus seeks to explain people's behavior and reflects a physical embodiment of the cultural capital embedded in their character.

22. Doxic Habitus

Doxic habitus is the collection of generally accepted traits and social behaviors. Through our perception of society and our perception of the world, these behaviors are no longer critically questioned and are taken for granted as social behavior in our subconscious.

23. Reflexive Habitus

In contrast, reflexive habitus are behavior and traits which come out of a thinking process. Through conscious reflection of our behaviors and understanding of the world, we realize the existence of multiple perspectives and knowledges. The skepticism towards our own beliefs allows us to reflect on prejudices and allocate our behaviors as an outcome of our experiences and location in the society and in the world.

24. Organizations vs. Institutions

Organizations are collectively organized groups of agents, such as companies or nations with shared goals and identity. Organizations can be public or private and are often associated with external bodies like government departments. Organizations are often confused with institutions. Institutions are systematically organized informal or formal collectives that pose social constraints to society, such as laws, conventions and rules. In the democratic system institutions can change. They have three core aspects: regulative, normative and cognitive.

25. Populism

Populism is a political movement building upon ideas and rhetoric which appeals to the majority of people by exploiting their current needs and desires. It is often connected to nationalistic, totalitarian and fascist dogmas.

26. Embodiment

Embodiment is understood as the role that the body (the interplay of sensory, motoric and perceptual experiences) plays in influencing and enacting thoughts, feelings and behavior. Embodiment is made up of the whole of bodily, cognitive and lived experiences within inhabited worlds. It is generally understood amongst social psychologists that people think, feel, and act inside their bodies.

27. Common Sense

Common sense is an intuitive judgement, based on a sum of the emotional sense and rationality that we use in everyday life. It is independent from specialized knowledge.

28. Institutional Discrimination

Institutional discrimination is a form of discrimination that is built into the system as unjust and discriminatory mistreatment and unequal selection of either individuals or groups, based on a certain characteristic.

29. Diaspora

A group of people who share a common heritage or home country and spread from their original country or territory to another place.

30. Eurocentrism

Eurocentrism denotes a worldview which perceives European values and history as superior to non-European ones. Eurocentrism enables and justifies Europe's dominant position in the global capitalist system.

Notes

1. Sa'adi, Persian poet who lived in the eighth century. Here translated by Farida Ahmadi. Printed on wall of the UN Headquarters in New York, United States. Nasa sent this poem as one of many thousands of languages into space as human civilization and culture.

Notes to chapter 1

1. This book is a qualitative study based on qualitative facts concerning the health of minorities. Facts alone cannot tell anything about the causes behind the numbers. Silent Cries gives an explanation of why minority women have the pains they have and confirms that the pains are real both bodily and physically.
2. This is about institutional power and structural discrimination, which I will come back to later in this book. It is also about symbolic power, as described by Pierre Bordieu.
3. Dagsavisen, 7. January 2006.
4. See Natta Ansari and Naushad Ali Qureshi 1998.
5. Marianne Gullestad 2004: "Blind Slaves of our Prejudices", Ethnos, p. 177-203, Routledge Journals. Marianne Gullestad, who belongs to the majority, explains that the mechanism for marginalization lies in the hegemony of the majority. And this hegemony lies in the power to define what separates "us" and "them". This thought lies deeply embedded in the European nationalistic self, originating from the colonial era.
6. Tordis Borchgrevink. Grete Brochmann and Jon Rogstad 2002. The term "matter out of place" is borrowed from Mary Douglas.
7. "I argue for a universalizing dis- course that would recognize the basic integrity of the human be- ing and the indispensable value of respect for human rights." See Unni Wikan 2002.
8. Magne Flemmen in DN, Wednesday 2. May 2007.
9. Gunilla Brattberg 1995.
10. It should be a basic right to have a condition of health that makes you able to function as a human. WHO defines health as "a human optimal condition"? By health is meant lack of pain and discomfort.

As Arne Johann Vetlesen says: "The positivity of health is based on the (absolute) negativity of pain, so that the most ambitious goal of health is achieved when pain, the enemy of, and contradiction to health, is defeated to the degree that it is removed" (see Arne Johan Vetlesen 2004).

11. I join Toril Moi's definition of social fields: an arena filled with competing relations, where some lose and some win. See Moi 2002.

Notes to chapter 2

1. The data in this report are taken from the HUBRO study (2000), a quantitative survey examining the health status of the population in Oslo. The survey includes all in- habitants in Oslo as of 3-3-2000 who are born in 1924-1925, 1940- 1941, 1955, 1960 and 1970.
2. The authors of the study take this into account and say they use the category under doubt.
3. Figure 4 and 5 are equal to figure 65 and 66 in the HUBRO study (page 73-74).
4. Central Bureau of Statistics, register-based employment statistics, fourth quarter 2006.
5. Http://www.ssb.no/vis/magasinet/analyse/art-2006-12-18-01.html
6. Central Bureau of Statistics, register-based employment statistics, fourth quarter 2006.
7. The HUBRO study 2002. For di- abetes, see page 43, for accidents and injuries and mental health, see page 51, for suicide, see page 28.
8. Interview with Edvard Hauff in *Minoriteter og psykisk helse. Et informasjonshefte fra rådet for psykisk helse* (Minorities and mental health. An information booklet from the Council for Mental Health), page 14, 2006.
9. The same place.
10. See Abdelmalek Sayed 2004. In her book *The suffering of the immigrant* (2004) she writes about illness among immigrants in French society. Sayed thinks we have to look at the immigration condition

as a disease to under- stand this type of disorders that are so closely connected to social problems.

11. Kirsti Maltrud in the article "Subjektive symptomer uten objektive funn", (Subjective symptoms without objective findings), see Malterud (editor) 2001.

12. Report to the Storting no. 49 (2003- 2004) Mangfold gjennom inkludering og deltakelse. Ansvar og frihet, (Diversity through inclusion and participation. Responsibility and freedom) page 180.

13. Margaret Lock has criticized the multiculturalist way to look at things in the health care system in Canada, see Lock 1990. Her arguments are that multiculturalism hides class perspectives in society.

14. Joaquim J.F. Soares and Giorgio Grossi have compared the experiences of muscle related pain among immigrants and Swedes. They show how many of the pa- tients use passive coping strategies as an important cause of pain. See Soares and Grossi 1999.

15. Belquis doesn't manage to meet the daily demands or what the Quran says she should do. She feels like a loser on both these most important arenas of her life. She uses religion as an "aid", but the result is that her life becomes even more filled with conflict. It is important to note that it was the Norwegian institution she sought, the Jacob Center, which gave her these excerpts from various reli- gious texts that she read over and over again.

16. For a good description of bound- ary markings between "us" and "the others", see Marianne Gullestad 2001.

17. The theory of Mary Douglas con- cerning what is alien as threatening and contagious – "matter out of place" – is highly relevant in this connection.

18. For a more extensive and very good description of what pain is, see Arne Johan Vetlesen 2004.

19. Aftenposten, 12.9.2007. A comment to the ambulance from Ullevål Hospital leaving seriously injured Ali Farah in the Sofienberg Park in Oslo in august 2007.

20. The same place.

Notes to chapter 3

1. Scheper-Hughes and Lock 1987.
2. Zygmunt Bauman 1998, 2004.
3. Gullestad 2001, 2004.
4. Bauman and Vecchi 2008:8.
5. https://snl.no/Mulla_Krekar
6. Hall 2000: 210f.
7. Gullestad 2002.
8. Eide and Simonsen 2007:9.
9. Axel Honneth doesn't mention multiculturalism, but I still think it is interesting to try out his theory in relation to this. Honneth belongs to the Frankfurter school in Germany and is influenced by the philosophy of Feuerbach. Feuerbach was interested in the contradictory relation between master and slave and how their contradictory interests in society lead to conflict. This is what Feuerbach calls the dialectic of contradiction. To him these clashes of interests, lead to social conflict. Honneth develops this idea further by stating that everybody has the same need. This concept also inspires Karl Marx in his theory concerning the contradictory interests of workers and capitalists.
10. Sana'i (1080-1131 / 1141)
11. Rumi (1207-1273)
12. Comaroff and Comaroff 1991.
13. Said 2003.
14. Gullestad 2002.
15. Gullestad 2002.
16. Gellner 2006.
17. Anderson 1983, my emphasis.
18. This Persian poem is analogous to the symbolism concerning the Leaning Tower of Pisa.
19. Borchgrevink 1999.
20. Gullestad 2004.

21. White paper nr. 49 (2003- 04): 36.
White paper nr. 49 (2003- 04): 180.
White paper nr. 49 (2003- 04): 65.
22. Wikan 2002.
23. Also Fuglerud 2001:127 shows how the use of categories like "immigrant" and national categories like "Pakistani" and "Somali" or "second generation immigrants" are widespread in Norwegian politics and public discourse.
24. Brochmann 2003.
25. Brochmann 2003: 83.
26. Aftenposten, 26.7.2006.
27. Wikan 2002: 2: "(…) a conspir- acy of silence that (…) has been wreaking havoc with the lives of many immigrants and their children".
28. The example is taken from the institution I call the Jacob Center.
29. Thorbjørnsrud 2007.
30. Thorbjørnsrud 2007.
31. Nilsen, C. H., 2019
32. Deveaux, M. 2010
33. Aftenposten 13. aug. 2020. https://www.aftenposten.no/norge/i/jd6GLo/kvinneopproer-i-den-somaliske-moskeen-vi-er-lei-av-aa-vaske-og-lage-m
34. Aftenposten 30. apr. 2010. Kjøreregler for religion i arbeidslivet (Do's and dont's of religion in the working place): https://www.aftenposten.no/norge/i/dlQVw/kjoereregler-for-boenn-paa-jobben?
35. Capurri, 2006
36. Langvasbråten (2008)
37. Einar Øverenget (2003) Hannah Arendt
38. In 1919, Afghanistan gained independence. In 1920, the sitting king was taken down from the throne, as he was against the English. Sharia was established at this time and the family of

Sibghatullah Mojaddedi opposed Afghanistan's independence and participated in this establishment.

39. Kari Vogt, Islam på norsk
40. https://www.youtube.com/watch?v=sAVhd2E9BqE
41. https://tv.nrk.no/serie/debatten/202009/NNFA51090320
42. https://www.vg.no/nyheter/innenriks/i/m6p85q/frp-forslag-vil-forby-boennerop-fra-moskeer-i-norge

Notes to chapter 4

1. Angarudd is a Persian word meaning "mix of everything" and "messy". But the word can also be positively charged when one speaks about herbs/ plant medicine.
2. Maezon is Persian for "harmonic".
3. This deals with human capabil- ities and possibilities in real life. See Nussbaum 1999 and Sen 1999, who describe in more detail what these capabilities are. Actually, this deals with children not having the opportunity to de- velop their inner capabilities.
4. This was the Jacob Center (a pseudonym). I return to this center later in the book.
5. See Report to the Storting no. 49 (2003-04):186.
6. I am particularly interested in Pierre Bourdieu's concept of class, because he shows how class con- tains so much more than what is material. With class background I mean different "access to and control over the basic material and non-material resources that sustain and promote life at a high level of satisfaction", see Baer, Singer and Johsen 1986:95.
7. In her book *Klassereise (Class Trip)* Kari Sveen defines "closeness to risk" as an additional factor in her definition of class. In my view the definition extension of Sveen is very interesting and highly relevant in connection to the relation- ship between class and illness.
8. Sveen 2001:80.
9. Most of my respondents lived in such areas.
10. Carlbom 2003.
11. Bourgeois 1995.

12. Carlbom 2003.
13. HUBRO study 2000-2001.
14. Blom 2002:3f.
15. Kjeldstadli 1996.
16. Ahnstrøm has ten points concerning segregation and ethnic concentration in Oslo. Those I refer to here are just a small selection.
17. Ahnstrøm 1996.
18. Dunin-Woyseth 1996.
19. Dunin-Woyseth 1996.
20. Hylland Eriksen 1996.
21. Carlbom 2003.
22. Larsen 2006.
23. Amartya Sen claims in his book *Development as Freedom* (1999) that one has to separate between substantial freedom and what he calls negative freedom, which he defines as absence of force. Sen thinks substantial freedom is closely connected to a life of quality and should be a more general goal for the development of societies. Therefore substantial free- dom is a basic principle for public political practice, see 1999:37.

Notes to chapter 5

1. Babrak Karmal was the Afghan president during the Soviet oc- cupation and leader of the pro- Soviet party Parcham. Gulbuddin Hekmatyar was the leader of Hezb-i-Islami, the fundamentalist party that received the most eco- nomic and military support from the West and Pakistan.
2. From Ayaan Hirsi Alis' *Mitt liv, min frihet (My life, my freedom)*, page 110.
3. Marjene Satrapis' *Persepolis*, for example, is about this.
4. Sverre Varvin interviewed by Kari Andresen in *'Minoriteter og psykisk helse'. An information brochure from the Norwegian Council for Mental Health*, page 10 and 11, 2006.

5. The poem and the text under the poem are borrowed from: *Det brente hjertet*, 1999, Aschehoug forlag, Oslo. The poems were written in cooperation with Inger Elisabeth Hansen.
6. Maryam Azimi's unpublished poem, translated by Johannes Gjerdåker and Farida Ahmadi.
7. Again, I refer to Axel Honneth. The women's need for recognition is ignored in the justice system, among fellow humans, and in love. The German philosopher, Axel Honneth, compares recognition with language. For a language to work, we need grammar. In the same way recognition needs grammar to work. This Honneth calls the moral grammar. We need an ethic. For Germany to function as a nation, and for people to have the opportunity to live a good life, it is a prerequisite with an ethic that prioritizes the need for recognition both in private and public life. I must add that we need a con- science. And this conscience must be global, not national.

Notes to chapter 6

1. See Boyd and Grieco 2003.
2. Aftenposten, 27.5.06.
3. Vogt 2000:24
4. Bourgois (1995) shows in his anal- ysis of the situation among immigrants from Puerto Rico in New York, USA, that we have to look at the subtle dynamics between agency and structure to understand the social field humans live in.
5. Carlbom 2003. Carlbom shows explicitly the consequences of multi-culturalism on the living environ- ments of minorities in Sweden.
6. A rural landscape is characterized by relations that are multiplex with different social dynamics than in urbane contexts where the relations to a large extent are uniplex. Multiplex relations are relations where persons know each other in the capacity of different roles and across contexts. The rural landscape in Grønland and the rest of the ghetto areas in Oslo are in addition marked by close kinship and new close bonds that arise in Norway.
7. See Sayed 2004.

8. The dissolution of identity and belonging strike immigrants and minorities in particular, but is also a general problem for postmodern society as such. This is especially true in a fluid modern reality where identity is basical- ly problematized; see Baumann 2004. It is also important to re- member how Norwegians set- tled down in their new country when they emigrated to the USA.
9. White paper nr. 49 (2003-2004):180
10. Giddens 1991, Bauman 2004.
11. Douglas 1966 and Scheper-Hughes and Lock 1987.
12. Dagsavisen, 13.11.2005, page 8.
13. See Wikan 2002 and Gullestad 2002.
14. See Wikan 2003:265.
15. Gullestad 2002:302.
16. Leirvik 2005.
17. See Khader 1996.
18. See Melhuus 2001.
19. Etymologically *sjærm* is connected to *sjærm-gah*, which means the outer parts of the female sex organ.

Notes to chapter 7

1. Eide and Simonsen 2007:9.
2. The same place.
3. Alghasi 1999.
4. Eide and Simonsen 2007:177.
5. Eide 2004.
6. Report to the Storting no. 49 (2003-2004):65.
7. Belquis, like many others, look at bin Laden as pure spirit. He is light, invisible, transparent and divine - and can therefore hide in the mountains in spite of the ad- vanced intelligence equipment of the Americans: Nobody can find a pure spirit.
8. Giddens 1991:27.
9. Sayed 2004.

10. Mahshar is the Day of Doom in Islamic teachings, a time of chaos and great fear, when nothing works.
11. This poem is at the top of the UN building in New York; see the first and the last pages of this book.

Notes to chapter 8

1. As Sayed (2004) has shown with empirical data from France, this is very common in the meeting between immigrants and institutions in the host nation.
2. NRK P2, 2 December 2007.
3. The Norwegian Equality and Anti-Discrimination Ombud, for example, relates to both these definitions.
4. Conversations with Ronald Craig, the fall of 2007, see also Craig 2006.
5. The center is a Norwegian institution I must keep anonymous because of the women I interviewed. What is interesting with this institution is that it had as a stated goal to help minority women.
6. The leader of the Jacob Center decided that I only was allowed to be in the Quran Group and on the weekly internal meetings, even if I wanted to be in the circumcision and forced marriage group. I was also allowed to participate in the Arabic course in the weekend. I imagined that through these groups, I could gain access to data about the social aspects of pain. I had never imagined that the Quran Group would be so rich with information about pain.
7. Vetlesen 2004.
8. Brochman 2002:76.
9. New York Times, 28.01.2006.

Notes to chapter 9

1. Soares and Grossi 1999.
2. Sayad 2004 and Monsen 1999.
3. Soares and Grossi 1999:262.
4. General Health Questionnaire (GHQ) from a selection of people.

5. *Den generende forskjellighet. Danske svar på den stigende multikulturalisme (The annoying difference. Danish answers to the increasing multiculturalism)* (1999).
6. He is supported by Birte Siim (2003:19), who writes about the "existing difference and social control over ethnic minority women's sexuality and reproduction within the private sphere" in Denmark.
7. Lock, Margaret 1990: "On being Ethnic: The Politics of Identity Breaking and Making in Canada, or Nevra on Sunday". In Culture, Medicine and Psychiatry 14: 237-254. Kluwer Academic Publishers.
8. 2004:110. GCSE is an academ- ic qualification in Britain and is used as an indicator of educational level and is one of the health indicators.
9. Sayed 2004 and Bourgois 1995.
10. Carlbom 2003.
11. The Democrats in the USA often use Scandinavia as an example of what they are trying to achieve.
12. Widding Isaksen, Lise 2006: "Tilpasning til tomme rom. Om globale omsorgskrisers relasjons-økologi (Adaptation to empty spaces. On the relation ecology in the global caring crisis)" In Periodical for gender research 12: 20-35.
13. Widding Isaksen 2006:10.
14. This concept means that human needs and social relations, for example the love between mother and child, are hidden by the need for profit in the market.
15. Widding Isaksen 2006:21.
16. Wikan 2003:267f.

Notes to chapter 10

1. Brochmann, Borchgrevink and Rogstad 2002
2. The same place.
3. Knut Kjeldstadli 2006: "Mulige fremtider - Norge som et flerkulturelt samfunn" (Possible futures. Norway as a multicultural society). Paper at the conference "Challenges in multicultural

dissemination" at the Center for Multicultural and International Work (SEFIA) at Oslo University College 2. March 2006.

4. Report to the Storting no. 49 (2003- 2004): 63.
5. Http://www.rbnett.no/article/20071211/LOKALNYTT/257494903/1122
6. Vetlesen 2004.
7. Published in Dag og Tid 09.01.07
8. 2003-2004: 180.
9. The Swedish doctor, Jørgen Malmquist, points out that social problems are increasingly considered as health problems - and therefore are medicalized. Research shows how the pharmaceutical industry exploits the idea that what are actually social problems, are medical ones, and produce large amounts of drugs based on this assumption. Malmquist criticizes this trend of the medicalization of social problems and urges the authorities to do something about them. Malm- quist, Jørgen 2000: *Föreställningar om sjukdom: somatisering, medikalisering, prioritering*. Lund: Student literature.
10. Hahn 1995.
11. Kleinman, Arthur 1985: "Inter- preting illness experience and clinical meanings: How I see clinically applied anthropology". In Medical Anthropology Quarterly 16(3): 69-71.
12. One example is the project "Aktiv på dagtid (Active in daytime)"

Notes to chapter 11

1. This slogan was first used in the French newspaper "*Révolutions de Paris*" in the 19th century. It was later used in 1898 in Dublin. It originally dates back to the 16th century and (the modified) words of writer and judge Etienne de La Boetie (1530–1563) and was first published in 1576. Prudhomme, Louis-Marie (1789). "Révolutions de Paris: dédiées à la nation et au district des Petits Augustins" (in French). Prudhomme. Accessed 5 August 2019.
2. According to Nussbaum, all people need substantial freedom to act. Nussbaum, Martha 1999: Sex and Social Justice. Oxford

University Press. Retrieved from:
   http://people.wku.edu/jan.garrett/nussbaum.htm
3. Bauman, Zygmunt and Benedetto Vecchi, 2004: Identity: Conversations with Benedetto Vecchi. Cambridge: Polity Press.
4. Partnership for Peace Consortium of Defense Academies and Security Studies Institutes Islamic State and al-Qaeda's Foreign Fighters Author(s): Maja Touzari Greenwood Source: Connections, Vol. 16, No. 1 (Winter 2017), pp. 87-98 Published by: Partnership for Peace Consortium of Defense Academies and Security Studies Institutes Stable URL: https://www.jstor.org/stable/10.2307/26326473
5. Walton, 2012
6. Kio, 2013
7. Walton, 2012
8. Pressemelding 17.06.20
9. Haug (2019)
10. Catholic Information Services
11. Seierstad, Åsne; 2018: Two Sisters, (Little Brown).
12. Linge and Bangstad, 2020
13. Salafisme I Norge (Salafism in Norway). Linge og Bangstad (2020)
14. The Dirty War on Syria, (Global Research Publishers, April 2016).
15. Kaspar Colling Nielsen. Den danske borgerkrig 2018-24 (The Danish Civil War 2018-2024). Cappelen Damm, 2013.
16. Loretta Napoleon. The Islamic Phoenix. Seven Stories Press, 2014.
17. Prime minister Ariel Sharon and President Bush of the U.S.A.
18. https://en.wikipedia.org/wiki/List_of_ongoing_armed_conflicts Retrieved 28.07.19
19. Samira Laakel, 2015.Le bonheur est parti avec toi (The happiness has left together with you),
20. Nadine Rosa-Rosso, 2018. Plus qu´hier et moins que demain. Contre le racisme, le colonialisme et la guerre (More than yesterday and less than tomorrow. Against racism, colonialism and war).

21. Dag Hoel, 2017. Fred er ei det beste (Peace is not the best). Spartacus.
22. https://www.aftenposten.no/verden/i/yvAQ7x/Shamima-Begum-19-angrer-ikke-pa-at-hun-sluttet-seg-til-IS-Na-har-hun-utlost-en-hissig-debatt-om-retur-av-fremmedkrigere
23. https://www.facebook.com/dw.persian/videos/761506210910426/?v=761506210910426
24. Sa'adi, Persian poet who lived in the eighth century. Here translated by Maryam Azimi and Farida Ahmadi.

List of References

Ahnstrøm, Leif 1996: *"Differensiert byutvikling"*, Plan. Tidsskrift for samfunnsplanlegging, byplan og regional utvikling 3/96. *("Differentiated urban planning" in 'Journal of community planning, urban and regional development')*

Alghasi, Sharam 1999: *Slik er de, slik er vi og slik er verden...: En kultursosiologisk studie av "innvandring", fremstilt i aktualitets- og debattprogram på NRK og TV2 I tidsrommet 1989-1997. (So are they, so are we and so is the world...: A cultural sociological study of "immigration", depicted in current affairs and talk shows in NRK and TV2)* Unpublished Master's Thesis, Oslo University.

Alghasi, Sharam 2011: *Kjære Onkel Napoleon: Noen refleksjoner rundt Vestens rolle i Midtøsten. (Dear Uncle Napoleon: Some reflections around Western involvement in the Middle East)* Internasjonal politikk 04/2011 (69): 710-715.

Ali, Ayaan Hirsi 2007: *Mitt liv, min frihet (Infidel: My Life)*. Oslo: Cappelen.

Ali, Ayyan Hirsi 2006: *Krev din rett. Om kvinner og Islam (The Caged Virgin: An Emancipation Proclamation for Women and Islam)*. Oslo: Cappelen.

Anderson, Benedict 1983: *Imagined Communities: Reflections on the Origin and Spread of Nationalism*. London: Verso.

Ansari, Natta and Naushad Ali Qureshi 1998: *Kolleger eller alibier. En studie av politikere med minoritetsbakgrunn. (Colleagues or Alibies. A Study of Politicians with Minority Backgrounds)* Oslo: Høgskolen i Oslo. (Oslo University College)

Ardener, Edwin 1975: "Belief and the problem of Women". Shirley Ardener (editor): *Perceiving Women*. London: J.M. Dent Sons Ltd.

Azimi, Maryam and Inger Elisabeth Hansen 1999: *Det brente hjertet. (The Burnt Heart)* Publisher: Aschehoug Forlag Oslo.

Baer, H.A., M. Singer and J.H. Johnsen 1986: "Towards a Critical Medical Anthropology". *Social Science and Medicine* 23(2): 95-98.

Baier, Annette 1994: *Moral Prejudices: Essays on Ethics*. Cambridge: Harvard University Press.

Barer, Robin, Justine Fitzpatrick and Cheikh Traore 2004: *Health in London*. London: London Health Commission.

Barry, Brian 2001: *Culture and Equality: An Egalitarian Critique of Multiculturalism.* Harvard University Press, Massachusetts.

Barth, Fredrik (editor) 1969: *Ethnic Groups and Boundaries: The Social Organization of Culture Difference.* Bergen: Universitetsforlaget (Publisher)

Bauman, Zygmunt and Benedetto Vecchi 2004: *Identity: Conversations with Benedetto Vecchi.* Cambridge: Polity.

Bauman, Zygmunt and Benedetto Vecchi 1998: *Globalization: The Human Consequences.* Cambridge: Polity Press.

Baybrooke, David 1976: The Insoluble Problem of the Social Contract, *Dialogue,* vol. XV, no. 1: 3-37.

Bell, Rae Frances et al. 2004: *Retningslinjer for smertebehandling (Guidelines for the treatment of pain).* Arbeidsgruppe nedsatt av Sentralstyret i Den norske legeforening. (Working group appointed by the board of the Norwegian Medical Association)

Bendelow, Gillian 2000: *Pain and Gender.* Pearson Education Ltd.

Berry, John W., Ype H. Poortinga, Marshall H. Segall, Pierre R. Dasen 2002: "*Cross-Cultural Psychology*". Arthur S. Reber and E. Reber (editor): *The Penguin Dictionary of Psychology.* 3rd ed. London: Penguin Books.

Blom, Ida and Sølvi Sogner (editor) 1999: *Med kjønnsperspektiv på norsk historie. Fra vikingtid til 2000-årsskiftet. (A gender perspective on Norwegian history. From the Viking age to the year 2000)* Oslo: Cappelen Akademisk Forlag.

Blom, Svein 2002: *Innvandrernes bosettingsmønster i Oslo (Immigrant settlement patterns in Oslo).* Oslo: Statistisk sentralbyrå. (Central Bureau of Statistics).

Borchgrevink, Tordis 1999: *Multikulturalisme: tribalisme- bløff- kompromiss? Debatter om det flerkulturelle samfunnet. (Multiculturalism: tribalism - bluff or compromise? Debates on the multicultural society.)* Oslo: Institutt for samfunnsforskning. (Institute for social sciences)

Bourdieu, Pierre 1984: *Distinction: A Social Critique of the Judgment of Taste.* Translated by Richard Nice. London: Routledge and Kegan Paul.

Bourdieu, Pierre 1977: *Outline of a Theory of Practice.* Translated by Richard Nice. Cambridge: Cambridge University Press.

Bourgois, Philippe 1995: *In Search of Respect: Selling Crack in El Barrio.* Cambridge: Cambridge University Press.

Boyd, Monica and Elizabeth Grieco 2003: *Women and Migration: Incorporating Gender into International Migration Theory.* Migration Information Source. Washington, D.C.: Migration Policy Institute.

Brattberg, Gunilla 1995: *At möta langvarig smerta (To face prolonged pain).* Stockholm: Liber AB.

Brinkmann, Johannes and Thomas Hylland Eriksen 1996: *Verden som møteplass. Essays om tverrpolitisk kommunikasjon. (The world as a meeting place. Essays on cross-party communication)* Bergen: Fagbokforlaget.

Brochmann, Grete, Tordis Borchgrevink and Jon Rogstad 2002: *Sand i maskineriet. Makt og demokrati i det flerkulturelle Norge. (Sand in the machine. Power and democracy in multicultural Norway)* Oslo: Gyldendal Akademisk.

Capurri, Valentina 2006: Women as individuals and members of minority groups: How to reconcile human rights and the values of cultural pluralism. *GeoJournal* 65(4): 329-37.

Carlbom, Aje 2003: *The Imagined versus the Real Other: Multiculturalism and the Representation of Muslims in Sweden.* Doctoral Thesis. Lund: Sociological Institute, Lund University.

Carr, Daniel B., John D. Loeser and David B. Morris 2005: *Narrative, Pain, and Suffering.* Seattle: IASP Press.

Comaroff, Jean and John Comaroff 1991: "Africa Observed: Discours- es of Imperial Imagination". *Of Revelation and Revolution: Christianity, Colonialism and Consciousness in South Africa,* vol. I. Chicago: The University of Chicago Press.

Craig, Ronald 2006: *Systemic discrimination in employment and the promotion of ethnic equality.* Thesis. University of Oslo.

Crisson, J.F. and F.J. Keefe 1998: "The relationship of locus of control to pain coping strategies and psychological distress in chronic pain patients". *Pain* 35: 147-54.

Csordas, Thomas J. 1988 "Embodiment as a Paradigm for Anthropology". (Winner of the 1988 Stirling Award paper for contributions in Psychological Anthropology.) *Ethos* 18:5-47.

Csordas, Thomas J. 1993: Somatic Modes of Attention. *Cultural Anthropology* 8:135-156.

Danielsen, Kirsten 1990: *De gammeldagse piker. Eldre kvinner forteller om sitt liv. (Old fashioned girls. Elderly women tell about their lives)* Oslo: Pax Forlag.

Das, Veena 1995: *Critical Events: An Anthropological Perspective on Contemporary India.* Delhi: Oxford University Press.

Deveaux, Monique 2006: *Gender and Justice in Multicultural Liberal States.* Oxford: Oxford University Press.

Douglas, Mary 1966: *Purity and Danger: An Analysis of Concepts of Pollution and Taboo.* London: Ark Paperbacks.

Dunin-Woyseth, Halina 1996: "Segregering i den fragmenterte by" (Segregation in the fragmented city) *Plan. Tidsskrift for samfunnsplanlegging, byplan og regional utvikling (Journal of community planning, urban and regional development)* 3/96.

Eriksen, Thomas Hylland 1999: "Universalistisk pluralism" (Universalistic Pluralism). Roar Engh (editor): *Skolen i mulighetenes årtusen. Undringer underveis. (The school in the millennium of opportunity. Contemplations along the way).* Oslo: Cappelen Akademisk Forlag.

Eriksen, Thomas Hylland 1996: "Det er ikke noe galt med gettoen". (There is nothing wrong with the ghetto) *Plan. Tidsskrift for samfunnsplanlegging, byplan og regional utvikling (Journal of community planning, urban and regional development)* 3/96.

Eriksen, Thomas Hylland and Halvor Finess Tretvoll 2006: *Kosmopolitikk. En optimistisk politikk for det 21. århundre. (Cosmopolitics. An optimistic policy for the 21st century)* Oslo: Cappelen.

Eide, Elisabeth and Anne Hege Simonsen 2007: *Mistenkelige utlendinger. Minoriteter i norsk presse gjennom hundre år. (Suspicious foreigners. Minorities in the Norwegian press through a century)* Kristiansand: Høyskoleforlaget.

Eide, Elisabeth and Anne Hege Simonsen 2004: *Å se verden fra et annet sted. Medier, norskhet og fremmedhet. (To see the world from another place. Media, Norwegianness and foreignness)* Oslo: Cappelen Akademisk Forlag.

Fraser, Nancy and Axel Honneth 2003: *Redistribution or Recognition? A Political-Philosophical Exchange.* London, New York: Verso.

Fuglerud, Øyvind 2001: *Migrasjonsforståelse. Flytteprosesser, rasisme og globalisering. (Understanding migration. Relocation processes, racism and globalization)* Oslo: Universitetsforlaget.

Gauthier, David 1986: *Morals by Agreement.* Oxford: Oxford University Press.

Gellner, Ernest 2006: *Nations and Nationalism.* Malden, Mass.: Blackwell.

Giddens, Anthony 1991: *Modernity and Self-Identity: Self and Society in the Late Modern Age.* Stanford, California: Stanford University Press.

Grønhaug, Reidar 1975: "Fremmedarbeidere i Norge. Etnisitet og klasse". (Immigrant workers in Norway. Ethnicity and class) *Sosialt forum/sosialt arbeid, (Social forum/social work)* pages 556-564.

Gullestad, Marianne 2006: *Plausible Prejudice: Everyday Experiences and Social Images of Nation, Culture and Race.* Oslo: Universitetsforlaget. Gullestad,

Marianne 2004: "Blind Slaves of our Prejudices: Debating 'Culture' and 'Race' in Norway". *Ethnos*, vol 69: 2, June: 177-203.

Gullestad, Marianne 2002: *Det norske sett med nye øyne. (Norwegians seen through fresh eyes)* Universitetsforlaget Oslo.

Gullestad, Marianne 2001: "Imagined Sameness: Shifting Notions of 'Us' and 'Them' in Norway". Line Alice Ytrehus 2001 (editor): *Forestillinger om "den andre" / Images of otherness*. Kristiansand: Høyskoleforlaget.

The web page of HL-senteret (The Center for Studies of the Holocaust and Religious Minorities). www.hlsenteret.no.

Hahn, Robert A. 1995: *Sickness and Healing: An Anthropological Perspective*. New Haven & London: Yale University Press.

Hall, Stuart 2000: "Conclusion: The Multicultural Question". Barnor Hesse (editor): *Un/Settled Multiculturalisms: Diasporas, Entanglements, Transruptions*. London & New York: Zed Books.

Haug, Kenneth 2019: *Kidnapper kristendommen. (Kidnapping Christianity)* Vårt Land (Our Country). Retrieved from: https://www.vl.no/nyhet/kidnapper-kristendommen-1.1567061?paywall=true

Haugli, Liv and Eldri Steen 2001: *Kroniske muskel/skjelettsmerter og selvforståelse. Utvikling og evaluering av en læringsmodell som vektlegger kroppen som meningsbærer. (Chronic muscle/skeletal pain and self understanding. Development and evaluation of a learning model that emphasizes the body as a carrier of meaning)* Oslo: Institutt for allmennmedisin og samfunnsmedisinske fag, Institutt for medisinske atferdsfag, Pedagogisk forskningsinstitutt, Universitetet i Oslo/Unipub.

Hertting, Ann S. 2000: *"Smärta ock trötthet. Ohälsa i tiden". (Pain and fatigue. Poor health today)* Lund: Studentlitteratur (Student literature).

Hervik, Petter 1999: *Den generende forskjellighed. Danske svar på den sti- gende multikulturalisme. (The annoying differenceness. Danish answers to increasing multiculturalism)* Copenhagen: Hans Reitzel Forlag.

Hobbes, Thomas 1985 [1651]: *Leviathan*. C.B. I: Macpherson, C.B. (red.) London: Penguin Books.

Honneth, Axel 2006: *Kamp om anerkjennelse. Sosiale konflikters moralske grammatik. (Struggle for recognition. The moral grammar of social conflicts)* Copenhagen: Hans Reitzels Forlag.

Honneth, Axel 2003: *Behovet for anerkjennelse. En tekstsamling. (The need for recognition.)* Edited by Rasmus Willig. Copenhagen: Hans Reitzels Forlag.

Hussein, Khalid 1986: *Pakkis*. Oslo: Tiden Norsk Forlag.

Jehovas vitner 2005: *Hva er det Bibelen egentlig lærer? (What is the real teaching of the Bible?)* New York: Watchtower Bible and Tract Society of New York Inc.

Jupp, James, John Nieuwenhuysen and Emma Dawson: *Social Cohesion in Australia*. Melbourne: Cambridge University Press.

Kale, Emine 2007: "Hvordan smerter kommer til uttrykk i psykiatrien". (How pain is expressed in psychiatry) Arild Aambø (editor): *Smerter. Smerteopplevelser og adferd. (Pains. Experiences of pain and behavior)* Oslo: Cappelen Akademisk Forlag.

Keefe, F.J., D.S. Caldwell, S. Martinez, J. Nunley, J. Beckham and D.A. Williams 1991: "Analyzing Pain in Rheumatoid Arthritis Patients. Pain Coping Strategies in Patients Who Have Had Knee Replacement Surgery". *Pain* 46: 153-160.

Keefe, F.J., J.C. Crisson, B.J. Urban and D.A. William 1990: "Analyzing Chronic Low Back Pain: The Relative Contribution of Pain Coping Strategies". *Pain* 40: 293-301.

Khader, Naser 1996: Ære og skam. Det islamske familie- og livsmønster- fra undfangelse til grav. *(Honor and shame. The Islamic family and life patterns - from conception to the grave)* Copenhagen: Gyldendals bogklubber.

Kjeldstadli, Knut 2006: *"Mulige fremtider - Norge som et flerkulturelt samfunn." (Possible futures - Norway as a multicultural society)* Innlegg på konferansen "Utfordringer i flerkulturell formidling" ved Senter for flerkulturelt og internasjonalt arbeid (SEFIA) (Lecture at the conference "Challenges in multicultural dissemination") at the Center for Multicultural and International Work (SEFIA) at Oslo University College, 2. March 2006.

Kjeldstadli, Knut 2005: "Skal integrering være målet? En politikk for forskjell og fellesskap". (Should integration be the goal? A policy for difference and community) *SAMORA* 3:17-23.

Kjeldstadli, Knut 1996: "Den delte byen". (The shared city) *Plan. Tidsskrift for samfunnsplanlegging, byplan og regional utvikling (in Plan. Journal of community planning, urban and regional development)* 3/96.

Kjos, Ingeborg 2013: "Anders Behring Breiviks manifest - En idéanalyse". (Anders Behring Breiviks manifesto – an analysis of ideas) Master's thesis, University of Oslo.

Kleinman, Arthur 1985: "Interpreting Illness Experience and Clinical Meanings: How I See Clinically Applied Anthropology". *Medical Anthropology Quarterly* 16(3): 69-71.

Kleinman, Arthur and Joan Kleinman 1997: "The Appeal of Experi- ence: The Dismay of Images: Cultural Appropriation of Suffering in Our Times".

Kleinman, Arthur, Veena Das and Margaret Lock (editor) 1997: *Social Suffering.* Berkeley: University of California Press.

Kleinman, Arthur, Veena Das and Margaret Loch (editor) 1997: *Social Suffering.* Berkeley: University of California Press.

Koenig, Mathias 2005: "Introduction". In *Canadian Diversity / Diversit / Canadienne,* autumn 2005. Association for Canadian Studies.

Kultalahti, Olli 2006: "An Analytical Framework of Research on Migration Pressure: Concepts and Approaches.": O. Kultalahti, I. Karppi and H. Rantala (editor): *Europe in Flux. Transitions and Migration Pressures.* Turku: Institute of Migration.

Kumar, Loveleen 1997: *Mulighetens barn. Å vokse opp med to kulturer. (The child of opportunity. Growing up with two cultures)* Oslo: J.W. Cappelens forlag.

Larsen, Øyvind 2006: *Helsekonsekvensutredningen. (The health consequence report)* Michael. Publication Series of the Norwegian Medical Society, vol. 3/4.

Leirvik, Oddbjørn (2005): "Christianity and Islam in Norway: Politics of Religion and Interfaith Dialogue". In *Canadian Diversity / Diversit / Canadienne,* vol. 4: 3, autumn 2005.

Linge, Marius og Bangstad, Sindre 2020: *Salafisme i Norge.* (Salafism in Norway) Oslo: Frekk Forlag.

Lock, Margaret 1990: "On Being Ethnic: The Politics of Identity Break- ing and Making in Canada, or, *Nevra* on Sunday". *Culture, Medicine and Psychiatry* 14, s. 237-254.

Locke, John 1689: The Second Treatise of Government.

Macey, Marie 2009: *Multiculturalism, Religion and Women: Doing Harm by Doing Good?* UK: Palgrave McMillan.

Majid, Shazia 2019: *Ut av skyggene.* (Out of the shadows) Oslo: Aschehoug & Co.

Malmquist, Jörgen 2000: *Föreställningar om sjukdom: somatisering, medikalisering, prioritering. (Ideas about illness: somatization, medicalization, prioritization)* Studentlitteratur, (student literature) Lund University.

Malterud, Kirsti 1999: "Kvinners ubestemte´ helseplager - medisinske og velferdspolitiske utfordringer". (The undefined health problems of women - medical and welfare policy challenges) *Tidsskrift for Den norske Lægeforening (Journal for the Norwegian Medical Society)* 119: 1790-1793.

Malterud, Kirsti (editor) 2001: *Kvinners ubestemte helseplager. (The undefined health problems of women)* Oslo: Pax Forlag.

Malterud, Kirsti and I. Okkes 1998: "Gender Differences in General Practice Consultations: Methodological and Interpretative Intricacies". *Family Practice* 15: 404-410.

Melhuus, Marit 2001: "Hvilken skam uten ære? Eller: Finnes den skamløse æren?" (What shame without honor? Or: Does shameless honor exist?) Trygve Wyller (editor) 2001: *Skam: Perspektiver på skam, ære og skamløshet i det moderne. (Shame: Perspectives on shame, honor and shamelessness in the modern)* Bergen: Fagbokforlaget.

Melzack, Ronald and Patrick D. Wall (editor) 1984 (1965): *Textbook of Pain.* Edinburgh: Churchill Livingstone.

Melzack, Ronald and Patrick D. Wall 1996 (1982): *The Challenge of Pain.* London: Penguin Books.

Moi, Toril 2002: "Å tilegne seg Bordieus feministiske teori". (To acquire the feminist theory of Bordieu) Irene Iversen (editor): *Feministisk litteraturteori. (Feminist literary theory)* Oslo: Pax Forlag.

Monsen, Nina K. 1999: *Kultur eller kjønn? Motsetningsfylte verdier og politiske valg i relasjon til tradisjonsbundne, muslimske innvandrerkvinner. En filosofisk analyse. (Culture or gender? Conflicting values and political choices in relation to Muslim immigrant women bound by tradition. A philosophical analysis)* Oslo: Kommunal- og arbeidsdepartementet (Municipal and Labour Ministry).

Nortvedt, Finn and Per Nortvedt 2001: *Smerte- fenomen og forståelse. (Pain - phenomenon and understanding)* Oslo: Gyldendal Akademisk.

Nussbaum, Martha 1999: *Sex and Social Justice.* Oxford University Press.

Oslo kommune og Statens folkehelseinstitutt (Oslo Municipality and the State Institute of Public Health) 2000- 2001: *Helseundersøkelsen i bydeler og regioner i Oslo (Health study in neighborhoods and regions in Oslo)* (HUBRO-study).

Okin, Susan Moller 1999: *Is Multiculturalism Bad for Women?* Princeton University Press.

Prathiba, Jain 2008: *Balancing Minority Rights and Gender Justice: The Impact of Protecting Multiculturalism on Women's Rights in India.* Ashgate.

Raja, Abid Q. 2008: *Talsmann. (Spokesman)* Aschehoug.

Raja, Abid Q. 2010: *Dialog. (Dialogue)* Cappelen Damm.

Rawls, John 1971: *A Theory of Justice.* Belknap: Harvard University Press.

Rosseau, Jean-Jacques 1762: *The Social Contract.*

Sachs, Lisbeth 1987: *Medicinsk antropologi. (Medical anthropology)* Stockholm: Liber.

Said, Edward 2003: *Orientalism.* London: Penguin Books.

Sayed, Abdelmalek 2004: *The Suffering of the Immigrant.* Cambridge: Polity Press.

Scheper-Hughes, Nancy and Margaret Lock 1987: "The Mindful Body: A Prolegomenon to Future Work in Medical Anthropology". *Medical Anthropology Quarterly* I: 6-31.

Scott, James: 1990: *Domination and the Arts of Resistance: Hidden Transcripts.* New Haven and London: Yale University Press.

Seierstad, Åsne 2016: *To søstre. (Two sisters)* Oslo: Kagge forlag.

Sen, Amartya 1999: *Development as Freedom.* New York: Random House.

Shoshan, Nitzhan 2016: *Management of Hate.* Princeton University Press.

Siim, Birte 2003: *Medborgerskabets udfordringer - etniske minoritetskvinders politiske myndiggjørelse. (Citizenship challenges - the political empowerment of ethnic minority women)* Århus: Den danske magtudredning. (The Danish report on power)

Siim, Birte 2000: *Gender and Citizenship: Policy and Agency in France, Britain and Denmark.* University of Cambridge Press.

Snow-Turek, A.L., M.P. Norris, G. Tan 1996: "Active and Passive Coping Strategies in Chronic Pain Patients". *Pain* 64: 455-462.

Soares, Joaquim J.F. and Giorgio Grossi 1999: *Experience of Muscoloskeletal Pain: Comparison of Immigrants and Swedish Patients.* Scandinavian University Press.

Staunæs, Dorthe 2006: "Køn, etnicitet og skoleliv". (Gender, ethnicity and life at school) *Tidsskrift for kjønnsforskning (Journal for gender studies)* 1-2: 103-105.

Storhaug, Hege 2006: *Men størst av alt er friheten. (But the greatest thing of all is freedom)* Oslo: Kagge Forlag.

Sveen, Karin 2001: *Klassereise: et livshistorisk essay. (Class Trip: A Life Historical Essay)* Oslo: Oktober Forlag.

Sveaas, Nora 1997: *Flukt og fremtid. Psykososialt arbeid og terapi med flyktninger. (Escape and future. Psychosocial work and therapy with refugees)* Oslo: Ad Notam Gyldendal.

Taras, Raymond 2012: *Challenging Multiculturalism: European Models of Diversity.* Edinburgh University Press. Retrieved from: https://www.jstor.org/stable/10.3366/j.ctt20q22fw [opened: 16.06.2020]

Thorbjørnsrud, Berit S. 2007: "Frihet, rettigheter og ortodokse presters kjønn. (Freedom, rights and the gender of orthodox priests) Thomas Hylland Eriksen and Arne J. Vetlesen (editor): *Frihet.* Oslo: Universitetsforlaget.

Tracey, Irene 2005: "Taking the Narrative out of Pain: Objectifying Pain through Brain Imaging". Daniel B. Carr, John D. Loeser and David B. Morris (editor): *Narrative, Pain, and Suffering.* Seattle: IASP Press.

Turner, Victor 1996: "Betwixt and Between: The Liminal Period in Rites de Passage". In Thomas Hylland Eriksen (editor): *Sosialantropologiske grunntekster. (Social anthropological basic texts)* Oslo: Ad Notam Gyldendal.

Turner, J.A. and S. Clancy 1986: "Strategies for Coping with Chronic Lowback Pain: Relationship to Pain and Disability". *Pain* 24:355- 364.

Varvin, Sverre 2003: *Flukt og eksil. Traume, identitet og mestring. (Escape and exile. Trauma, identity and coping)*

Vetlesen, Arne Johann 2004: *Smerte. (Pain)* Lysaker: Dinamo Forlag.

Vetlesen, Arne Johann 2003: *Menneskeverd og ondskap. Essays og artikler (Human dignity and evil. Essays and articles) 1991-2002.* Oslo: Gyldendal Akademisk.

Vogt, Kari 2000: Islam på norsk. Moskeer og islamske organisasjoner i Norge. (Islam the Norwegian way. Mosques and Muslim organizations in Norway) Oslo: Cappelen.

Wadel, Cato 1991: *Feltarbeid i egen kultur. En innføring i kvalitativt orientert samfunnsforskning. (Fieldwork in their own culture. An introduction to qualitative oriented social science)* Flekkefjord: SEEK.

Walton, Stephen J. 2012: "Antifeminism and Misogyny in Breivik's "Manifesto"". *NORA - Nordic Journal of Feminist and Gender Research* 20(1): 4-11

Werner, Anne 2005: *Kampen for (tro)verdighet. Kvinner med "ubestemte" helseplager i møtet med legen og dagliglivet. (The fight for credibility/dignity. Women with "undefined" health problems meeting their doctor and daily life)* PhD thesis at the Faculty of Medicine, Oslo University.

Widding Isaksen, Lise 2006: "Tilpasning til tomme rom. Om globale omsorgskrisers relasjonsøkologi". (Adapting to empty rooms. About the global relational ecology of the caring crisis) *Tidsskrift for kjønnsforskning (Journal for gender research)* 1-2: 20-35.

Wigers, Sigrid Hørven 2002: "Fibromyalgi- en oppdatering". (Fibromy- algia - an update) *Tidsskrift for Den norske Lægeforening (Journal of the Norwegian Medical Association)* 122: 1300-1304.

Wikan, Unni 2003: *For ærens skyld. Fadime til ettertanke. (For the sake of honor. Fadime for contemplation)* Oslo: Universitetsforlaget.

Wikan, Unni 2002: *Generous Betrayal: Politics of Culture in the New Europe.* Chicago & London: University of Chicago Press.

Ødegaard, Ørnulf 1932: *Immigration and Insanity: A study of Mental Disease Among the Norwegian born Population of Minnesota.* Copenhagen: Levin & Munksgaards Publishers.

Yetkin, Murat 2017: "We owe radical Islamist militancy to Brzezinski". Daily News. Retrieved from: https://www.hurriyetdailynews.com/opinion/murat-yetkin/we-owe-radical-islamist-militancy-to-brzezinski-113639

Newspapers:

Aftenposten, 26.7.2006
Aftenposten, 27.5.2006
Aftenposten, 10.5.2005
Aftenposten, 12.9.2007
Dagens Næringsliv, 2.6.2007
Dagsavisen, 19.1.2006
Dagsavisen, 7.1.2006
Dagsavisen, 13.11.2005
Dagsavisen, 24.3.2005
Le Monde Diplomatique nr. 12, December 2005
The New York Times, 28.1.2006

White papers:

Report to the Storting no. 49 (2003-2004) *Mangfold gjennom inkludering og deltakelse. Ansvar og frihet. (Diversity through inclusion and participation. Responsibility and freedom)* Oslo: Det kongelige kommunal- og regionaldepartement (The Royal Norwegian Department of Municipal and Regional Affairs).

Websites:

Katolsk Informasjonstjeneste (Oslo) (17. januar 2008). (Catholic Information Services) http://www.katolsk.no/nyheter/2008/01/17-0001

Pressemelding (17.06.20). (Press release) https://www.google.com/url?q=https://www.regjeringen.no/no/aktuelt/vil-veilede-kommuner-og-nav-i-kampen-mot-radikalisering/id2711321/&sa=D&ust=1598188659950000&usg=AFQjCNEkNBbvmPj4gK9vhe9Co6hKkcr0bQ

Ursula von der Leyen replies to political leaders and warns ex-Right that EU values are not for sale, retrieved from: https://www.youtube.com/watch?v=sAVhd2E9BqE Opened: 21.09.2020

About the Author

Farida Ahmadi was born in 1957 in Kabul. She came to Norway in 1991 as a refugee from Afghanistan. She studied social anthropology at Oslo University.

Farida Ahmadi is the founder of Global Happiness and works as an international lecturer. She has dedicated much of her life to working for peace.

"When women's needs are misinterpreted and ignored, their pain and needs are delegitimized. They are unseen, yet objectified. People have strong opinions about them, without really knowing them. This is a book that shines the spotlight on life as a woman in those dark corners where no one visits, and where loneliness and pain reside. Farida Ahmadi gives these unseen women a face, listens to their silent screams, and gives them a voice."

Hisako Ishitani (Chairperson)

Refugee Empowerment, Japan

About the book

"Farida's book is born out of a deep engagement with the lives of refugee Muslim women who cannot find the means to make their pain knowable within the institutional structures that define the social service sector in Norway. How does a modern state committed to the preservation and enhancement of life manage to produce the conditions under which the singularity of these women's lives is extinguished. Farida Ahmadi provides a complex and nuanced ethnography that should be read by anthropologists, social workers and policy makers.

Veena Das
Prof. Anthropology,
John Hopkins University

"It shows great passion for humanity and its most vulnerable victims of tyranny and violence."

Roger Griffin
Prof. History,
Oxford Brookes University

"Farida put a spotlight on life of woman's dark corners of their loneliness and pain reside. Also, listens to their silent screams and gaves them a voice".

Loveleen R. Brenna
Leader of SEEMA

www.ingramcontent.com/pod-product-compliance
Lightning Source LLC
LaVergne TN
LVHW061609070526
838199LV00078B/7218